Dear Reader:

803 - 365 07 84

The book you are about to read is the latest bestseller from St. Martin's True Crime Library, the imprint *The New York Times* calls "the leader in true crime!" Each month, we offer you a fascinating account of the latest, most sensational crime that has captured national attention. *The Milwaukee Murders* delves into the twisted world of Jeffrey Dahmer, one of the most savage serial killers of our time; *Lethal Lolita* gives you the *real* scoop on the deadly love affair between Amy Fisher and Joey Buttafuoco; *Whoever Fights Monsters* takes you inside the special FBI team that tracks serial killers; *Garden of Graves* reveals how police uncovered the bloody human harvest of mass murderer Joel Rifkin; *Unanswered Cries* is the story of a detective who tracked a killer for a year, only to discover it was someone he knew and trusted; *Bad Blood* is the story of the notorious Menendez brothers and their sensational trials; *Sins of the Mother* details the sad account of Susan Smith and her two drowned children; *Fallen Hero* details the riveting tragedy of O. J. Simpson and the case that stunned a nation.

St. Martin's True Crime Library gives you the stories *behind* the headlines. Our authors take you right to the scene of the crime and into the minds of the most notorious murderers to show you what really makes them tick. St. Martin's True Crime Library paperbacks are better than the most terrifying thriller, because it's all true! The next time you want a crackling good read, make sure it's got the St. Martin's True Crime Library logo on the spine—you'll be up all night!

Charles E. Spicer, Jr.
Senior Editor, St. Martin's True Crime Library

The Coed Call Girl
MURDER

Fannie Weinstein & Melinda Wilson

St. Martin's Paperbacks

THE COED CALL GIRL MURDER

Copyright © 1997 by Fannie Weinstein and Melinda Wilson.

Cover photograph of Tina Biggar by Beverly Raburn.
Cover photograph of motel by Taro Yamasaki.

ISBN: 0-312-96357-2

Printed in the United States of America

St. Martin's Paperbacks edition/July 1997

10 9 8 7 6 5 4 3 2 1

AUTHORS' NOTE

The material in this book derives from personal interviews, public records, and news reports.

The dialogue was reconstructed from documents, courtroom testimony, and personal recollections by participants.

Pseudonyms were used for the following individuals, solely at the authors' discretion, to protect their privacy: Valerie Brady, Sandra Brown, Nancy Chandler, Elite Desires, Carol Esposito, Mark Hawthorne, Luke Jackson, Steve Malone, Peter Nelson, Theresa Simmons, and Paul Tranchida.

Finally, neither were monetary inducements offered, nor editorial promises made, to sources in exchange for information.

ACKNOWLEDGMENTS

I owe many people my deepest gratitude.

First, thanks to my agent Jane Dystel and my editor Charles Spicer for believing in me and in this project;

To the following for their contributions to the Tina Biggar story I reported for *People*: Giovanna Breu, Jack Friedman, Ann Guerin, Richard Jerome, Mary Ellen Lidon, M.C. Marden and Taro Yamasaki;

To friends and acquaintances of Tina Biggar, and members of the Oakland University community, for the time and help they so generously provided;

To sources who asked not to be named, for their invaluable assistance;

Lastly, special thanks to Laura Berman and Ruth Coughlin (their editorial wisdom is unmatched), Paul Engstrom, Mark Lee and Maria Slowiaczek, without each of whom this book—and little else—would be possible.

F.W.

This book could not have been written without the help of many people, who were not only kind, but candid and generous.

Special thanks goes to *Detroit News* Publisher Robert H. Giles for giving me the time and support I needed to complete this work.

I also owe a debt of gratitude to the Southfield, Farmington Hills, and Michigan State Police Departments, specifically Chief Bill Dwyer, Deputy Chief Marty Bledsoe, and detectives Ron Shankin, Bob Tiderington, Patrick Comini, and Al Soderlund of Farmington Hills; in Southfield, Police Chief Joe Thomas, Deputy Chief Lloyd Collins, detectives Michael Cischke and Mark Zacks, and police officers Ken Rochon and Bill Pylkus, and Ted Monfett of the Michigan State Police.

Attorney Michael Modelski and Oakland County Assistant Prosecutor Donna Pendergast were giving of their time and memories.

Salutes to Joe Rokicsak for his horticultural knowledge and to Paul Altavena for his computer assistance. A number of private citizens in Oakland County shared their homes and memories with me, for which I am grateful, including Jerry Holbert.

Personal thanks to Ellen Wilson and Debra Kulesza; to Michael Green, who helped out with the photography and lifted my sometimes flagging spirits; and to my two daughters, Amelia and Lily, who had to forego my undivided attention for months on end but who loved and supported me unfailingly, anyway.

M.G.W.

I forgive you . . .

One man knew.

But he wouldn't tell. It was his special secret, one he reveled in during stolen visits to the grassy lot where he'd hidden her lifeless body.

As summer changed to fall, he came at least twice, once before sunrise, and again late in the night, each time standing over her, calling out her name.

Forgive me, he begged. Again and again, he asked the same thing. Until finally, one day she answered.

And when the words came, strong and clear and, of course, audible only to him, they were exactly what he had been waiting to hear: I forgive you. I'm happy now. I forgive you.

PROLOGUE

As Farmington Hills, Michigan, Police detectives Al Soderlund and Patrick Comini padded through the knee-high weeds and grass, pushing aside cobwebs and fallen branches, an occasional ray of sun streaked through the trees to warm the tops of their heads.

It was September 21, 1995, the first day of fall. But a chill had bitten through the warm autumn air, a prelude to the cold winter ahead.

Having divided the half-acre field behind the small white house into strips several feet wide, the two detectives were walking the vertical rows end to end, starting in one direction and returning in the other.

As their eyes scanned the ground, they were alert for any smells that didn't blend with the goldenrod, wild raspberry bushes, and towering elms and maples scattered through the wooded patch.

When the dense underbrush yielded nothing after more than a half-hour of careful searching, they started back toward their car, Comini first, Soderlund following behind him.

From the corner of his eye, Comini spotted what he thought might be a pile of discarded clothing behind a tall raspberry bush near a young walnut tree. Obscured by the bush, the strange heap was nestled against a chain-link boundary fence grown over with grapevines that separated the woods from the volleyball court of a college fraternity house.

"Al, you better come over here," Comini called out to his partner, his voice thick with apprehension as he moved toward the suspicious pile.

Nothing in the detective's short career prepared him for what he saw next. It was a woman. Or what was left of one. Had it not been for the overpowering stench and clothing, Comini wouldn't have been certain what he had found.

She was lying on her left side in a fetal position, knees pulled to her chest. Her shirt, tan and short-sleeved, had been pulled over her head, exposing a dark-colored brassiere. She wore denim shorts, belted, and sandals. Decomposition was so advanced that her jaw had detached from her skull, as had her long, blond hair, still gathered into a ponytail by a black cotton band.

Although the grass and the raspberry bush had grown tall around her, little or no attempt had been made at covering her body. As a result, what time and the elements hadn't erased of her flesh and organs, small forest animals had. Very little but bone and clothing remained.

Soderlund, who'd come up behind Comini, stood with his partner for several seconds. Both men looked down at the horrific sight, holding their hands over their mouths and noses in a futile attempt to block out the overpowering stench.

They backed away, saying nothing.

There was little to say, really.

They both knew who they were looking at.

Soderlund went to his car to get his mobile phone.

"We have a body here," he told his boss, giving him the address of the small white house. "I think it's her."

No further explanation was necessary.

For three weeks, the FBI, the Michigan State Police, and other local law enforcement agencies had been hunting for the woman. Police helicopters equipped with special body heat–sensing equipment had buzzed landfills and excavation sites. Cadaver-sniffing dogs had rooted through fields and backyards not too far from this one.

Comini knew finding her was something of a coup. But he

felt more heartsick than proud as he paced the gravel driveway in the few quiet minutes left before hordes of technicians
and police and news media would descend upon the quiet
field.

His discovery would extinguish the hopes of so many.
Comini himself had a little girl, a precious three-year-old. He
couldn't imagine the horror and hurt the dead woman's parents would feel when the news reached them. The young
woman in the woods had once been their beautiful little girl.

Later, the young detective would say the image that
haunted him from that day was her feet. For weeks, whenever
he closed his eyes at night, he saw their dark leathery flesh
tucked inside a pair of summer sandals.

It was unthinkable to anyone who knew Tina Biggar that this
would be her cruel fate.

Until she disappeared on August 23, 1995, she seemed to
have it all.

Tina was 23 and about to start her senior year at Oakland
University, a mid-sized college in the well-to-do Detroit suburb of Rochester. She was tall, with wavy blond hair that
cascaded below her shoulders. She had sparkling brown eyes
and a 1,000-watt smile. Tina personified in a young woman
the carefree coed so often pictured in college brochures studying on the lawn outside an ivy-covered building or simply
walking through campus, textbooks clutched tightly against
her breast.

"She was radiant," confirms Tina's live-in boyfriend,
Todd Nurnberger, who never stopped believing, even after
she was missing for weeks, that he and Tina would spend the
rest of their lives together.

Tina thrived at Oakland. One of the psychology department's most promising students, she loved figuring out what
made people tick. As a junior, she jumped at the chance to
work with her favorite professor on a research project. She
had even started talking about becoming a psychology professor herself someday.

More than anything, Tina was determined to get into a

good graduate school. Her grades alone—she boasted a 3.43 grade point average—probably would have been enough. But Tina was ambitious. She wanted to stand out. So she came up with an idea for her own research project. She submitted it for approval twenty-four hours before she was last seen alive.

Tina would have made a great psychologist. She was easy to talk to and a good listener. She also had a way of making people feel good about themselves, even customers at the steakhouse where she waited tables for close to three years. That Tina's tips were routinely higher than any other wait-person's came as no surprise to anyone who ever saw her work a table.

As much as school meant to Tina, and as much as she loved waitressing, both took a back seat to her number-one priority: her family. Dad Bill, a Coast Guard commander, Mom Connie, a registered nurse, her four younger brothers, and her younger sister were the center of Tina's universe. She called home at least twice a week, just to make sure she didn't miss out on even the smallest bit of family news. She made the four-hour drive to Traverse City, Michigan, where Bill was stationed, as often as her hectic schedule permitted.

Because of Tina's devotion to her family, friends and co-workers refused to believe that she'd simply taken off when they heard she'd disappeared. The Tina they knew would never go away without telling her parents. The Tina they knew had talked nonstop for months about going back to school in the fall and getting her research project off the ground. But as the mystery surrounding Tina's disappearance began to unravel, they were left wondering if they really knew Tina at all.

No one denied she had her faults. Over the years, those she'd allowed to get close to her—mainly Todd and a few girlfriends—caught glimpses of a side she kept hidden from her family and the rest of the world. A distrustful side. A vengeful side. A side that had no use for rules. A "bad girl" side that ran contrary to her strict Catholic "good girl" up-bringing.

Everyone who saw Tina in the weeks leading up to her disappearance noticed something wasn't right. She wasn't the same old Tina. She was stressed out, irritable, even bitter.

Still, no one who knew her was prepared for the shocking truth her disappearance would bring to light: not only had she led a double life for close to a year, but she had managed to keep it completely hidden as well. So complex was the web of deceit she'd spun, even the man she lived with had been wholly fooled.

Only days before she disappeared, Tina's mountain of lies was on the verge of collapse. She hinted to Todd there was something she needed to tell him, something that would explain why she hadn't been herself lately. But no one will ever know whether she really intended to come clean. It was a secret that Tina took to her grave.

CHAPTER
1

Farmington Hills Detective Ronald Shankin was rifling through reports from the night before. It was Friday, August 25, 1995. Thirty years old and a detective for just eight months, Shankin was working the day shift, assigned to commercial break-ins, work that involved talking to business owners about burglaries and employee thefts, hardly the stuff of crime novels. To date, his headiest assignment had been nabbing an armed robber for a string of retail thefts, a suburban crackhead from a so-called nice family who knocked over 7-Elevens and gas stations to feed his habit.

The report that caught his eye on this particular morning had to do with a missing person. Cases like missings, stalkings, and domestic assaults were the kinds of miscellaneous matters that landed on Shankin's desk in addition to his burglary duties, parceled out by higher-ups, according to workloads and schedules.

Since Shankin worked days, he often got assigned cases that had come in the previous night but which needed more time or attention than either patrol officers or the few detectives who worked nights could afford. This was one of those. A young college student living in Muirwood Apartments named Tina Biggar had disappeared. Her father and boyfriend had come to the station the night before to fill out a routine Missing Persons Verification Form. It's a procedure in which police simply take down a person's age and birth date and a dispatcher enters the information into the two computer networks circulated to police nationwide: LEIN, the Law Enforcement Information Network and NCIC, the National Crime Information Center.

Police don't generally pay much attention to missing person reports during the first few days after they've been filed. People take off for any number of reasons, from adolescents looking to escape overbearing parents to women fleeing domestic abuse situations. The Farmington Hills Police average about sixty missing persons reports a year, the overwhelming majority of which are people whose whereabouts become known within forty-eight hours after they've been reported gone. Many who report missings never even bother to check back with the police to let them know that their loved one has turned up. Some are embarrassed; others just forget.

When Shankin drew the Tina Biggar case, his first thought was that he might be able to wrap it up with a few telephone calls. In the past, he'd made quick work of missings, tracking down the person, usually through friends, and persuading them to call their mate or parent. He hated the idea of someone spending a sleepless night worried about a missing when a quick telephone call could quell their fears. A few months earlier, he'd tracked down a man who'd split from his longtime lover in Farmington Hills. He even had the Tampa Police go out and confirm that the man was alive and well, just to allay his jilted partner's fears.

As far as Shankin was concerned, Tina Biggar might also be off on a lark, but he wanted to talk to her family and friends first.

Boyishly handsome, with blond good looks and small-boned features, Shankin, in appearance and manner, was the antithesis of the stereotypical hard-nosed, doughnut-dunking detective made popular on television by cops like Detective Andy Sipowicz of *NYPD Blue* fame.

Polite and articulate, Shankin was dogged, but quietly so. He was learning the ropes and he knew it. Too young to have developed the thick hide and outsized ego typical of some veteran detectives, Shankin was still kind and enthusiastic—

a boy scout, as some of his fellow officers good-naturedly ribbed him. As if his fresh-faced good looks and sincere nature weren't affront enough to some of his grizzled colleagues, Shankin's diet also drove them crazy: He never drank coffee; he always ate salads; preservatives rarely touched his lips; and he worked out religiously. Not many of his fellow cops, male or female, could boast of such a trim waist. Spending time on an early missing persons case was just the kind of thing Shankin's colleagues would hammer him about and he knew it—Shankin the saint. He didn't care. He called Bill and Todd at Tina and Todd's apartment and asked them to come into the station.

If Shankin had any misgivings about wasting his time or taxpayers' money on a routine missing who would turn up in a few days, they vanished when he met Bill Biggar.

Eyes made swollen from crying and lack of sleep, his broad shoulders slumped with worry and grief, Bill was a man who commanded respect. As a helicopter pilot with the U.S. Coast Guard, he had logged hundreds of miles flying search-and-rescue missions. Now the considerable skills Bill had honed in the military were focused laserlike on finding his daughter.

With little prompting, Bill laid out Tina's background, her recent mental state, a loan allegedly coming from an unknown guy named Ken, the friends and family who figured into her life. He gave the detective names and telephone numbers of Tina's closest friends and confidantes: a Professor Harrison at Oakland University and a woman named Danielle Lentine, who lived in Georgia.

Todd added that he talked to Tina every day and that he always saw her when he came home from work.

"If she wasn't going to be home, she always called me to say she had to work late," Todd told Shankin. "This just isn't normal," he said.

Her car was gone: a silver 1987 Honda, license number EKD 246. Other than that, she'd left everything behind in the apartment that she would have needed for an overnight stay: her birth control pills, her glasses, her makeup bag—something she never traveled without. The only things Todd and

Bill could find missing from home were her laptop computer and her schoolbag.

Tina was an honors student at Oakland University, majoring in psychology, they explained. As part of a research project, she'd been gathering information on the impact of AIDS on prostitutes. Some of the research had taken her to a jail in a rough section of Detroit. It was yet another thing they were worried about.

"It wasn't your usual course of study," Shankin recalled later. "We just sort of left it at that, but it didn't sit right with me."

Shankin opened a case file. Tina's life was now a number: 95-22969.

He noted the basics on an incident report: Name: Biggar, Tina Susan [a misspelling; it was actually Suzanne]. Age: 23. Height: 5' 7". Weight: 150 [that would also change, too, negotiated downward, to 145 pounds, at Todd's suggestion]. Hair: Blond. Length: Shldr. Eyes: Brown. In the section marked narrative, Shankin summed up what the two men had told him:

R/P [reporting person] states that the above missing was last seen on 8-23-95, and missing was very upset/nervous in regards to a loan. R/P states that missing was to borrow $20,000 from a male known as "Ken." R/P states missing didn't take any clothes, nothing in her apartment to indicate that she had planned to leave. Glasses/contact lens case still inside one of her bags.

His report may have been bare bones, but Shankin again went over in depth Tina's last few days with Todd, information Bill had obviously covered with his daughter's boyfriend as well.

He learned that Tina had come home late Tuesday night, the day before she disappeared, and that when Todd left the house Wednesday morning, Tina was still sleeping. She wasn't there when Todd got home from work Wednesday. When it got late and he got worried, he called the restaurant where she waited tables. He was told she hadn't worked there since June 3, further heightening his fears.

Shankin asked to talk to the two men separately. Todd was in a position to know more about the intimate details of Tina's life than Bill. And Shankin had a hunch that Bill might be more forthcoming about Todd out of earshot of the young man.

He was right. Alone with the detective in a conference room, Bill revealed that Tina and Todd were splitting up. Todd had painted his relationship with Tina as being extremely close, so Shankin was interested to hear that her father had a different view.

Bill assured Shankin that he didn't think Todd had done anything to hurt Tina. He thought Todd was responsible, hardworking. Still, Tina had definitely indicated to her family that Todd was on his way out of her life. For just that reason, Bill had planned to travel to Detroit that weekend to help Tina move out of her and Todd's apartment and into a place in Ferndale, in southern Oakland County.

Throughout the interview, Shankin could sense that Bill was mentally sizing him up, registering, no doubt, reservations about his age and experience. Who is this young kid, anyhow? Does he have what it takes to find my daughter?

The effect was more motivating than intimidating. Shankin wanted to prove Bill wrong, to show him that he handled every case with care and diligence, whether it was a daughter of a Coast Guard higher-up or a Jane Doe off the street.

Shankin was delicate while questioning Bill, who was obviously distraught about his daughter. But he was more direct with Todd, now that he knew he had a soon-to-be-estranged boyfriend on his hands.

"Have you ever hit her?" he asked Todd. No, he assured Shankin, their relationship wasn't violent. He said he and Tina fought, like most couples, but they'd never come to blows. Even their breakup was amicable, and not at all final—in his mind, anyway. Tina just said she needed some time to think things over. It was a trial separation, meant to last six months or so. They still planned on seeing each other after she moved out, Todd explained.

"How was your sex life?" Shankin quizzed Todd. The young detective wasn't prying. He wanted to find out if Tina was seeking companionship she might have lacked at home.

"Great," Todd assured him. "Best sex I've ever had in my life."

Geez, give me a break, thought Shankin. I wasn't looking for a performance rating, just some idea of how frequently they made love. He made a mental note: Tina likes sex, whatever that had to do with anything. For that matter, so did he. So did most people he knew. So what?

Shankin didn't doubt Todd was telling the truth. He didn't look like a man hiding something. He watched Todd's hands and his eyes while he questioned him. He didn't fidget or move about. No signs of nervousness. Still, he was someone to watch. They were breaking up. He was one of the last people to see Tina. Shankin got the feeling he wasn't hearing the whole story about why their romance was fizzling.

Actually, the two men had raised a number of red flags for Shankin. For months Tina had been pretending to work at a restaurant when she was actually somewhere else. Why? What was she doing that she couldn't tell her boyfriend and family about? Her fractured relationship with Todd might have had something to do with it, but then so might her recent friendship with this "Ken" guy.

Todd said he never hit Tina, but who knew what people did behind closed doors? On top of all of that, her college studies had taken her into dangerous waters.

Any one of those circumstances in and of themselves could have put her in harm's way. Taken together, they left Shankin with a tight knot in his stomach and a whole lot of leads to chase down. So much for a simple missing, wrapped up with a few phone calls.

Bill hadn't shared any specific doubts about his daughter's well-being, but Shankin got the general impression the Coast Guard commander was ready for the worst. He hoped Bill was wrong.

Certainly Tina's life left room for a range of possibilities as to why she was missing, not all of which were sinister. She might have gotten into a fight with Todd and left him—possibly for this Ken guy. She just hadn't bothered to tell her family, he theorized. Or she could have run off with a totally different man, someone she'd been seeing all those nights that Todd thought she was out waitressing. She was young, pretty. She could be with Danielle or another friend in some other state. The weekend was coming. Maybe she would turn up. But if she didn't, he couldn't imagine Bill sitting still all weekend. The military commander clearly wanted police assistance—he would damn well demand it, in fact. But if the police or anyone else weren't going to help him, they better get the hell out of his way. With or without them, he was going to find his daughter.

CHAPTER
2

"**A** woman would run through fire and water for such a kind heart."

These words, which appear under Bill Biggar's senior picture in his high school yearbook, proved more prophetic than his admiring schoolmates ever could have imagined. For when it came to solving the mystery of his daughter's disappearance, Bill, too, was prepared to weather any elements that stood in his way.

Bill embodied small-town America and spent his life upholding the values and mores he was taught during his youth. The third of Eugene and Virgeana Biggar's children, William Morris Biggar was born July 26, 1950, in the tiny farming community of Aurora, South Dakota.

His great-great-grandparents, Thomas and Ellen Biggar, were Scots who emigrated to Canada in 1819. Half a century later, their son, Thomas, headed south to the United States. After a decade spent mining in California, he settled down on a farm just outside of Aurora.

Thomas Biggar eventually married a local schoolteacher named Belle. Together, they had two children: a daughter, Grace, and a son, Morris. Morris, and his wife, Matia, had eight children. One of them was Bill's father, Eugene, a farmer until he retired in the early 1980s.

Bill attended Elkton High School, graduating in the spring of 1968. A popular honor student, the handsome blond farm boy was elected president of his junior class and Homecoming King the year after that.

Tall, with an athletic build, Bill was a football standout, too. As a 170-pound junior guard, he earned All-Conference honors. The following season, he repeated that feat and was named honorable mention All-State as well.

Making Bill's accomplishments on the gridiron all the more impressive was the fact that the Elks managed only a single victory his senior year. Their poor performance, however, did little to dampen school spirit. The school's cheerleaders saw to that. Among them was a fresh-faced brunette by the name of Constance Sue Myers.

Connie was born May 8, 1951, in Milwaukee, Wisconsin and was still a toddler when her parents, Howard and Helen, left the nation's beer capital behind for Elkton.

Like Bill, Connie was an honor student and among the most popular students in her grade. A cheerleader, a Future Homemaker of America, and a member of several choral groups and the staffs of the school newspaper and yearbook, she was probably one of the busiest as well. Still, she found time to star in the class play her senior year: a comedy/mystery titled *I Was a Teen-Age Dracula*.

Wedding bells rang for the young sweethearts on August 21, 1970, at Elkton's Our Lady of Good Counsel Catholic Church.

Neither Bill nor Connie had strayed far from home after high school. There was no need to. South Dakota State University, the largest school in the state, was less than twenty miles away in the small college town of Brookings.

Bill was 20 when he and Connie wed, five semesters away from graduating with a degree in health, physical education, and recreation. Connie was 19. A physical therapy major, she had just completed her freshman year.

Bill and Connie's wedding made the social pages of the *Brookings Register.* The bride, the newspaper reported, wore "an empire dirndl skirted gown with chapel length train enhanced with Beauvois lace. Her jeweled neckline was enhanced with lace petals and a petaled tiara completed her bridal ensemble.'' Her bridesmaids wore ''empire waisted gowns of lavender Dacron voile.''

The church was decorated with lavender gladioli and white mums. Connie's bouquet was comprised of cymbidiums and stephanotis while the bridal party carried white and lavender daisies.

Seven months after Bill and Connie exchanged vows, Connie became pregnant with Tina.

On December 31, 1971, the young couple celebrated not only the New Year, but the birth of their first child, a girl they named Tina Suzanne.

Nine days before Tina's first birthday, on December 22, 1972, Bill graduated from SDSU. (Connie left school after Tina was born.) That same day, having completed the university's four-year ROTC program, he was commissioned as a second lieutenant in the U.S. Army.

A born leader, Bill was made for a career in the military. In the spring of 1973, he was ordered to report to Fort Jackson in Columbia, South Carolina. He went on from there to Alabama's Fort Rucker, where he trained to be an army pilot.

In the summer of 1975, Bill joined the 335th Aviation Co. at Fort Riley in Kansas. Connie, too, had her hands full. Tina was 3½ and by this time, she had two younger brothers: Aaron was born in October 1973, two months before Tina turned 2, and then there was the newborn Jason.

Bill was a model soldier. By 1979, he had risen to the rank of captain and had been awarded numerous honors. But in June of that year, four months after Connie gave birth to a baby girl she and Bill named Julie, he resigned his commission. He did not, however, abandon the military altogether. Not long after receiving his Army discharge, Bill joined the United States Coast Guard.

Bill's career switch had little effect on the Biggars' lifestyle. They still had to pick up stakes every few years, following Bill from one duty station to another. His first Coast Guard assignment was in Miami. Roughly four years later, he was transferred to the Coast Guard Air Station in Traverse City, a 125-man post that handles search-and-rescue missions on Lake Michigan, Lake Superior, and Lake Huron.

Situated at the southern point of northwest Michigan's breathtaking Leelanau Peninsula, Traverse City and its surrounding communities attract millions of tourists annually. From the spring through the fall, visitors can boat on Lake Michigan, explore the beaches and bluffs along the Sleeping Bear Dunes National Lakeshore, tour the region's vast vineyards and orchards, or visit Horton Bay, where Ernest Hemingway spent his boyhood summers. In the winter, sports enthusiasts flock to the area's popular ski resorts.

It didn't take long before Traverse City felt like home to the Biggar clan. Neither Bill nor Connie had ever warmed to Miami.

"They're not big-city people," Todd would later say.

They didn't care for the hot, sticky climate either.

Traverse City was another story entirely. With a population of roughly 16,000, it was about the same size as Brookings. It reminded them of the small South Dakota community.

Bill and Connie made friends quickly in Michigan. Devout Catholics, they were active members of their church, known for their tremendous generosity.

"I'll tell you what kind of person Bill Biggar is," a longtime friend told a reporter after Tina had disappeared. "I had a brain tumor. Every time I went for treatment he was there."

Bill and Connie socialized with other Coast Guard families as well. "Everyone liked being around them," another friend recalled. "That's just the kind of people they are."

Nothing, however, matched the joy Bill and Connie derived from spending time with their children.

"Whatever the kids were doing, they were there," the same friend remembered. "They never missed a game, recital, or play.

"It was obvious they were a very close, loving family."

In spite of their busy schedules, Bill and Connie made time for volunteer work, too, helping to guarantee the success of events like Traverse City's annual Cherry Festival.

Because of their deep religious faith, Bill and Connie opted to send Tina and her siblings to parochial schools whenever possible. In Traverse City, Tina attended Immaculate Conception Middle School. ICMS, like most Catholic schools, had strict rules regarding attendance and behavior. Dress was closely monitored as well.

St. Francis High School, where Tina spent ninth grade, had similar regulations. Some students rebelled. But the strict regimen brought out the best in Tina. She did well in school and participated in numerous extracurricular activities. She was a member of the student council, the drama club, and the forensics team. She also swam, ran track, and played softball.

Nineteen-eighty-six, however, would also prove to be a year in which Tina's faith in God and all that is good was shaken to its very core.

The year began with a joyous announcement: Connie was going to have a baby. Tina almost burst when she heard the news. It meant she'd have another little brother or sister to dote on. On November 9, the Biggars welcomed little Matthew John into the world. Bill and Connie, naturally, were thrilled. So, too, were Matthew's five siblings. (After Julie, Connie had given birth to another son, Christopher.)

But the family's happiness was short-lived; Matthew died suddenly when he was little more than a month old. The cause of death: Sudden Infant Death Syndrome, or SIDS. Full of sorrow, Bill and Connie returned home to Elkton to bury their tiny son. His funeral took place at Our Lady of Good Counsel, the same church where his parents had married sixteen years earlier.

Young Matthew's tragic death cast a pall over a household that had once been filled mostly with laughter. But as the Biggars struggled to come to terms with their unexpected loss, more change was on the horizon. In 1987, prior to the beginning of Tina's sophomore year of high school, Bill was transferred again.

Kodiak, Alaska, was the next place the Biggars would call home.

CHAPTER
3

Tina was fifteen when the Biggars moved to Kodiak.

By this time, changing addresses every few years had become a fact of life. She never had trouble making new friends, but she was reluctant to get too attached to people, knowing she'd eventually have to leave them behind.

"Tina had a lot of friends," Todd would later say. "But because she moved around so much, they weren't ones she had known her entire life. I think she missed that. I also think that's why she always put her family first."

Kodiak Island is a remote place, reachable only by air or ferry. It sits in the Gulf of Alaska, south of Cook Inlet and the Kenai Peninsula. Russian fur traders first reached the island, which is about the size of Connecticut, in 1763. They were driven away by the native Alutiiq, who have inhabited Kodiak and the islands that surround it for more than 7,500 years. Roughly twenty years later, the Russians returned and established Alaska's first European settlement. They remained in control of the island until 1867, when it was purchased by the United States.

Thousands of visitors make the trek to Kodiak each year. They come to hunt or to simply catch a glimpse of the island's most famous residents: the roughly 3,000 Kodiak brown bears who live in the Kodiak National Wildlife Refuge. Stretching across 2,491 square miles, or roughly two-thirds of the 3,670-

square-mile island, the refuge was established in 1941 by an Executive Order signed by President Franklin Delano Roosevelt, who was under pressure from conservationists to protect the bears and other wildlife.

Besides tourism, the main source of income on Kodiak Island is its fishing industry. Home to more than 700 vessels, the Port of Kodiak consistently ranks as one of the most productive in the United States. During the summer months, it also draws throngs of young people in search of high-paying jobs at one of the local canneries.

The year-round population of Kodiak Island is just over 15,000. About half the residents live in the city of Kodiak, at the island's southeastern tip. Another 2,000 make their home on the Coast Guard base, the country's largest. Bill and Connie did. They could have bought a house, but they didn't because Michigan was home and they didn't intend to stay in Kodiak after Bill's tour of duty ended.

As always, Bill and Connie's lives in Kodiak revolved around their children. "You'd always see them out together," said a former classmate of Jason Biggar's. "Or at church, or some school event.

"It was pretty obvious all the kids were close, too."

Tina entered Kodiak High School as a sophomore. There were roughly a hundred students in her class. Most had been going to school together since kindergarten. It didn't take long for Tina to find her niche. She fell in with the popular kids: the "pretty people," as they were called by the school's other cliques—the brains, the nerds, the stoners, the jocks.

"She was definitely one of the 'in crowd,' " one classmate recalled.

"But she wasn't one of those girls who thought she was better than everybody else," another former schoolmate said. "She was actually very friendly. She'd smile at people even if she didn't know them."

Tina was also considered one of the best-looking girls in her class.

"She was striking," the same schoolmate said. "And she

had these big, beautiful eyes. I don't think she even knew how pretty she was."

During the school year, a typical night out for Tina and her friends began with a basketball game or wrestling match at the high school gym. Afterwards, if it was warm enough, they'd retreat to a local beach, light a bonfire, and drink beer.

Tina lost her virginity around this time. Then, before she knew what hit her, she faced what was perhaps the most difficult decision she'd ever make in her life.

It wasn't long after Tina had her first sexual encounter that she discovered she was pregnant. The father was a local boy who, by this point, had faded out of the picture. Tina's strong Catholic upbringing meant an abortion was out of the question. That left her with two choices: keeping the baby or giving the child up for adoption.

Confused and torn, Tina hid her pregnancy from Bill and Connie, relying on baggy clothes to disguise her swelling stomach. She didn't doubt they would stand by her. She knew they would. It was more that she couldn't bear the thought of disappointing them. Especially Bill. Tina respected him more than she did anyone else. She knew he was proud of her, too. How could she let him down like this?

Tina realized she couldn't disguise her condition forever. She'd have to tell her parents eventually. Bill and Connie, naturally, were devastated when she finally broke the news. But they vowed to be there for her, even after she dropped her second bombshell: she was giving the baby up for adoption.

It wasn't a decision Tina made lightly. She'd wrestled with it night and day for months. She adored her younger brothers and sisters and dreamt of someday having a houseful of children herself. Bill and Connie adamantly opposed the idea. They wanted her to let them raise the baby while she finished school.

"She said 'No,' " a friend of her brother's remembered. "She said if she was going to be a mom, she wanted to be a full-time mom."

It was a sign of Tina's strong will and independence that, even as a teenager, she took matters into her own hands. She contacted an adoption agency and made arrangements to interview several sets of potential parents. She finally selected a childless couple who lived in a small town. They seemed to her like decent people; "very down-to-earth," she once said.

Tina made only one request of the couple who would be taking her baby into their home: that she be allowed to remain a part of the child's life. They agreed. Tina never saw her baby after the infant girl went home with her new parents. But she cherished the cards and photos that arrived in the mail several times a year.

In addition, while in college, she talked about wanting to write a book about her experience under the pen name "Sue Myers," her mother's middle and maiden names. She wanted to tell young girls who found themselves in the same position she had that adoption was an acceptable alternative to abortion.

Bill and Connie eventually came to terms with Tina's decision.

"They were very supportive," a schoolmate recalled.

Her friends in Kodiak stood by her, too.

"In a town this size, what she did wasn't easy," noted one. "People respected her for that. No one gave her any crap."

Tina did what she could to put the ordeal behind her. Over time, her life returned to normal. She even began dating again. Soon, she was in the throes of a serious relationship. But this one, too, had traumatic consequences.

Tina would never look at men the same way again.

Most of the girls at Kodiak High went out with guys from school. But some preferred to date the young Coast Guardsmen stationed on the island—"Coast Guard groupies," they were called.

"They liked the attention they got from those guys," one Kodiak High graduate explained. "But mostly they saw them as their ticket off the island."

Tina felt comfortable around the young men on the base. More than a few reminded her of her father. And like many young women, she was drawn to them for this very reason.

Tina knew it was taboo for daughters of officers to date guys from the base. She knew that Bill would be less than pleased with her if she did become involved with one, especially while she was still in high school. He may never have said so in so many words. It was more of an unwritten rule. But when it came to Luke Jackson, rules seemed to stop mattering.

Dark, muscular, and looking like he stepped off the pages of a *Gentleman's Quarterly* fashion spread, Jackson joined the U.S. Coast Guard Reserve in January 1989. Two months later, he went on active duty, assigned to the base in Kodiak. Jackson had just turned 20. Tina had celebrated her seventeenth birthday the previous New Year's Eve. That he was close to three years her senior did not matter a bit—Tina had always been mature for her age.

Tina fell hard for Jackson, a classic bad boy. She didn't care that he had a reputation as a troublemaker. In a way, this made him that much more attractive to her. She had never known anyone quite like him. Being with him was exciting. Dangerous.

Tina had a natural tendency to think more with her heart than her head. But it didn't take her long to figure out that maybe Jackson wasn't someone she wanted to share her life with. Her instincts about him proved correct. Sadly, she didn't act on them until it was too late.

Jackson was a drinker with an enormous jealous streak. He had an explosive temper. He was unpredictable, given to rages. And the longer he and Tina were together, the more possessive he became. Eventually, he became abusive. It reached the point where Tina was scared to be around him. She told Jackson she wanted out, but he insisted he wanted to marry her. He wasn't about to let her walk away.

Bill later told the police about an incident at Jackson's trailer. Tina had gone there to see the Coast Guardsman, but when she got up to go, he balked at her leaving. A terrified Tina managed to contact a friend who, in turn, got in touch with him, Bill said. He explained how he rushed over to Jackson's trailer, where the two men talked for a while. Finally, Bill convinced Jackson to let Tina leave with him.

Bill made Tina promise never to see Jackson again. She agreed she wouldn't. Bill believed his daughter. She didn't always make the wisest decisions, he thought. But he didn't think she'd lie to him. At least not about this.

Jackson was another story. What if he wasn't willing to leave Tina alone? What if he came looking for her again? As long as Tina was in Kodiak, Bill decided, she'd never be far enough away from Jackson. He knew she had to leave.

Despite her pregnancy and her tumultuous relationship with Jackson, Tina had managed to keep her grades up. As a result, she was able to graduate from Kodiak High in December 1989, half a year ahead of schedule.

She applied and was accepted to her parents' alma mater. By the fall of 1990, she'd left Kodiak for the relative calm of Brookings and SDSU. It broke Bill and Connie's hearts to watch their oldest child go. They couldn't help but worry about her. She had been through so much over the past few years. But they took solace in knowing that in Brookings, she'd be surrounded by family: her grandparents, aunts and uncles, cousins. Above all else, she'd be out of Jackson's clutches. Tina, they prayed, would never have to worry about him bothering her again.

CHAPTER
4

Although Tina missed her family, she was happy to be in Brookings. She had visited there often as a child. It had a familiar feel. In a way it was like going home.

A quintessential college town, Brookings was founded in 1879, at the very start of the "Great Dakota Boom." The little prairie community grew quickly. Within a decade, the population of Brookings and the roughly two dozen small townships that surrounded it doubled. Most of the newcomers were, like Bill Biggar's ancestors, first- and second-generation immigrants from northwestern Europe, farmers lured to the area by word of the region's rich, productive soil.

Over the last century, Brookings has managed to retain most of its small-town charm. The majority of residents still live in single-family homes on neat, tree-lined streets. It's also a safe place to live as well, consistently boasting one of the lowest crime rates of any city in the country.

Tina began her freshman year at SDSU by declaring biology as her major. Following in her father's footsteps, she also enrolled in Army ROTC.

Her classes that first semester included Military Science I, an ROTC course designed to give students a no-obligation look at career opportunities in the Army. Later in her freshman year, Tina studied Army history and Army customs and traditions, and learned how to read maps and provide first aid.

She also joined the corps' drill team, the Plains Riflemen.

Tina embraced the rigorous demands of the ROTC program. Lt. Jan Griesenbrock, one of her instructors, remembered her as an above-average student who exhibited strong leadership skills. And her fellow cadets, he added, liked and respected her.

"She would have made an excellent officer," Griesenbrock recalled thinking on more than one occasion.

In 1991, Bill was transferred back to Traverse City. Tina was thrilled, so much so that she decided to take a semester off. She'd rejoin her family in Michigan and catch up with old friends. But she stayed in South Dakota through the end of the summer, serving for four months as a U.S. Army Reservist assigned to the 323rd Chemical Company in Sioux Falls.

Tina began looking for a job as soon as she got back to Michigan. It didn't take long before she found one: a sales position at an American Eagle clothing store. Tina's friendly, outgoing personality helped her become the top-selling clerk in no time. After only a few months on the job, her bosses wanted to promote her to assistant manager. She was flattered, but said she had to pass. She was going back to school in January, she explained. They offered her more money. Tina again said no. She wanted to get on with her education. But what her bosses couldn't convince her to do—to remain in Michigan—Todd Nurnberger almost did.

The son of a postal worker and a registered nurse, Todd was born February 16, 1971, in Traverse City. The oldest of three children, he graduated from Traverse City High School in the spring of 1989 with a respectable near-"B" average. That fall, he enrolled at Northwestern Michigan College, where he hit the books and raised his grade point average to an A-minus. His hard work paid off. After two years at NMC, he applied and was accepted to the University of Michigan in Ann Arbor, where he planned to pursue a degree in chemical engineering.

Like most in-state U-M students, Todd made plans his first year there to go home over Thanksgiving break. It turned out, however, to be anything but a happy homecoming. The day before Thanksgiving, one of his closest friends from high school was in a serious car accident. Doctors gave him little chance of surviving. Todd returned to Ann Arbor the Sunday after Thanksgiving. Less than a week later, he headed back to Traverse City to bury his friend.

After the funeral, Todd's parents, hoping to take his mind off his grief, suggested a trip to the local mall. Todd, still reeling from his friend's sudden death, wasn't exactly up for shopping. But his parents meant well, so he took them up on their offer. Among the stores they visited that day was the American Eagle where Tina worked.

Tina approached Todd's mother and started chatting with her. Todd and Tina exchanged pleasantries. She seemed nice, he thought to himself. But he wasn't in the mood to make small talk. Tina spent about thirty minutes with Todd and his parents. Todd tried on and eventually settled on a few sweaters. Before they left the store, Tina gave him a tip.

"If you're going to wash the sweaters yourself, don't put them in the dryer," she said. "Let them dry naturally. Hang them over the back of a couch."

Todd nodded, managing a slight smile. He wasn't trying to be rude. It's just that his mind was a million miles away.

But riding home in his parents' car, Todd's thoughts drifted. That salesgirl was pretty, he thought to himself. She had this warmth about her, too. He'd always found that hard to resist in women.

The following day, Todd returned to the mall with his best friend, Steve Malone. As they walked by the American Eagle store, Todd peered inside. Maybe the girl who'd waited on him and his parents was working again that day. She was. He beckoned Steve to accompany him inside.

She recognized Todd immediately, greeting him with a smile.

"I need some gloves, too," he told her.

He didn't really, but he had to have some reason for coming back. Tina showed Todd the gloves the store had in stock. He took his time, finally choosing a pair. Tina directed him to the cash register. But before she moved on to her next customer, Todd tried his own sales pitch.

"I'm meeting some friends at the Sandtrap tonight," he told her, referring to the bar and restaurant that overlooks the golf course at the Grand Traverse Resort, just outside of Traverse City. Both Todd and Steve had jobs there before Todd moved to Ann Arbor. Todd, in fact, had worked at all seven of the resort's restaurants—busing, waiting, hosting, and bartending.

"Maybe I'll stop by," Tina said. She smiled—God, she has a great smile, Todd thought—then walked away.

To Todd's surprise, Tina showed up that night. He stood up to greet her.

"You know Steve," he said, greeting her. "And this is Valerie Brady."

The four of them clicked almost instantly. For several hours, they sipped cocktails, ate pizza, and played darts. Toward the end of the evening, Todd asked Tina for her phone number. He was clearly smitten. It was pretty obvious that Tina liked Todd, too. He was tall—six-foot-two; and strapping—200 pounds. He also knew how to turn on the charm.

Todd and Tina weren't able to get together again before Todd returned to Ann Arbor, but they talked by phone almost every night thereafter. And as soon as Todd finished his last final exam, he made the roughly four-hour drive north to Traverse City.

Over the Christmas holiday, Todd and Tina saw each other nearly every day. They'd meet at the mall, then spend a couple of hours shopping. Afterwards, they'd go out to dinner or catch a movie, double-dating most nights with Steve and Valerie.

Although they'd only just met and hardly knew each other, Tina invited Todd to spend part of Christmas Day with her and her family and vice versa. They exchanged gifts, too. He gave her a gold necklace. She bought him a Fossil watch.

By the time New Year's rolled around, it was clear that Tina and Todd's whirlwind romance was more than just a fling. But the start of winter semester was just around the corner. That meant Tina would be moving back to Brookings, while Todd returned to U-M.

Before Tina left Traverse City, she and Todd agreed they wanted to keep seeing each other. Other couples dated long-distance. Why couldn't they?

For four long months, they did just that. They talked incessantly, running up hefty phone bills. They also managed to see each other on four separate occasions. Tina visited Todd in Ann Arbor three times, and Todd spent U-M's spring break in Brookings. From time to time, they talked about one or the other of them transferring. Tina finally decided it made more sense for her to switch. By going to school in Michigan, she figured, she'd be closer not only to Todd but to her family as well.

Tina checked out several colleges before settling on Oakland University. She considered U-M, but worried she'd be just another face in the crowd on the giant Big 10 campus. Oakland, which had about a third as many students as Michigan, reminded her of SDSU. Oakland was attractive to Tina for other reasons as well. It was only an hour away from Ann Arbor—and Todd. It also had a strong program in physical therapy. Biology, she'd decided, wasn't for her.

In the spring of 1992, Todd drove to Brookings, where he and Tina packed up her belongings. They fit what they could in his car, shipped the rest, and left for Michigan, excited by the prospect of being in the same state again. Still, the romantic summer they'd pictured for themselves didn't quite pan out.

CHAPTER
5

Both Tina and Todd had lined up summer restaurant jobs in Traverse City, but their grueling schedules kept them apart more than they'd hoped. Tina also wanted to spend time with her parents and brothers and sisters before school started in the fall. Todd understood this. He knew how much she'd missed them after she went back to Brookings. But he wanted Tina to make him a priority, too. She, in turn, complained he spent too much time with his friends.

Even their sex life—or lack thereof—became a source of tension. Tina and Todd had been sleeping together for months. But back in Traverse City, both were living under their parents' roofs. It meant overnight stays were out of the question.

Despite the many strains on their relationship, breaking up wasn't something Tina and Todd ever considered. They focused, instead, on the fall and on the promise of the coming school year.

Just prior to her first semester at Oakland, Tina moved into an apartment that was just a few minutes from campus. She shared the three-bedroom apartment with two roommates, both Oakland students. At the same time, Todd used a restaurant connection to help Tina secure a job at the Rochester Chop House and Oyster Bar, an eatery known for its steaks and bins of oysters, clams, and mussels. Because Tina was putting herself through school, she needed to earn as much money as possible.

That fall, Tina and Todd managed to see each other at least two or three times a week. They got to spend weekends together as well, falling into a happy rhythm. Tina was walking on air. Things were working with Todd, she felt challenged at school, and she loved her job at the Chop House, where she sometimes pulled in more than $100 a night in tips alone.

"She was an incredible waitress," said Chop House manager Aimee Vermeersch, a close friend of Tina's. "It didn't matter how many hours she'd just spent at school or how many tables she had. She'd come in and blow everybody out of the water."

Tina and Todd were so busy they barely noticed the fall fly by. Before they knew it, the holidays were around the corner. They planned to spend Thanksgiving in Traverse City. Tina, however, couldn't get away until Thanksgiving Day itself, so Todd drove north alone the day before. That night, he got together with some high school pals. Over drinks, they reminisced about their friend whose fatal accident had taken place exactly one year ago to the day. On the way home, about a mile from his parents' house, Todd ran out of gas. He pulled over to the side of the road, lifted his hood, and turned on the car's emergency lights. Surely someone would come by and realize he needed help. But that someone turned out to be a Grand Traverse County sheriff's deputy. Smelling liquor on Todd's breath, the officer asked him to take a Breathalyzer test. He agreed, failed, and was arrested for Driving While Impaired.

Todd felt like an idiot. He knew he never should have gotten behind the wheel. But he truly believed he was sober enough to make it home safely. Making matters worse was the fact that he'd served as a reserve officer with the sheriff's department while attending Northwestern Michigan College. As a result, he knew everyone at the station where he was booked. When Todd told Tina about his arrest, she blew up.

"What were you thinking?" she demanded to know.

*   *   *

Todd's arrest made for changes in his and Tina's relationship. With his restricted license, he could drive only to and from his job at Robby's at the Ice House, a downtown Ann Arbor restaurant. That meant whenever he and Tina wanted to get together, she'd have to come to Ann Arbor. Before Todd's arrest, they'd taken turns making the hour-long commute. Now the responsibility for making the effort fell entirely on Tina's shoulders. She was hardly thrilled with the situation. But she didn't have much of a choice. In the spring, much to Tina's relief, Todd got his license back. It wouldn't be for long.

One weekend in July, Todd drove up north to meet some friends at a wine festival. On the way back, he was stopped by a cop for driving erratically. This time he faced a more serious charge: Operating Under the Influence of Liquor.

Todd was arrested. Later that summer, he served a two-week sentence in the Leelanau County Jail. Tina was furious when she found out that he'd been busted again. She told him she had "no intention" of visiting him while he did his time. She softened, however, and made the trip after all. Their meeting in the jail was an emotional one.

"We both just sat there and cried," Todd later recalled.

In the fall of 1993, Tina moved into a new apartment with one of her roommates from the previous year. Todd also got a new address. He had been living with four buddies, but wanted more privacy than that arrangement provided. He moved into a smaller place—a two-bedroom apartment he shared with a single roommate, a PhD student who was more an acquaintance than a friend.

Although Todd's jail time was behind him, he wasn't through paying for his mistake. His second arrest had cost him his license altogether. He was forbidden to drive anywhere for a full six months. This meant Tina, again, had to make all the effort if she wanted to continue seeing Todd.

"She used to bust her butt for him," Vermeersch recalled. "She'd work on a Saturday night, then jump in her car and drive all the way to Ann Arbor."

Actually, at this point, nothing was going right for Todd.

Business was off at the restaurant where he worked. Tips, as a result, were down. At the Chop House, on the other hand, Tina continued to earn top dollar. So when she and Todd did go out, she usually ended up footing the bill, which was sometimes considerable. Both Tina and Todd had a tendency to spend their money as fast as they earned it, whether they could afford to or not. Both liked dining in upscale restaurants. They liked expensive wine, too. It wasn't unusual for them to run up $100 dinner tabs.

By late fall, Tina and Todd's relationship was more strained than ever. Tina began resenting the hours she had to spend on the road because Todd had screwed up. She was tired of paying for everything they did.

Todd was drowning in guilt. As fall turned to winter, he became increasingly depressed. But instead of getting his life together, he only made things worse. And again, he'd have no one but himself to blame.

Not long after Todd first arrived at the University of Michigan, a buddy from his dorm hall introduced him to a fellow student named Nancy Chandler. Todd was attracted to Nancy, who was tall and pretty. Nancy liked Todd, too. But she already had a boyfriend, so neither she nor Todd acted on their feelings. They did, however, become good friends. By early January, Todd and Tina's relationship was in serious trouble. More than once they'd talked about splitting up. Tina resented Todd more than ever. Todd, meanwhile, was starting to feel less guilty and more angry himself. He was tired of Tina blaming him for all their problems. He knew he had screwed up. But he began wondering: Was she ever going to stop throwing it in his face?

Todd wasn't exactly looking forward to the upcoming semester either. In particular, he dreaded a French class he had to take in order to graduate. Not wanting to blow his overall grade point, he asked Nancy to tutor him. At first, their relationship was platonic. But neither tried to hide the amorous feelings they had for one another. One night, following a late-night tutoring session, one thing led to another and Todd and Nancy ended up in bed. Over the next two months, they slept together five times. After each of his romps with Nancy, Todd swore it would never happen again.

By the end of February, the affair was over. Todd considered telling Tina, but he feared if he did, she'd dump him for good. He knew how jealous Tina could be. He'd found out firsthand not long after they first started dating.

In the winter of 1992, while Tina was still at SDSU, Todd visited an old friend who was going to school in Ohio. When Tina learned about the trip, she was furious and accused Todd of cheating on her. He swore nothing had happened, but she refused to believe him. She struck back by sleeping with a friend in Brookings. She even called Todd to boast to him about it.

Because of the way Tina had reacted then, Todd thought long and hard about confessing his affair to Tina. In the end, he decided to keep his mouth shut. The long, cold Michigan winter was about to end. Spring was around the corner. And, best of all, he'd soon have his driver's license back.

By the summer of 1994, Tina and Todd's relationship was back on track. Convinced they had a future together, Todd asked Tina to move in with him. There was no point, he argued, in their continuing to pay two rents. Tina, with the memory of the past six months still fresh in her mind, wasn't so sure. And although she had yet to renew her lease, she'd pretty much planned to stay put.

Todd, though disappointed, accepted Tina's decision. It turned out, however, not to be as final as he thought. One night in late July, at around 2 A.M., Todd's phone rang. It was Tina. She'd thought it over and had changed her mind: She wanted to move in with him. Immediately after hanging up the phone, an elated Todd rushed to a twenty-four-hour supermarket, where he picked up an apartment guide with listings for rentals halfway between Ann Arbor and Oakland. The very next day, he and Tina found a place: a one-bedroom apartment in the Detroit suburb of Farmington Hills.

The lease at Tina and Todd's new apartment didn't begin until September 1. Tina was able to arrange to stay at her old place until then. Todd, however, had to be out of his by mid-August. So Todd moved in with Tina and her roommate for two weeks. One day, while Todd was out, Tina began un-packing some of his boxes. Inside of one, she found a sexu-ally suggestive greeting card addressed to Todd. Her eyes quickly moved to the signature at the bottom. It was Nancy's.

Furious, Tina immediately picked up the telephone and called Todd's old roommate.

"Did Nancy ever spend the night at your apartment?" she demanded.

He said she had.

Tina exploded. Not only had Todd slept with Nancy, he'd lied to her about it. Earlier that summer, Tina and Todd had been driving in the car, talking about their relationship. Some-how, the subject of infidelity came up.

"I've thought about it," Tina confessed. "And I've had the chance. But that's it. Have you ever cheated on me?"

"No," Todd swore.

As soon as Todd came back to the apartment that August night, Tina confronted him with the card.

"I know you slept with Nancy," she declared.

Todd admitted he had. Tina, he later said, "went ballistic."

Later that night, once Tina had calmed down, Todd men-tioned something about their upcoming move.

"Live with you?" Tina said incredulously. "I don't even know if I still want to see you."

An uneasiness filled the air over the next week or so as Tina weighed her options. One day, she'd hint she could put Todd's affair behind them. The next, she'd imply they were through. One night, Todd noticed Tina wasn't wearing the sapphire and diamond ring he'd given her.

"What happened to your ring?" he asked.

"I threw it out the car window," she said, looking him straight in the eye.

Less than a week before they were to move, Tina told Todd she'd made up her mind.

"I'm willing to give you another chance," she said, "but I'm not making any promises."

She also made it clear to Todd he wasn't off the hook entirely, warning him, "You're going to have to put up with a lot of shit."

Todd wasn't exactly sure what Tina meant by that. But he found out soon enough. A few days later after Tina had agreed to go ahead with the move, she and Todd went to a party at a friend's apartment. They'd only been there a few minutes when Todd bumped into an old friend and stopped to catch up. After a while, he went looking for Tina. He eventually found her out by the complex's pool, kissing a well-dressed, forty-ish man Todd didn't recognize. This time it was Todd who flew into a rage. He stormed away, then marched back. Moments later, he and Tina were screaming at each other.

"Don't you dare compare what I'm doing to what you did," she yelled.

"At least I didn't do it right in front of your face," Todd shouted back.

When friends asked her about the fight several days after the fact, Tina brushed their concerns aside.

"She said she was going to pay him back for what he did to her," Aimee Vermeersch would later recall. "She wanted to see him suffer."

CHAPTER
6

On September 1, 1994, Tina and Todd moved into their new place, a comfortable one-bedroom unit they filled with contemporary furniture. A typically large Midwestern complex with many amenities, Muirwood had an outdoor swimming pool, multiple lighted tennis courts, and acres of winding jogging and hiking paths. Residents also had access to the Muirwood Health Club, which featured an indoor wave pool, a sauna, and an exercise center.

But it was hardly a love nest. For the first couple of months, Todd bent over backwards trying to make amends for his infidelity.

"He kissed her ass all the time," says Vermeersch.

He also attempted to convince Tina's friends to put in a good word for him.

"We were all at this one party and for two hours he sat there telling me how much he loved her and how sorry he was," recalls Vermeersch. "I said, 'Todd, don't tell me. Tell Tina.'"

Chances are it wouldn't have made any difference. Tina refused to cut Todd any slack. If he happened to be running late, or wasn't where he said he was going to be at a given time, an accusatory Tina gave him the third-degree. But whenever Todd queried Tina about her schedule, she'd blow up and make a snide comment about Nancy. Eventually, a weary Todd just stopped asking.

Because of the flare-ups at home, Todd didn't mind that his busy schedule kept him away from the apartment most days and some evenings. In August, he'd begun working in Ann Arbor as a chemist for Warner Lambert–Parke-Davis' pharmaceutical research division. His job was to help develop methods for testing yet-to-be-released drugs and those already on the market. Todd juggled the job with a full course load at U-M and a couple of wait shifts a week at D. Dennison's Seafood Tavern, a Farmington Hills restaurant not far from his and Tina's apartment. Tina's schedule was equally hectic. She, too, was going to school full-time and working even more than Todd: typically five 4 to 11 P.M. shifts weekly at the Chop House.

By now, Tina had changed her major again, from physical therapy to psychology. The reason: a course she'd taken the year before with a psychology professor named Algea Harrison. Harrison became a mentor to Tina, who had decided she wanted to go on to graduate school and eventually become a psychology professor herself. It was also through Harrison that Tina became involved in the project that set in motion a series of events that ultimately resulted in her death.

That September, Tina was one of eight Oakland students who volunteered to assist Harrison in a research project on AIDS awareness funded by the Centers for Disease Control (CDC). The group was assigned to interview female prostitutes incarcerated for short-term sentences at the Dickerson Detention Center in Hamtramck, a tiny, self-governing municipality located within Detroit city limits. First, the students from Oakland would ask the women what they knew about AIDS and HIV, the virus that causes AIDS. Then, students from Wayne State University in Detroit would visit the center and teach the women about the disease: how it's transmitted and how they could protect themselves from contracting it. Afterwards, the Oakland group would return to the center and reinterview the women in an attempt to gauge how much of the information they'd retained. The students and prisoners were under observation at all times by detention center personnel. Under the study's rules, the students also were prohibited from having contact with the women outside the jail structure.

Tina spent that first semester learning how to conduct the interviews and other tasks related to the project. She also attended training sessions during which she and the other volunteers were given clear and sternly worded warnings against becoming personally involved with the subjects.

Eventually, Tina began going to the jail with a woman named Danielle Lentine, a senior at Oakland, Harrison's chief assistant, and Tina's officemate. Tina would observe Danielle conducting interviews. Later, they switched roles: Tina would do the interviewing while Danielle observed. Danielle was responsible for ensuring that Tina followed the correct protocol.

The detention center was not the most hospitable environment, but Tina wasn't the least bit fearful. To her, it was a lot like ROTC: a challenge she was determined to meet.

"Tina was a very, very strong person," said Vermeersch. "She wasn't intimidated by anything."

As the fall wore on, Tina and Danielle grew closer. In November, they roomed together during a trip to CDC headquarters in Atlanta. Along with Harrison and other students involved in the project, they attended a conference related to the research. The trip was authorized and paid for by the university.

Tina and Danielle soon began spending time together outside the classroom, too. Danielle later told police that they hadn't been friends long when Tina confided she and Todd were having problems. Tina told Danielle she'd found out about Todd's affair, and that their relationship was "on the rocks." She wanted to get "revenge" against him by having an affair herself, Tina said.

But by November, it was beginning to look—to Todd, at least—as though Tina's resentment toward him was starting to fade. They were getting along better than they had in quite some time, he thought. Their lives, it seemed to him, were returning to normal.

Although school and work took up most of their time, Tina

and Todd maintained a healthy social life. They threw dinner parties at their apartment, with Todd, a gourmet chef, preparing his signature salmon with lobster cream sauce. They saw a lot of Steve and Valerie, who'd moved to the Lansing area, about ninety minutes away. And they made frequent trips to Traverse City, usually at least once a month.

Todd's infidelity, however, remained a point of contention. That November, Tina and Todd went to Chicago with Steve and Valerie to help the latter celebrate their engagement. Heading home, after four days of nonstop partying, Todd began thinking that maybe he and Tina were going to make it after all. He was sadly mistaken. About two hours into the drive, Tina threw a fit.

"How could you fuck another woman and not have the gall to tell me?" she screamed at him.

Not wanting to exacerbate the situation, Todd simply sat there in silence. Steve and Valerie, who were aware of the problems Tina and Todd had been having over the past several months, also said nothing.

Tina would also bring up the affair when she and Todd were alone. But instead of the bitter girlfriend, she sounded more like an insecure lover.

"I want to marry you," she'd said once. "But I'm afraid when I'm pregnant and ugly you'll go out and have an affair."

For months, Tina ran hot and cold. But through it all, the one aspect of Tina and Todd's relationship that never suffered was their sex life. Even when it seemed like they were on the verge of breaking up, they never stopped being intimate. This, perhaps more than anything, convinced Todd that he and Tina still had a chance.

When it came to sex, Tina and Todd weren't beyond a little experimentation either. One Friday night, not long after the Chicago trip, Todd and Tina and Steve and Valerie went to see a band at a club in East Lansing. Dreading the ninety-minute drive home and the prospect of crashing at the house Steve shared with several roommates, Todd and Tina decided to get a motel room. Steve and Valerie agreed to join them.

They ended up renting a single room with two double beds. At around 1 A.M., Todd and Steve left on a beer run. They returned a short time later to find Tina and Valerie sitting next to each other in one of the beds. The two women had a blanket pulled over them. It was obvious, though, that beneath the blanket they were both naked.

The two couples had shared a room while traveling together many times before. And each had made love in their bed while the other pair slept or did the same. They had even joked among themselves about having a foursome.

Already buzzed, Todd and Steve began playing a popular college drinking game. The rules were simple: Every time either of them guzzled a beer, they got to remove a single article of clothing. Tina and Valerie egged them on. By the time the sun came up, they'd all had sex numerous times. They'd tried every possible combination, with the exception of same-sex pairings.

The foursome ended up sleeping together again on only one other occasion: one night, the following spring, at Tina and Todd's apartment. Again, it was a drinking game—this time, strip poker—that got the evening rolling.

CHAPTER
7

January brought not only a new year, but a new semester as well. Buoyed by encouragement from Harrison, Tina immersed herself in the CDC project.

"At work, it was all she ever talked about," recalled Aimee Vermeersch. "To me. To the cooks. To the bar staff. To other waitresses. She was just so excited about it."

Tina gushed about Harrison as well.

"She loved her," Vermeersch said. "She wanted to be her."

Vermeersch wasn't the least bit surprised that Tina got swept up in the project. In a way, it was tailor-made for her.

"Tina," she said, "was an incredible listener. She made you feel like you could talk to her about anything. And no matter what kind of problem you had, you never felt like she was judging you. She'd say, 'Everybody has a skeleton or two in their closet, including me.' "

By this time, Tina needed three more semesters' worth of credits to earn her bachelor's degree. Graduate school was next, she'd decided. She was convinced, though, it would take more than good grades to get into a top program. She knew the work she'd done on the CDC study would look impressive on an application. But what else could she do, she asked herself, to ensure she'd stand out from other applicants? The answer: her own research project.

One day, Tina and Danielle were at work in their office

when Tina began thinking out loud. She told Danielle she'd been reviewing the interviews she'd conducted for the CDC study and that she'd found herself wondering whether "high-price call girls"—women who worked for escort agencies and tended to service a somewhat more upscale clientele—were any more knowledgeable about AIDS than women who worked the streets. She said she suspected they were, and that as a result, fewer were likely to test positive for HIV.

"I bet they make their customers wear condoms, too," Danielle said.

Tina snapped back.

"Of course they do," she said in an uncharacteristically testy tone. "Those girls are high class."

That spring, Tina became obsessed with spending the following fall semester conducting her own research project. Since she'd had little trouble getting the women from the CDC project to open up to her, she was confident she could also convince women who worked for escort services to confide in her. She began calling services that advertised in the *Metro Times*, a free, weekly alternative newspaper distributed around metro Detroit. If an answering machine picked up at the other end, she simply left a message explaining who she was and what she wanted. She also called several services whose phone numbers she'd obtained from women at the jail.

The women she'd interviewed liked Tina. She didn't look down at them. They even joked with her about turning tricks herself.

"They told her all the time how attractive she was," Aimee Vermeersch said. "And that she'd do really well as an escort because she was so smart."

It was in the spring of 1995 that Tina first approached Harrison about her honors project. She was thrilled when Harrison agreed to serve as her faculty sponsor and immediately began drafting a proposal. But before she could begin doing fieldwork, the proposal needed to be approved by the university's Institutional Review Board, whose primary role is to protect the rights of human subjects participating in research projects.

Tina hadn't felt this good about herself in a long time. She and Todd were getting along better than they ever had. Yet, as August rolled around, their relationship reached a crossroads. With the lease on their apartment about to expire at the end of the month, they had to start thinking not only about their future living arrangements but about their future in general. In the past, they'd talked about getting married. Todd still believed they would someday. They'd even looked at a few houses together. But Tina had her doubts, especially since her relationship with Todd had been punctuated by so many ups and downs over the years.

Tina told Todd that before she could make a lifelong commitment to him she needed to live on her own for awhile.

"There are some things I need to straighten out," she said. "I'm not saying I want to break up. But I'll understand if you do."

Tina's pronouncement didn't exactly surprise Todd, but it brought to mind a conversation they'd had a couple of weeks earlier.

Todd had a habit of letting things slide until the last minute. This drove Tina crazy. So from the day they began living together, Tina put herself in charge of paying the bills. As a result, Todd hardly ever looked at them. One day, however, he happened to pick up a recent telephone bill. He noticed what seemed like fairly regular calls to an Indianapolis number. He didn't know anyone who lived there. He didn't think Tina did either.

When he asked Tina about it, she told him the number belonged to a man named Peter Nelson. He was in his early thirties and worked with computers. One day, while in Detroit on business, he had dined at the Chop House, Tina explained. They'd struck up a conversation and Peter had said he would call her the next time he was in town. They ended up going out several times. But only, she was quick to note, as friends. She confessed, however, that if had shown interest in her, she might have reciprocated.

Todd tried not to let it bother him. After all, nothing had actually happened, he told himself. The only reason Tina had told him about Peter was to make him jealous.

Todd agreed to give Tina the space she was asking for and immediately began looking for a place for himself in Ann Arbor. Although he'd be graduating from U-M with a degree in chemistry in less than a month, he wasn't leaving school. He was still in the process of meeting the requirements for a chemical engineering degree. Then there was his job at Parke-Davis.

Tina, on the other hand, put off looking for a new place to live. Instead, she concentrated on finishing her proposal. She finally did, and on July 31, submitted it to Harrison.

Titled "Survey of Sexual History and Health Practices Among Women Employed as Escorts," Tina's proposal included an abstract in which she characterized the project as "a descriptive study aimed at assessing sexual histories and health practices among women working in the commercial sex industry as escorts." Tina went on to note that she planned to use her findings to make recommendations about ways to educate this little-studied population about sexually transmitted diseases and the transmission of HIV, the virus that causes AIDS.

Tina detailed how she planned to either interview twenty women who worked as escorts for one of two services, or to have them fill out questionnaires. She identified the operations as Fantasy Fun Capital I and Fantasy Fun Capital II, but added that these were pseudonyms for actual escort services. The point of using aliases, Tina wrote, was "to protect the confidentiality of all parties involved."

She went on to explain that she planned to select her subjects at random from employee lists provided by the two services. The women chosen would be told about the study and then asked if they were interested in participating. The actual interviews would be conducted at the escort service offices and last approximately 30 to 45 minutes.

Questions about sexual experiences prior to the age of 16, the subject's use of alcohol, cigarettes and controlled substances, sexual experiences over the past two years, and how the subjects viewed themselves were included in a fourteen-page questionnaire attached to the proposal. They were typical of those the women would be asked to answer. The subjects would also be asked to take a true-false quiz attempting to determine how much they knew about AIDS.

Harrison eventually signed off on the proposal, which Tina ultimately submitted to the IRB. The fact that Tina and Harrison followed through on the proposal, however, came as a troubling surprise to Oakland Psychology Professor and IRB Chairman Dean Purcell.

Earlier in the summer, Purcell happened to bump into Harrison in a campus parking lot. According to Purcell, Harrison told him, ''I'm going to be sponsoring a new project that's related to the CDC study. Does the proposal have to go through the full IRB approval process again?''

''Does it differ from the original?'' Purcell asked.

''It's going to be a study of high-class call girls,'' Harrison responded.

''That sounds different. How is the student going to access this population?''

''She knows some of the girls.''

Purcell didn't like the sound of it.

''I would never supervise an undergraduate project like that,'' he said. The conversation ended then and there.

A faculty member at Oakland since 1974 and chair of the eight-member IRB since January 1995, Purcell had several immediate concerns. For one, he questioned the wisdom of sanctioning an undergraduate student to become involved with subjects who participated in ongoing criminal activity.

Purcell also found it hard to believe that the escort services Tina had contacted were so willing to help her out.

''I don't know what an escort service office is like,'' he would later say. ''It may be a perfectly tame place that welcomes research. But my gut feeling was that these people were not, with a capital 'N,' going to want a student mucking around in their business.''

Purcell also was uncomfortable with the fact that Tina had

made preliminary contact with the escort services prior to obtaining approval for the project from the IRB.

It turned out that Purcell wasn't the only faculty member troubled by Tina's proposal. When Purcell mentioned it to several colleagues, they, too, expressed serious reservations.

"They all agreed it seemed like a pretty far-out thing for an undergraduate to be doing," he later said.

Once the proposal officially landed on his desk, Purcell voiced his concerns to Don McCrimmon, Oakland's director of grants, contracts, and sponsored research.

"I think you're probably right," McCrimmon told Purcell after hearing only a brief description of Tina's proposed project. McCrimmon, in fact, was concerned enough that he suggested they consult a lawyer about the subjects' rights and about any possible liability the university might face if the study went awry.

Purcell was confident a lawyer would recommend against approval. And while he couldn't say for sure how the IRB's eight board members would vote when presented with the proposal, he was certain about one thing: it would not get his vote.

CHAPTER
8

Around this same time, Todd began noticing that Tina seemed depressed and high-strung. He knew she was anxious about her project and about receiving approval from the IRB. But something told him it was more than that. The proposal alone, he remembers thinking at the time, couldn't be the sole reason behind her extreme mood swings.

Out of nowhere, Tina began apologizing for the way she'd treated him when they first moved in together.

"Why don't you leave me?" she asked him more than once. "You deserve someone better."

But before Todd even had a chance to respond, she'd say something hurtful. Or just plain mean.

Todd wasn't sure what to make of Tina's behavior. But he didn't see any point in calling her on it. At least not yet.

One of the things Tina had been complaining most about was her car. It needed new brakes, but she was short of cash. Todd figured his car could use a new set, too. So he bought shoes and pads for both and said he'd install them himself on his day off. However, the day he planned to repair the cars, he got called in to work. When he told Tina, she got mad.

"I'll have Ken do it," she huffed.

Although he'd never met Tina's friend Ken, Todd didn't have a very good feeling about him. He owned the Q Club, a bar in Pontiac, not far from the Chop House. Tina had been picking up occasional wait shifts there since the winter.

Ken had called the apartment a couple of times looking for Tina. But if Todd happened to answer the phone, he was incredibly abrupt. One call, in particular, had struck Todd as especially strange. One morning, while Tina was showering, the phone rang. Todd picked it up. He didn't recognize the voice on the other end.

"Is Crystal there?" the man asked.

"Who?" asked Todd.

"Crystal."

"There's nobody here by that name."

"Oh, I mean, Tina."

"She's here. But she's in the shower."

"Will you tell her Ken called?"

Todd said he would. He hung up the phone and went to give Tina the message.

"Why would he call you Crystal?" he asked her.

"I don't know why," she said. "He's weird."

Tina assured Todd that she wasn't the least bit interested in Ken as anything other than a friend. He was older, she said. And not very good-looking. And he stammered when he spoke.

Todd didn't understand why Tina couldn't just wait for him to work on her car. He left the apartment that day less than thrilled with the prospect of Ken doing the job. When he finally returned home that night, at around 10 P.M., he planned to tell Tina exactly how he felt. But she wasn't there and didn't arrive for another ninety minutes.

Tina was barely inside the apartment before she warned Todd that she wasn't in the mood for a fight. Ken, she complained, had taken forever to fix her brakes. Afterwards, as a way of saying thank you, she took him out to dinner. But while they were eating, some people Ken knew happened to come into the restaurant. He then proceeded to buy them drinks on Tina's tab.

"I'm going to bed," Tina announced. Todd followed a short time later. The subject of the brakes never came up again.

Tina's mood swings continued over the next couple of

weeks. Especially puzzling to Todd was her behavior following a traffic accident she had on August 14. It happened only
a few minutes from Muirwood, on the I-696 Expressway. It
had been raining and the road was slick. Tina lost control of
her car, spun off into a ravine, and hit a small tree. Uninjured,
she managed to hitch a ride to D. Dennison's, where Todd
was working at the time. Tina was clearly shaken from the
accident. But oddly enough, she was as upset about having
to cancel an appointment to see an apartment—she'd started
looking—as she was about any damage to her car, a Honda
Accord she'd owned for about two years.

"She was extremely clingy that day," Todd said later.
"She kept saying over and over, 'I'm so glad you're here.
I'm so lucky to have you.'"

Todd arranged to get off early that night. He drove Tina
back to her car. It wouldn't start, so they called a nearby
garage for a tow. The police also came by. Making matters
worse, they gave Tina a ticket for not immediately reporting
the accident.

The car's body appeared to have escaped serious damage,
which was a big relief to Tina. She'd been complaining for
weeks about how broke she was. The next day, though, she
learned the suspension had been totaled. Fixing it would cost
$500. "Do whatever you have to," she told the man at the
garage, "and bill it to my credit card."

The accident and the cost of repairing the car seemed to
leave Tina more stressed out than before. Then, suddenly,
only a few days after the accident, Tina told Todd her car
problems had been solved. She'd been by the Q Club and had
talked to Ken. When she mentioned the accident, he asked
her why she didn't just buy a new car. She'd told him she
couldn't afford to. Out of the blue, she said, he offered to
make her a loan. He explained he'd recently inherited a large
sum of money. She could borrow "however" much she
needed, he said. Once she got her finances straightened out,
she could start paying him back.

Tina admitted she was a bit apprehensive at first. She wondered, for example, what would happen if Ken decided he

wanted all the money back at once. But after thinking it over, she'd decided to accept Ken's offer.

Tina told Todd she and Ken had gone by the dealership where she'd purchased her last car to see what was on the lot. She picked out a 1993 Honda Accord. It cost about $15,000. If everything went according to schedule, the car would be hers Monday, August 21.

Todd was suspicious. It didn't make any sense that the owner of a club where Tina hardly ever worked was willing to lend her so much money. But whenever he brought it up, Tina got angry.

"I'm not supposed to talk about it," she said. "Ken doesn't want anybody to know about the loan because he doesn't want other people asking him for money, too."

Bill Biggar also had reservations about the loan. Tina had told her parents about her boss's offer. Bill said he didn't know if it was a good idea for her to accept such a large sum of money from someone she barely knew.

"Are you sure you know what you're doing?" he asked his daughter. "Is this all on the up and up?"

Tina managed to convince Bill that Ken was legitimate and that he didn't have any ulterior motives. He simply wanted to do her a favor because she had helped him out in the past by picking up shifts.

A few days later, Tina told Todd that she'd gone back to the dealership to complete all the necessary paperwork. The money, she said, was in the process of being transferred from a bank in England. It was being sent to Ken by his mother-in-law, the mother of his late wife. According to Ken, his wife had been killed by friendly fire during the Gulf War. Once the money arrived, all he'd have to do is exchange it for American currency. Then, he'd give Tina a cashier's check that would cover not only the cost of the car, but a few overdue bills she'd talked about needing to pay.

Maybe the car would be enough to pull Tina out of her funk, Todd thought to himself. But then she did something around the same time that was so totally out of character, his concern, which had been ebbing, turned to alarm.

One of Tina's brothers was flying into Detroit. Bill and Connie had arranged to meet him at the airport. They told Tina about their plans and she agreed to come as well. But on the evening of his arrival, Todd received a call from Connie. She was worried. Tina hadn't shown up.

"Is everything okay?" Connie wanted to know.

Todd said he hadn't heard from Tina.

"Something must have come up," he told Connie. "I'll have her call you as soon as she comes home."

Later that night, when Tina finally did return to the apartment, Todd asked her why she hadn't gone to the airport. She insisted she had. She just hadn't been able to find her parents or her brother there. This made absolutely no sense to Todd. Tina had been to the Detroit airport many times. Even if she had gotten lost, why hadn't she had them paged? To Todd, these were legitimate questions. But Tina seemed stressed enough already. He didn't press the matter further.

Tina's behavior grew increasingly peculiar. Not long after the airport incident, Tina told Todd she'd found an apartment in Ferndale, a suburb just north of Detroit. She described the apartment, about a twenty-minute drive from the Oakland campus, as a "fixer-upper." Because of its condition, the landlord was willing to give her a short-term lease. He had agreed to rent it to her for $450 a month, which she thought was pretty reasonable. She'd also made a deal with the landlord to deduct the cost of any repairs or improvements she made from the rent.

"Maybe my luck is finally changing," she told Todd. Maybe, Todd thought to himself, that's all it was. Maybe he had been overreacting.

But only a few days later, Tina was distraught again. The night of the twenty-first, she walked in the door just before 11 P.M. She was livid, she announced.

Ken's mother-in-law was having trouble transferring the money for the car. Instead, she was going to bring it here herself. She and Ken were supposed to meet her at the dealership at 7 P.M., but the woman never showed. Three hours later, Tina told Ken she was through waiting.

"Call me when you have the money," she told him.

*   *   *

The following morning, Todd got up and went to work at Parke-Davis. When he got home, at around 4:45 P.M., he found Tina sitting in the living room in front of the television. It was obvious she wasn't paying any attention to whatever was on. In fact, she seemed even more upset than she had been the night before.

"What's wrong?" he asked.

Tina told him she and Ken had been painting her new apartment when the ceiling in another apartment in the same building collapsed. The entire structure had been condemned.

"My whole life is going to shit," Tina yelled.

"Is there any news about the car?" Todd asked.

"I don't want to talk about it," she said glumly. "But it's going to be a miracle if this deal ever goes through."

Todd went into the bedroom, changed for his shift at D. Dennison's, then went back into the living room. He knew Tina had been counting on moving into the apartment in Ferndale. She'd even arranged for her parents to come down from Traverse City the weekend of the twenty-fifth to help her move.

Todd told Tina she could stay with him at his new apartment in Ann Arbor until she found a new place. He also admitted how worried he'd been about her.

"It's just that you've seemed so unhappy lately," he said. "What's going on?"

Tina stared off in the distance.

"Please, just tell me what's going on," Todd pleaded. "Whatever the problem is, we'll work it out together."

"Can you find someone to work for you tomorrow night?" she asked. "There is something I need to tell you."

Todd said he'd try to find a sub. Just before 6 P.M., he left for work.

It was sometime between 11 and 11:30 P.M. that Todd returned home. Tina was gone. Todd went to sleep about an hour later. When he woke up the following morning, at about 6 A.M., Tina was in bed beside him. Todd got up, took a shower, and got ready for work. Before he left, he stuck his head back in the bedroom to tell Tina he was leaving. She was still sound asleep.

CHAPTER
9

On Wednesday, August 23, Todd worked his normal nine-hour shift. The day, however, seemed to last forever. Todd was anxious to go home. That night, he kept thinking, he'd finally find out what had been making Tina behave so strangely.

By early afternoon, Todd had found someone to work for him at D. Dennison's that night. He called Tina at the apartment to let her know, but the answering machine picked up. Todd tried reaching her via her pager and her cellular phone, but she never called back. Todd left Parke-Davis at about 4 P.M., stopping on the way home to pick up some carpeting he'd ordered for his new place. It was around six when he got back to Muirwood.

Tina still wasn't home. Todd tried her pager again. No luck. He started to become concerned. Tina usually returned his pages right away. But he'd been beeping her all afternoon and he'd yet to hear anything.

He didn't know what else to do, so he simply sat waiting for Tina to return home. He spent most of the night staring at the television, unable to focus. When, by 11 P.M., Tina still had neither returned his pages nor come home, he decided to call the Chop House. Maybe she'd agreed to work at the last minute and was too busy to get back to him.

The first time Todd called, the person who picked up told him Tina wasn't working that night.

"Was she there at all?" he asked.

Whoever answered the phone wasn't sure. But if she had been there, she'd already left. Forty-five minutes later Todd tried the Chop House again. This time, he was told she hadn't worked there for three or four months.

How could that be? Todd thought to himself. Tina hadn't said anything to him about quitting, or even about cutting back her shifts. And if she wasn't at the Chop House all those nights she said she was, where had she been?

The realization that Tina had been lying to him for months made Todd sick. But he was more worried than anything else. It was close to 1 A.M. In all the time they'd lived together, Tina had never stayed out so late without calling. Todd waited up as long as he could fight off his exhaustion, then finally fell asleep. He awoke Thursday morning at roughly 6 A.M. Tina had not come home at all. Todd checked the answering machine. There were no messages from Tina or anyone else.

Todd didn't know what to do next. So he left for Parke-Davis, arriving at around 7:30 A.M. As soon as he got there, he told his supervisor what was going on.

"Do you think I should be worried?" he asked her.

She suggested he call Bill and Connie.

He reached Connie first. It was around 8 A.M.

"Tina didn't come home last night," he told her.

Connie, alarmed, called Bill at work. Over the next two hours, Todd spoke to both Connie and Bill several times. He also called the Michigan State Police and the Farmington police. But neither had taken any reports on anyone who matched Tina's description. Todd tried the Chop House again, and then the Q Club. No one had seen Tina.

Todd asked his supervisor if he could have the rest of the day off. He left Ann Arbor just after 10 A.M. Before going home, however, he stopped at the Honda dealership. He spoke with a salesman named Phil Black. Black confirmed that Tina and a male friend had been in several times over the past week and that she'd settled on a used Honda Accord. At Todd's request, he went over Tina's file. The man Tina had come in with was named Ken. Todd asked Black for a description of Ken. He also gave Black his pager number and asked the salesman to beep him if he heard from either Ken or Tina.

Next, Todd drove to the Oakland campus. He headed straight for Harrison's office. Maybe Tina was out doing some kind of research. If that were the case, Harrison would definitely know.

Because fall classes didn't begin for another two weeks, all the doors to the psychology building were locked. Todd managed, though, to pry one open. Once inside, he found Harrison working in her office. He told her Tina had disappeared.

Harrison said she'd last seen Tina two days before, on Tuesday, the twenty-second, at about 12:45 P.M. Tina had come to her office to show her some notes she'd compiled for the CDC project. Harrison looked over Tina's work, made a few corrections, and asked her to produce a final, clean copy. A short time later, Tina returned to Harrison's office with the finished product.

Harrison said she had mentioned to Tina that she seemed very tense. Tina had admitted she was. She explained that she was in the middle of moving, that her bills were piling up, and that a friend who'd agreed to lend her $20,000 to buy a new car was having problems getting his hands on the money.

"This car deal had better go through today," Tina had told Harrison.

Harrison admitted to Todd she wasn't exactly sympathetic, telling Tina she had "ten seconds to feel sorry for herself." This wasn't the first time Tina had mentioned the loan to Harrison.

"Something's wrong with this deal," she had warned Tina previously. "No one gives you something for nothing. What does this man want?"

"He only wants to help," Tina had told her professor. "He said he's tired of me coming to work, hyperventilating, and saying, 'I have to make $100 in tips tonight so I can pay my rent.' "

Harrison asked Tina if she'd told her parents about the loan. Tina said she had.

"What did they say?" Harrison asked.

"They said it was okay."

At that point, the conversation ended.

Harrison told Todd that before Tina left her office on the twenty-second, she'd also asked if it would be OK if another student faxed the notes she'd just turned in to Harrison to the CDC. She was in a hurry.

Moreover, Harrison said she'd since learned that Tina had delivered the proposal for her research project to the IRB office on that very same day.

Todd was still at Oakland when his pager went off. It was Bill.

Bill and Connie had decided after hearing from Todd that Bill should drive down to Farmington Hills. At around 2:30, Todd met Bill at a Burger King not far from his and Tina's apartment.

Todd shared what he'd learned so far with Bill. The two men then headed for the apartment to search for clues that might tell them where Tina was or who she was with.

While not exactly close, Bill and Todd respected each other. In many ways, Bill and Connie were a lot like Todd's parents. Both Bill and Todd's father, a postal worker, were civil servants. And Todd's mother, like Connie, was a nurse.

Bill never concealed the fact that he didn't approve of Tina and Todd's living together—once he found out, that is. When Tina finally agreed to move in with him, Todd shared the happy news with his parents. But Tina had chosen not to tell Bill and Connie about the new arrangement. She let them believe instead that she was living by herself. She knew her parents would object to her sharing an apartment with Todd, and she hated the prospect of Bill, in particular, being disappointed in her. How she looked in her father's eyes meant everything to Tina. When he praised her, she swelled with pride. When he criticized her, she crumbled.

It only took a couple of months before Bill and Connie discovered—it was clear that Todd was there all the time—the truth about their daughter's living situation.

"They never made too much of an issue out of it," Todd would say later. But Bill did send Tina an article from *Catholic Digest* warning against the evils of cohabitation. Attached to the clipping was a brief note. "Please read this," it urged.

Todd suspected, though, that Tina may have told them about his affair. If she had, it would explain why Bill seemed somewhat cool in recent months. Connie, on the other hand, had been treating Todd the same way she always had.

Back at Tina and Todd's apartment, Bill and Todd rifled through Tina's belongings. Nothing struck them as especially revealing. They called around to her friends, but no one they talked to had seen her. Todd also tried the Q Club, hoping to catch up with the mysterious Ken. No one answered.

Eventually, they reached Aimee Vermeersch. She told them that Tina had begun cutting back on her shifts at the restaurant around the first of the year and that she'd quit altogether at the beginning of June.

"Didn't you know?" she asked Todd.

Todd said nothing.

He then asked Aimee, who had a friend who waitressed at the Q Club, if she knew anything about the owner, Ken.

"Ken?" Aimee said, puzzled. "The owner's name isn't Ken."

Another lie.

Aimee, meanwhile, experienced a sinking feeling as she hung up the telephone.

"My heart dropped," she'd later recall. "Something was obviously wrong. I was absolutely sick."

Aimee wanted to believe Todd was holding something back. Maybe he and Tina had argued. Maybe that's why she had run off. But the more Aimee considered the possibility, the less likely it seemed.

"Even if Tina and Todd had a really big fight and she needed some space, she never would just take off without telling her family where she was going," Aimee said. "She would have called her mom and dad and said, 'Todd and I are having some problems and I need to get away for a few days.'"

Nine o'clock came and went. Tina was still nowhere to be found. Bill decided it was time to go to the police. The two men drove to Farmington Hills police headquarters. A vaguely sympathetic officer filled out a report. At the same time, the desk sergeant on duty warned Bill and Todd not to expect the department "to do back flips over Tina's disappearance."

"Missings" are not given much priority, he explained. Most people turn up within forty-eight hours.

Tina, he seemed to be suggesting, probably would, too.

It was still before noon the following day when Bill and Todd returned from meeting with Farmington Hills Detective Ron Shankin.

The two men agreed that Tina and Todd's phone bills might hold the key to Tina's disappearance. The only problem was that Todd, who hadn't looked at a bill in close to a year, had no idea where Tina kept them. He searched and searched, but came up empty-handed. Frustrated and believing there was no time to waste, he called the telephone company and asked to have copies of all of his and Tina's bills, dating back to January, faxed to him.

He thumbed through the first batch as soon as they arrived. They'd sent him every bill but August's. He called the telephone company back and asked if they could fax him a list that covered the past three weeks. August was a problem. That bill had yet to be compiled. But grasping the urgency in Todd's voice, they agreed to generate a list of all calls made from the apartment through August 23.

Bills in hand, Todd and Bill began dialing all the numbers Todd didn't recognize. Probably because it was Friday afternoon, they reached quite a few answering machines. Some numbers simply rang and rang. Todd called the phone company a third time. He wanted to know if there was any way he could get names to go with the numbers. He was told the only way that was possible was if he claimed he'd been improperly billed on every call. So he did.

By late afternoon, Bill and Todd had names to go with the numbers Todd couldn't identify. When Todd compared the two lists, there were two things that struck him as odd. One was an inordinate number of calls placed to someone named Debbie Lawson, calls Tina had made from outside the apartment but had charged to her calling card. Todd was certain he'd never heard that name before and couldn't remember Tina ever mentioning someone by that name.

Tina had also made repeated calls to two Detroit area escort agencies. One was named L.A. Dreams; the other, Calendar Girls. The fact that Tina had been calling the services didn't trouble Todd in and of itself. He knew she had contacted a bunch of them while trying to find escorts willing to be interviewed for her project. But what didn't make sense to Todd was the time the calling card calls were placed: sometimes as late as midnight and, in many cases, right after Tina had called the apartment.

Todd picked up the phone and placed a call to the mysterious Debbie Lawson. The number that matched her name was located at a private residence in Dearborn, a city of roughly 90,000 that borders Detroit on the west. After a few rings, a woman picked up.

"Hi," Todd said. "I'm calling to see if you know a Tina Biggar."

"Sorry," the voice on the other end responded.

Over the next couple of hours, Todd tried Lawson's number several more times, hoping someone different might answer. But each time he called, the same woman answered. Each time they'd have the same exchange. Todd would ask if she knew anyone named Tina Biggar. He'd explain that Tina was missing and that he and her father were trying to find her. The woman would deny knowing Tina. She also claimed over and over again that she'd never heard of anyone named Debbie Lawson.

A few hours later, Bill gave the number a try. Again, a woman answered.

"I need to know if anyone there knows a Tina Biggar," he asked. This woman, too, pled ignorance.

"You must have the wrong number," she said. But this time, instead of hanging up, she added a caveat.

"I have two daughters," noted the woman who said her name was Donna. "Maybe one of them knows her."

"How old are they?" Bill asked.

"One's twenty-one and one's twenty-three."

"That's possible," said Bill.

Donna told Bill to call back in an hour. Her younger daughter would be home then. He could ask her himself if she knew Tina.

Buoyed by what they thought was a solid lead, Bill and Todd waited anxiously for an hour to pass. As soon as it had, Bill picked up the phone.

This time, the woman who answered at the Dearborn number identified herself as Shelly. Bill told Shelly the same story he'd told her mother: his 23-year-old daughter had disappeared and he was calling around to numbers that appeared on her phone bill.

Shelly was silent for several seconds.

"I'm sorry," she apologized after the long pause. "I don't know her."

Frustrated, Bill hung up. There was obviously more to Tina's calls to Debbie Lawson than he was hearing. Just how much more, he intended to learn.

CHAPTER
10

Over the weekend, Todd began to search painstakingly through Tina's belongings. Maybe there was something he had missed.

There was.

Tina had already begun packing for her move. And buried in a box she'd left in the living room along with other belongings was a red Esprit-brand duffel bag. Todd felt certain he'd never seen it before. Inside he found unused condoms, lubricants and jellies, and a stack of blank credit card receipts. He also found a couple of envelopes preaddressed to a company named Elite Desires. In the upper left-hand corner, where the sender's return address normally goes, was the name Crystal. It was the same name, Todd realized, that Tina's friend, Ken, had used when he called her at the apartment.

From the moment Tina disappeared, evidence that her involvement in escorting was more than academic had begun to mount. The late-night calls to L.A. Dreams and Calendar Girls. Her pretending to be working at the Chop House when she'd already quit. But the contents of the duffel bag confirmed Todd's worst fears: Tina hadn't just been studying prostitutes; she'd been working as one, too.

Todd's mind raced. So many things began to make sense. Sometime around Christmas, Todd had asked Tina why she'd started buying dressier and more expensive clothes. She claimed that in addition to waitressing, she was sometimes working as floor supervisor at the Chop House.

Then there were things Todd had never given a second thought because they seemed innocent enough. Around the beginning of the year, for example, he noticed that Tina was washing fewer and fewer of the aprons she wore at work. Now he knew why.

Even gifts Tina had given him suddenly seemed tainted. For Christmas, she'd purchased pagers for both of them. She said the pagers would make it easier for the two of them to stay in touch. As he sat there stunned, Todd realized the only reason Tina had wanted a pager was to help her maintain her cover. If a pager was the only way he could reach her, she could call him back, claiming to be at the Chop House or at school—or anywhere, in fact.

And what about all of his pages Tina had taken forever to return? Todd thought to himself. When she'd finally call back, he remembered, she'd say she hadn't heard the pager. It was in her book bag, or she'd accidentally left it in her car.

Todd suddenly wondered about Tina's job at the Q Club, too. Tina had insisted on two separate occasions that Todd stop by while she was working. Todd had no interest in going either time, but did anyway. Now he realized Tina had been lying to him about that job, too. Maybe she wasn't picking up as many late-night shifts there as she said she was. Maybe the reason she'd invited Todd there was to fool him into thinking she'd worked there more often than she really did. It was a perfect alibi.

Todd felt nauseous. He began searching the rest of the house. In one drawer, he found a garter belt and ten unopened packages of black stockings.

As long as he'd known her, Tina had a weakness for lingerie. She had something like six drawers full of garments from Victoria's Secret alone: bra and panty sets, teddies, camisoles. But black stockings were just not something Tina wore very often. At least not when she went out with Todd.

The stockings pushed Todd over the edge. He was dumbstruck. Tina had been living a double life—and deceiving him—perhaps for as long as the entire year they'd been living together. He was furious. He was embarrassed. He was a million emotions all rolled into one. Soon, he stopped thinking altogether and let his feelings take over.

He wanted to die.

Todd had hunted up north with friends for years. But because he also hunted with coworkers in the southern part of the state from time to time, he stored his 20-gauge shotgun at his and Tina's apartment. Tina, who was an excellent shot, had a 20-gauge shotgun, too. On more than one occasion, she'd gone pheasant hunting with Bill, a popular pastime in eastern South Dakota.

Todd also had a deer rifle. And, from his days as a reserve officer with the Grand Traverse County Sheriff's Department, a standard police-issue .357 Magnum revolver. Both of these guns were also at the apartment. Several times a year, Todd and Tina used them to target shoot.

Reduced to tears, Todd took the .357 out of its case, loaded it, and placed the muzzle inside his mouth. It wasn't so much that he wanted to end his life, he would later say. It was more that he was having trouble coming up with reasons to live.

Confused and on the verge of collapse, Todd put the gun down and called Steve and Valerie. It was close to 3 A.M. Though barely able to decipher his mumbled words, Steve and Valerie knew Todd was in trouble. They promised to be there as soon as they could.

"I was hysterical," Todd would say later, describing the state Steve and Valerie found him in when they arrived at the apartment. "But they managed to calm me down."

"Beyond that," he said, "I don't remember a thing."

By the following afternoon, despite only a few hours of fitful sleep, Todd had pulled himself together. Steve had to leave because he was scheduled to work, but Valerie could stay until Sunday. That night, with Valerie's help, Todd continued searching for clues to Tina's whereabouts. The two of them drove all over the Detroit metro area, stealing Yellow Pages phone books from hotel pay phones. Their goal was to compile a list of escort services operating in the metro area. One of them, they thought, might provide them with a lead or two.

One escort service Todd and Valerie contacted was Elite Desires. Pretending to be a prospective client, Todd told the woman who answered the phone that he wanted an appointment with an escort.

"What kind of date did you have in mind?" she asked him.

He described Tina.

"Blonde, curvy, someone in their early twenties."

"We don't have anyone who looks like that," he was told.

Todd called back a short time later and explained that a friend of his had gone out with the woman he'd described earlier and that his friend had recommended her to him.

"We did have a girl like that," the woman said this time. "But she's no longer with us."

When Todd next saw Bill, he told him about the duffel bag. Bill rummaged through it himself. His demeanor didn't change an iota.

"It doesn't look good," he admitted. "But we still don't know anything for sure."

CHAPTER

11

The morning of Monday, August 28, an obviously enraged Bill Biggar stomped into the detective bureau, flying past the receptionist to Shankin's desk.

He'd talked to the Ferndale police over the weekend trying to find out more about the apartment Tina was going to rent. One of the detectives there happened to mention that Tina was listed as a "voluntary missing" on the law-enforcement computer network.

"You and I know for a fact that Tina is not a voluntary missing," Bill said, his deep-timbered voice rising a level with every word.

Shankin pulled out the Missing Person Verification Form from the file to find out why Bill was so steamed. Bill snatched it from his hands.

"There, right there," he said, pointing to a box that had been covered over with white-out fluid.

"See, somebody changed it to voluntary. This is bullshit, Ron. As far as I'm concerned, this is fraud. I want to see your supervisor."

He was yelling now.

Bill was right. It had been changed. Shankin hadn't done it, but he knew why someone had. For police classification purposes, adults are almost always thought of as voluntary missings unless there is some visible sign of a struggle.

Tina had constitutional rights. If she was stopped by the

police and detained for no reason other than because her father wanted her to be, the police were liable. Unless someone witnesses a kidnapping or there is physical evidence of violence—a weapon, blood, etc.—police are left with little choice but to enter adult missings into the computer as voluntary.

Which is exactly what one of the officers working the desk the night Bill came in to report Tina missing had done, whiting out the box that Bill had checked and changing it to voluntary.

Shankin brought Bill in to meet Sergeant Doug Anderson, his next in command. The two officers let Bill do most of the talking. He obviously needed to get some things off his chest.

Listing Tina as a voluntary missing was evidence they weren't taking her disappearance seriously, something he'd suspected since he filed the report, he told them. They were treating this case as if Tina had just strolled away from everybody she loved, for no good reason. That wasn't what had happened, and they knew it.

Bill was also frustrated that they'd come in Saturday with the full name of the man who was going to loan Tina money for the car, Kenneth Tranchida. Nothing had been done about it. The officer at the front desk had merely taken down the information and noted that Shankin was looking into it.

"Two precious days have been wasted," Bill told Anderson. He hoped now that Shankin was back at his desk, things would start moving again.

"What is it going to take for you people to realize something is wrong?" Bill's voice started to break.

"We're going to do everything we can to find her," Anderson assured Bill.

Shankin took Bill back to his desk. That's enough venting, he thought. They had work to do. Secretly, though, Shankin was almost relieved that Bill had blown up. An angry Bill Biggar was a formidable force. There was a good chance Anderson would clear Shankin's caseload to work on nothing but Tina's disappearance—which is what he wanted. Bill's concern had pulled him in. So had his work ethic. It was apparent Bill and Todd had worked tirelessly over the weekend to find out more about Tina's last months. Starting with Kenneth Tranchida.

But Ken wasn't the only man in Tina's life Bill was worried about. There was also Luke Jackson. Luke and Tina had dated while she was in high school in Kodiak, Bill informed Shankin. One night, he tracked Tina to Luke's trailer. Luke was drunk.

Bill explained that after the incident, he had initiated statutory rape and court-martial proceedings against Luke because of his involvement with Tina. Tina had been the star witness in the case, ensuring Luke's court-martial, Bill told the detective.

Concerned Luke might be involved in Tina's disappearance, Bill said he would use his Coast Guard contacts to try to find an address for him. He wanted Shankin to try to track him down, too. There was a chance Tina might be with him—Bill knew his daughter could be erratic. Sure, Luke had frightened her in the past, but maybe he'd done something to win back her affections.

Bill told Shankin how he and Todd had gone over some old telephone bills that had numbers Todd didn't recognize. Some of the numbers were for escort services. Bill said it must have had something to do with Tina's research.

He also mentioned the duffel bag containing the sex products and credit card receipts.

Later, Shankin and other police would say Bill sought to manage the prostitution side of the investigation himself in the early stages, hoping he could keep that information about Tina away from the police and protect his daughter's reputation and his family's privacy.

In any case, police said later that Bill's cat-and-mouse game did them more harm than good. Everything Bill didn't tell Shankin, he and other detectives eventually found out on their own.

After Bill left, Shankin worked the telephones, starting with the numbers on Tina's old telephone bills that Todd hadn't recognized. One number in particular showed up repeatedly in late 1994 and early 1995.

"Elite Desires," said a woman who answered the number. She identified herself as "Sabrina," but declined to give her last name.

Shankin had reached an escort service in Grosse Pointe, she informed him. No, they'd never heard of a woman named Tina Biggar or a research project on AIDS and prostitutes. That wouldn't apply to them anyway, the woman explained haughtily. "We're strictly a legitimate service that sends model-type women to accompany professional men to social functions," she said.

What a crock, thought Shankin, who nevertheless played along, hoping to learn more. They were obviously a sex-for-hire business trying to trade on the tony reputation of Grosse Pointe, a lakefront suburb on Detroit's east side, home to auto scions like the Fords and other captains of industry.

Any cop with half a brain knew that escort services were thin veils for prostitution, usually run out of dingy offices equipped with a few telephones.

Still, Sabrina wouldn't budge. She had no idea why Elite Desires' number appeared on the November 1994 through February 1995 telephone bills of a missing college student named Tina Biggar.

Shankin didn't buy a thing she said, but he resolved to call her back later.

The detective finally reached Danielle Lentine in Georgia. Sadly, Tina wasn't with her. She'd already talked to Bill. She'd last seen Tina two months ago. Things weren't going well for Tina then, Danielle told the detective. Tina hadn't told Danielle anything about any escort services. But she had mentioned that she and Todd were on the outs. She'd gone out with other guys occasionally, including some businessman from Indiana named Peter, who she'd met in a local bar. At one point, she said she'd even marry Peter if he asked her. Danielle explained Tina was most depressed about her financial situation. She complained about having to get her car fixed and not having the money.

"She said her life was falling apart," Danielle told the detective.

The car loan again, Shankin thought as he hung up. This car deal must have meant the world to Tina. No wonder. Detroit, the auto capital of the world, has perhaps one of the poorest mass transit systems of any major U.S. city, built as it is around the sanctity of the personal automobile.

Detroit's suburbs sprawl fifty miles or more northward, with everything from entertainment to business to education spread over a huge area, connected largely by freeways, and only haphazardly by buses. Life without a car in Metro Detroit could be a commuting hell.

And then along came Ken Tranchida, who had apparently promised to fix all that for Tina with the snap of a finger. The only problem, Shankin discovered when he ran a criminal LEIN on Ken, is that Ken was the least likely person to help Tina—or anyone else for that matter—with money problems.

He had too many of his own.

Ken had an arm's-length list of petty property crimes in Michigan stretching from 1980 to 1991, when he'd been classified a fourth-time habitual offender. Bad checks. Burglary. Fraud. Forgery. Embezzlement. Breaking and entry. Larceny. Name a small-time con involving money and Ken Tranchida's fingerprints—or those of Mickey Bentley, an alias he sometimes used—were all over it. But not terribly adroitly. He'd gotten caught a lot. Certainly he wasn't the kind of guy who could bail you out of a jam, especially one involving money.

But then Tina would have no way of knowing that.

Paroled in August 1994 for good behavior, Ken apparently hadn't been able to keep his nose clean. Royal Oak, yet another Oakland County suburb, had an outstanding warrant on him from June 27 when he hadn't shown up for a hearing on charges of driving with an expired license and possession of a stolen license plate.

Shankin also ran Ken on CLEMIS, an Oakland County-wide computer database that lists the names and addresses of people who've been involved in incidents requiring police attention in Oakland County.

He got a hit. Kenneth Ray Tranchida, with an address in Southfield, 27018 Shiawassee Street.

Bingo. Ken was close by. Indian Country, the cops called that area. A working-class neighborhood in the south end of Southfield near Eight Mile Road; the dividing line between the suburbs and the city of Detroit, it was crisscrossed with streets named after Native American tribes: Seminole, Poinciana, Negaunee.

Ken's extensive criminal history meant a lot of things.

It meant Ken knew the system, and that the system knew Ken. Ken had a parole officer, who would know how to track him down. It also showed that Ken Tranchida was a creature of geographical habit. All his crimes were in Oakland County.

No doubt, he was still around. And the Royal Oak warrant meant that if Shankin did find him, he could keep him—at least for a little while. Long enough to question him about Tina, anyway. Ken's criminal background also had a heartening side: He'd never been convicted of assaulting anyone. On paper, at least, Ken Tranchida didn't appear to be a dangerous man.

But the information on Ken's background still begged the same question: Why would Tina go anywhere near someone like him?

Shankin wanted to know more about the car deal. He called Phil Black, the car salesman Tina and Ken had talked to the week before.

He certainly did remember Tina Biggar and Ken Tranchida trying to buy a car, a 1993 used Honda Accord SE that sold for $14,900, plus tax and title. How could he forget? It had been one of the oddest almost-sales he'd ever made in his life, Black told Shankin.

Tina and Ken had been in the showroom two or three times looking at cars between August 16 and the previous Monday, August 21. During one of their visits Ken had told the salesman that he was on leave from the military, where he was stationed at Fort Knox. He also mentioned that he had once been married to a woman from England who was killed in the Persian Gulf War. His former mother-in-law, whom Ken had called "Mumsy," was going to give him money for the car, although it was going to be in Tina's name.

At first, Ken had said that "Mumsy" was going to transfer money from England to a local bank, which he would convert into a cashier's check to pay for the car. Then Ken called to say that the money had indeed arrived at Standard Federal, a Michigan bank chain, but it had come in the form of British pounds. For some reason, the bank wouldn't change it to U.S. currency, he'd told Phil Black.

The second time Ken and Tina came in, Ken told the salesman that "Mumsy" was instead coming to Detroit herself and would meet them at the dealership on the twenty-first with the money.

Tina and Ken showed up together that Monday night, but "Mumsy" never made it.

The two waited at the dealership from around 7 to 10 P.M., hanging out near the car Tina was set to buy. By then, Phil had completed all the paperwork, insurance, title, everything. All Tina and Ken had to do was hand over the money, at which time Phil would sign over the registration to Tina.

As the hours wore on and it became clear "Mumsy" was a no-show, Ken had made a flurry of telephone calls to a number he said was "Mumsy's" pager, trying to track her down.

Just as the dealership was about to close, Ken made a telephone call to another relative, who had some shocking news, he told a by then clearly frustrated Tina and an ever-more-wary Phil Black.

"Mumsy" had been shopping that day at Westland Mall—a shopping mall in Detroit's western suburbs—and had a heart attack. She'd been taken to a hospital in Pontiac.

The upshot was no money, no car. The two left the dealership together. Phil Black hadn't remembered them arguing, just that Tina seemed frustrated. That was the last time he'd seen them.

Phil paged Ken at home the next day to ask whether they

still planned on buying the car. Ken told him he'd just gotten the most horrible news. Mumsy had died, he informed the car salesman. No matter, everything was still set for the car. Ken assured him that he'd be in the next day to pay for it. Black said he hadn't heard a word from either Tina or Ken since.

What an incredible bullshitter Ken Tranchida is, Shankin thought as he got off the phone with Black. Mumsy? Desert Storm? Ken must be a pathological liar. And a pretty smooth one at that. His story was bizarre, but he'd obviously had Tina going. And Phil, the car salesman—at least to a point. Shankin knew from looking at Ken's criminal record that Ken's principal livelihood was petty thievery. It was doubtful he had a rich relative.

On top of that, Pontiac was almost fifty miles from Westland Mall. No reputable ambulance company would transport a seriously ill patient from Westland Mall to a Pontiac hospital.

Still, he called the hospitals in Pontiac. It was just as he expected. None of them had a death on the twenty-second matching the description of the "Mumsy" person Ken had described to Tina and Phil Black.

This Ken guy was beyond fishy. But more puzzling was Tina's friendship with him, Shankin thought. Bill had told him that Tina was an honors student at Oakland, a bright young woman with a promising future. Why in the hell would she go anywhere near someone like Ken Tranchida?

Maybe Ken would tell him. Shankin called Bill to tell him he had an address for Ken. Bill was thrilled. Finally a break. And an indication that someone besides himself was actually doing some legwork outside an office. The two men decided to go to the Shiawassee address together.

Bill had a photograph of Luke Jackson standing next to a pickup truck, holding up a bottle of Grizzly Bear Ale, shirtless and tanned. Ken had been described on CLEMIS as being dark-haired and olive-complected, weighing about 165 pounds. The two men reasoned that since they didn't yet have a mug shot of Ken—a formality, in a couple of days Shankin would be able to obtain one—they'd take along the photo of

Luke, who very roughly resembled Ken, to show people. It was off the mark, they realized. But it might give people an idea of the type of guy they were looking for.

When they got to Shiawassee, Bill's and Shankin's hopes sunk. There was no such address as 27108. Still, they canvassed both sides of the 27000 block to see if the computer could have been a digit or so off.

They knocked on nine or more doors in the neighborhood, on both sides of the street, and talked to a local convenience store owner. No one had seen anyone resembling the description they had of Ken Tranchida hanging around that area. Still, quite a few people weren't home. Perhaps something would pan out later.

One of the houses at which no one answered had been 27013 Shiawassee. Bill and Shankin had no idea that the unkempt, two-story blue and white wood-framed house with the thinning front lawn was owned by Gloria Johnson, the former mother-in-law of a friend of Ken's. Nor did they know Ken had been renting a room there for the past six months. Or that Tina Biggar had been inside that house a little over a week ago. The two men weren't going to get that lucky.

Not yet.

CHAPTER

12

B ack at the station, Shankin was able to track down several Tranchidas in the telephone book, including Joe, Ken's stepfather. Joe told him he hadn't seen Kenny in several months.

"And that's fine with me," Joe told Shankin testily. He wasn't surprised the police were poking around after Ken, he said. Having to run from the law was par for the course for Ken.

"When he does come around, all he does is steal from us anyway," Joe told him. "We don't want him here, and he knows it." Joe suggested that Shankin try Ken's uncle, Pete Tranchida.

"Pete's one of the only people in the family who'll still talk to him."

It wasn't easy getting information out of Pete Tranchida, a querulous 69-year-old who was suspicious of police and of almost everybody else. For Peter Tranchida, contacts with an outsider were a chance to rail against the injustices of the "system," meaning the courts and police and politicians, all of which had failed both Ken miserably and of which he "had proof."

After Shankin calmed Pete down, assuring him that they didn't want to harm his nephew, Pete conceded he'd seen Ken a week ago, on August seventeenth. Because of Ken's spotty living arrangements, Ken sometimes used his address for mail, the elderly man explained. That year, Ken had had his federal income tax return check sent to Pete. Pete had cashed it for Ken, who didn't have a bank account. He'd given Ken the money when he'd seen him that day, $350. Pete didn't know why Ken needed the cash.

Despite his reluctance, Pete agreed to take them to where Ken was staying. But he didn't want the police meeting him at his home. They chose a neutral location, an Uncle Ed's Oil Shoppe at an intersection near Ken's rented room.

Peter kept his promise. He led Shankin and another detective to 27013 Shiawassee, one of the houses Shankin and Bill had been to earlier that day where there had been no response. A couple of hours hadn't made a difference. There was still no answer from inside the tired-looking house.

Pete agreed to come back to the station with Shankin. He seemed to be warming to the young detective. He was cooperating, anyway, Shankin thought. At Shankin's desk, they came up with a plan they thought would get Ken to call them without frightening him off.

Pete would page Ken, putting in Pete's home telephone number. When Ken returned the call, Pete's wife would tell Ken to call Shankin's direct line, which Pete would then answer.

Oddly enough, it worked. Within five minutes, Pete was sitting at Shankin's desk talking on the telephone to Ken, a man Shankin very much wanted within his grasp.

"I was kind of startled at first. The bad guys usually don't call you," Shankin later recalled.

The detective had been right to use a circuitous route in contacting Ken. He could tell from Pete's conversation with Ken that Ken was spooked.

"It's okay to talk to the police, Ken," Pete was telling his nephew. "They don't want to do anything to you. They just need a little information."

Pete, who hadn't said a word about Tina, handed the telephone to Shankin.

"Hello, Ken. This is Detective Ron Shankin of the Farmington Hills Police." The detective was jumping out of his skin, but he purposefully kept his voice offhand, non-threatening. Casual.

"Where are you, Ken?" Shankin asked, cursing the fact that he didn't have caller ID on his telephone.

Surprisingly, Ken answered without hesitation.

"I'm at a pay phone at a Kmart in Clarkston. Why?"

Good, he's still close by, still in Oakland County, thought Shankin. A creature of habit.

"Ken, there's someone missing who you know, a young woman named Tina Biggar. Can you tell us where she is? Her family's awfully worried about her."

"No, I don't know where she is," he shot back. "I haven't seen her in about a week."

"Still, Ken, I'd sure like to get together and talk with you. How about tomorrow? Why don't you come over to the station?"

Ken interrupted.

"I don't have a way to get there. I don't have a car."

"No problem," Shankin reassured Ken, still trying to keep his tone feather-light. "We'll pick you up. Is 9:15 in the morning okay?"

That wouldn't be a problem, Ken replied. He'd be happy to answer any questions they had.

"See you tomorrow," Ken had closed with the detective, his voice shy and obsequious, a tone he'd honed to a science.

Shankin sent Pete Tranchida on his way, with a promise to call if he heard from Ken or if plans changed in any way.

Shankin leaned back in his chair to assess where he was with the case. After two of what felt like the longest days of his life, he had finally pinned someone who might have some answers about Tina. With any luck he'd meet Ken tomorrow. Still, he didn't feel in the least bit settled. Talking to Ken had been only the tiniest of victories.

There were still so many loose threads, so many men in Tina's life whose names were followed by question marks: Todd, Luke, Ken, this Peter person from out of state she'd dated briefly.

There was also the escort service business. Somehow it all tied together, although he had no idea how.

Still, the more Bill talked to him about Tina, the more convinced he was that something was horribly wrong. Tina wouldn't take off without talking to her family first. They may have had their differences in the past, but they were family, not unlike the one he'd come from: big, Irish Catholic.

Even when things got rocky, you stuck together. Surely, Tina wouldn't intentionally hurt them in this way.

And Tina was the bottom line. She was still out there somewhere.

CHAPTER
13

While Shankin worked the case, Bill and Todd worked the street and the phones looking for Tina on their own.

Bill told Todd he wanted to talk to Shelly again, the young woman he had reached at the Dearborn number that was listed under the name Debbie Lawson. Someone at that number, he was convinced, knew something they weren't saying. He dialed the number. A woman picked up.

"Shelly isn't here right now."

"Please," Bill said. "My daughter's missing. I know she's been leading a secret life. Can somebody please meet me at a restaurant?"

There was silence on the other end for several seconds.

"Okay," the woman finally said, making no attempt to hide her reluctance. She told Bill that Shelly would meet him at a nearby Denny's.

After being seated at a table with Shelly, who'd brought along a twenty-something male cousin, Bill and Todd again explained that Tina was missing. They were contacting anyone they had reason to suspect she may have been in contact with.

Shelly insisted she didn't know why the Dearborn number appeared so many times on Tina and Todd's phone bill.

"Can you tell me what you do for a living?" Bill asked Shelly.

"I work in a hospital blood lab," she replied.

Todd pondered Shelly's response. He knew Tina had, on her own volition and against project regulations, taken some of the prostitutes she had interviewed for the CDC project to a clinic to be tested for AIDS after they had been released from jail. Maybe that was Tina's connection to the Dearborn number. But that didn't make any sense, he told himself. Why would Tina call someone who worked at the clinic at home?

It was then that Bill handed Shelly a list of names he had written down on a piece of paper. It included several Todd had obtained from the telephone company but did not recognize. At the bottom of the list were two names Bill was especially curious about. The first was Ken Tranchida, the friend who was supposed to be loaning Tina the money she needed for her new car. The second was Mickey Bentley. The Farmington Hills Police had told Bill that Ken had a criminal record and that Mickey Bentley was an alias Ken used from time to time.

Shelly agreed to take the list home to see if her mother or her sister recognized any of the names on it.

"Bill, can I talk to you alone for a minute?" Shelly then asked.

Bill nodded. Todd and Shelly's cousin excused themselves from the table. While Bill and Shelly lingered inside, Todd found himself standing outside with a man he still didn't know by name.

The two of them stood there in silence for several minutes. Then Shelly's cousin spoke.

"My aunt is Debbie Lawson and she runs an escort service," he told Todd. "Here's her number. You should call her."

Todd could barely believe what he was hearing. He had felt certain for days that Debbie Lawson was someone who could answer a lot of his and Bill's questions. Moments later, Bill emerged from the restaurant. As he and Todd drove back to the apartment, Bill told him that Shelly had indicated she might have some additional information for him and that she was going to call him in a few hours. Todd, in turn, told Bill what he had learned. Although he didn't say as much, Todd got the impression that Bill also thought that, at last, they were making some real progress.

Back at Muirwood, Todd tried without luck to reach Debbie Lawson at the number he'd been given. He was disappointed. But at least, he thought to himself, he knew who she was and what she did. Besides, Shelly's cousin had told him to call. That had to mean that Lawson had something she wanted to tell him.

While Bill waited for Shelly to call, Todd checked out the address for Elite Desires listed on the envelopes he'd found in the Esprit bag. He picked up a friend who had just finished his shift at D. Dennison's and they headed for Mack Avenue, a major thoroughfare that stretches from downtown Detroit into Grosse Pointe. Todd came upon the address about two blocks into the elite suburb. But the building that matched the number on the envelope housed a dentist's office. Todd assumed the service used the Mack address as a mailing address. The business itself was probably run out of an office somewhere else.

Todd dropped his friend off and returned to Muirwood, where Bill was waiting. He planned to try to reach Lawson again. But as soon as he walked in the door, Bill told him that wouldn't be necessary.

While Todd was out, Bill had received a call not from Shelly but from Shelly's mother. Her name was Donna Mehdi. Together with her sister, Debbie Lawson, she owned and operated four Detroit area escort services.

Tina, she confirmed, had been working for two of them since May.

CHAPTER
14

Many women become escorts, police and other experts say, because they buy into the *Pretty Woman* myth. They convince themselves they're at less risk than street prostitutes because they cater to a more upscale clientele; princes like Richard Gere in the film *Pretty Woman*, ready to sweep them off to million-dollar castles.

Did Tina believe in this kind of fairy-tale ending? Aimee Vermeersch thinks that she very well may have.

"They make it seem like it's a big game, like all you have to do is go out to a nice social event with some guy and he'll buy you jewelry or a car or put you up in a penthouse," Vermeersch said not long after Tina's body was discovered. "But you really don't know who you're going to meet up with."

A former escorting colleague of Tina's echoed Vermeersch.

"A client is a client, whether he's a street bum or a $1,500-a-suit executive," said the woman, who once worked in the office of a Metro Detroit service. "The minute you lose that perspective, you're going to get hurt."

Class systems have existed among prostitutes since ancient Greece, when women in Athenian brothels were divided into three distinct groups: deikteriades (showgirls), auletrides (flute players and dancers), and the highest caste, the hetairai. The hetairai were succeeded by the courtesans, who captivated bankers, princes, and cardinals from the fifteenth century on.

Researcher Carol Jacobsen, who interviewed more than 100 Detroit prostitutes in the late 1980s and early 1990s for a documentary video, confirms that a class system still exists today among women who sell sex for money.

"It's subtle, but it's there," Jacobsen said. "And the women on the street are at the bottom of the ladder." As a result, she explained, escorts "may feel a little bit safer" than their less-fortunate colleagues. But in reality, it's a false sense of security. Like street prostitutes, escorts can't go to the police if they're assaulted or raped by a customer. If they did, they'd have to incriminate themselves at the same time.

Industry insiders say that while some escorts work for services that are more exclusive than others, a common denominator links them all.

"Every one of them could tell you a story of heartache, a story of how she's been hurt by a man," said Tina's onetime colleague. "They see making a man pay for their time as a way of getting even with the entire gender."

Most clients, the woman added, have an equal disdain for women.

"The majority of them do not know how to have a normal relationship with women, so they end up resenting them. They use escort services because to them paying for sex is a way of demeaning women."

In recent years, police agencies in and around metro Detroit have cracked down on some local escort agencies. Among the most publicized cases was the arrest, in November 1992, of Barbara Eaton of Rochester Hills, who prosecutors said grossed nearly $1 million over a three-year period.

Services like Eaton's, called Centerfolds, advertise in newspapers and in the Yellow Pages as escort and massage providers.

Eaton, who opened Centerfolds in 1989 and whose client list consisted of more than 2,000 names, employed as many as thirty women at any given time. They provided services ranging from legal party entertainment, such as exotic dancing, to sexual intercourse.

At the same time Eaton was arrested, so, too, were six women who worked for her as "escorts." Each allegedly charged $250 an hour for sex and made as much as $100,000 a year. The women, who ranged in age from 21 to 39, wore pagers and met their clients at private residences in order to ensure they weren't cavorting with undercover police officers. Later, prosecutors dropped charges against some of the women in exchange for their testimony and the others pled guilty or no contest.

Eaton was charged with pandering, or enticing a person into prostitution, and with accepting the earnings of a prostitute. She was acquitted on the first charge, but found guilty on the second and sentenced to thirty days in jail, two years on an electronic tether, and 100 hours of community service. Both Eaton and the state appealed the outcome of her trial. As of the time of this writing, those appeals were pending.

During her October 1994 trial, Eaton's lawyer argued that Eaton was unaware of any illegal acts that may have been committed by her employees. She even made the women who worked for her sign a document in which they promised not to have sex with their clients, a former employee testified. Even so, the woman added, Eaton was well aware Centerfold escorts and their customers were engaging in sexual activities.

The former escort's story was not an atypical one. A one-time topless dancer, she said she went to work for Eaton to escape an abusive spouse and to make money to support herself and her baby. What did set the woman apart from other former coworkers was her willingness to testify. Many of Eaton's employees, like Tina, led double lives. More than a few were businesswomen with day jobs who viewed escorting as a quick, easy way to supplement their income.

Another police sting made headlines in August 1994. For three months, police officers, posing as customers, contacted various escort services and asked to book an appointment. The service would ask for their name and for a telephone number and then call back fifteen minutes later to say that an escort was on her way. Once the woman arrived, she would ask for the client's driver's license, then call her employer to confirm the customer's identity. The escorts, all of whom wore pagers—some carried cellular phones as well—accepted cash or credit cards.

One service even had a six-page set of rules employees were expected to abide by. A copy of the document, obtained by the *Detroit News*, indicated women could buy condoms from the service at a cost of $2 each; that the service had a dress code; and that telephone pagers, garters and stockings were required gear.

Moreover, the newspaper reported, escorts who violated any of the rules were subject to fines ranging from $50 to $175. If, on the other hand, they recruited a new employee, they would receive a $200 bonus.

CHAPTER
15

In the escort business, it's called "starving a woman out." It's when a service lets an escort believe clients are being told she's available when, in fact, the service has no intention whatsoever of booking any appointments for her.

This is what happened to Tina at Elite Desires.

The Grosse Pointe service hired Tina sometime around November 1994. It was the owner who dubbed her "Crystal." She always chose exotic-sounding names, names that wouldn't remind clients of their mothers or wives or daughters.

But by mid-March 1995, Tina had worn out her welcome. She'd been warned numerous times about failing to call in after being paged, about being late for some bookings and about not showing up for some appointments at all. Following each admonition, she'd apologize profusely and swear it would never happen again.

Tina ultimately proved unable to live up to her promises.

After going more than a week without any bookings, Tina called the Elite Desires office and was put through to Sabrina.

"I haven't had anything for a week," said Tina, who previously had averaged about six bookings a week: two a night, three times a week. "What's going on?"

"I'm glad you called," Sabrina replied. "I need to talk to you."

In Detroit escort circles, Elite Desires is considered one of the industry's Cadillacs. While Tina was working there, clients—politicians and CEOs among them—were charged either $300 or $250 an hour, depending on the escort. Escorts were paid $175 if they were booked for the higher fee, $150 if the rate was $250.

Of the service's stable that comprised about a dozen women, the higher-priced escorts were, in the words of one industry insider, "dead gorgeous with flawless bodies." The "$250 girls"—Tina included—"were attractive but had more of an average, everyday look."

Elite Desires had a very strict dress code for its escorts. Elegant but conservative was the required look. Dresses or skirts were a must. Pants were forbidden. So, too, were scarves and necklaces—anything that a client could use to strangle an escort.

Elite Desires was one of the busiest services in metro Detroit, booking as many if not more appointments than any other local agencies. This enabled the service's top earners to pocket as much as $90,000 annually, tax-free. They were tipped handsomely, too; sometimes as much as $1,000 an hour. Not surprisingly, some of Elite Desires' escorts lived extremely upscale lifestyles. One, in particular, had a habit of flying off to New York simply to shop at Gucci.

Elite Desires refused to hire anyone under the age of 21. Women younger than that simply didn't have the level of maturity the job called for, the service believed.

The oldest escort ever employed by Elite Desires was 51. Some clients specifically requested older escorts. They were older men who felt uncomfortable around younger women because they reminded them of their daughters. In other instances, they were younger men who simply preferred to be with someone older and more experienced.

The service offered variety in terms of type, too. At one point, clients had a choice of escorts ranging from a six-foot-seven blue-eyed blonde to a five-foot-tall 99-pound brunette. The more variety, the conventional wisdom goes, the more appointments a service is likely to book.

The escorts employed by Elite Desires came from all walks

of life. About one-quarter of the women who worked for the service were professional escorts. Escorting was how they made their living. The service's part-timers ranged from stockbrokers to homemakers to factory workers.

About half of Elite Desires' escorts were either married or had boyfriends. Some, like Tina, kept their escorting careers secret from their significant others. Others had spouses who not only knew what they did but encouraged it because it was so lucrative.

Sabrina met Tina face to face for the first time in early February 1995. She had asked Tina to meet her at a bar in Novi, west of Detroit. The owner of Elite Desires wasn't happy with Tina's job performance. She was unreliable.

From the moment she first laid eyes on her, Sabrina was disappointed with Tina's physical appearance. Tina, who Elite Desires described to clients as an "All-American-type girl with a Colgate smile," was heavier and had a larger frame than Sabrina had expected. And while she was attractive, Sabrina thought, Tina certainly wasn't a knockout like some of Elite Desires' other escorts.

She didn't mince words, telling Tina that if she didn't get her act together, she'd be fired.

"I will terminate you," Sabrina warned Tina. "I have the authority to do that."

Tina offered a series of excuses for every time she'd been late or missed an appointment. She was sick, she explained. Her pager batteries had died. Her boyfriend came home unexpectedly just as she was about to leave for a date.

Then there was the excuse Sabrina found to be the least believable of all. Tina claimed she had volunteered to take part in a study on birth control pills. She wasn't very specific, but she said that because of her participation, she sometimes bled between periods. As a result, she explained, there were days she didn't feel comfortable seeing clients.

"I don't want to hear it," Sabrina told her. "It has to stop."

Sabrina wasn't Tina's biggest fan. Prior to their meeting, she'd spoken to her on the phone a number of times. She couldn't quite put her finger on it, but something about Tina's involvement in escorting just didn't sit right with her. At the bar in Novi, she figured out just what it was.

In the midst of their conversation, Tina had pulled out a daily planner. Written on a page inside was a list of questions.

"Do you think I could meet with some of the other escorts?" she asked Sabrina.

"This isn't a sorority," Sabrina said, with a hint of derision. Besides, she added, "We don't believe in that. Everyone's entitled to their privacy."

Despite Sabrina's tone, Tina continued to prod.

"Can I come to the office?" she asked.

This girl is trouble, Sabrina thought to herself. And she told the service's owner just that when she arrived at the office the morning after her meeting with Tina.

"She's done," Sabrina declared, throwing her briefcase down on her desk.

"What are you talking about?" the owner demanded.

"I want to get rid of her," Sabrina replied. "She doesn't want to be an escort. She's a college student. She wants to do research."

"You don't know what you're talking about," Sabrina's boss shot back. "I hired her. We book her real good. She stays."

"It's your call." Sabrina shrugged. "You do what you want to do."

But the owner changed her tune after Tina missed three appointments in a single evening.

Tina called in one day she was scheduled to work and was given the names and addresses of three clients she'd been booked to see. But she failed to show up for the first appointment—and the second and third, for that matter—and didn't respond to any of the service's pages that night.

The following morning when Sabrina arrived at the office, the service's owner was livid.

"Get a hold of her," she ordered Sabrina after informing her of Tina's latest transgression. "Do what you have to do. Fine her ass. Whatever."

Sabrina tried, without luck, to page Tina. Several days later, Tina finally called in with what Sabrina considered a lame excuse.

"Even if that's true, the very least you could have done was call," she reprimanded her. "This just isn't acceptable. Things are going to have to change. You're going to have to do better."

Tina apologized.

"I'm really sorry," she said. "I need to work. I need to make some money."

The following week, Tina kept the few appointments the service booked for her. But at a staff meeting, Sabrina recommended she be cut loose altogether.

"You guys are nuts," she said to her colleagues. "We've got to get rid of this girl. She's a college student who wants to do research. She's going to cause us nothing but problems and we don't need any problems."

The service's owner finally relented, telling Sabrina, "It's your call."

That was when Sabrina recommended they starve Tina out. A week later, Tina called in wanting to know if there was a problem.

"We're not going to need you anymore," Sabrina told Tina.

"Why?" Tina wanted to know, her voice cracking. "Why are you doing this?"

"You know very well why," Sabrina said. "You're always late. You don't check in when you're supposed to. And you blew those three appointments. Frankly, we don't need the aggravation."

"Can't you give me another chance?" Tina pleaded.

"No, that's it," Sabrina told her.

Tina was silent for several seconds.

"I just don't understand," she replied. Her voice had turned petulant.

Sabrina was quickly losing her patience.

"Well, if you must know, we've had some complaints from clients."

Sabrina wasn't trying to be hurtful. Some clients had complained. One had said Tina seemed disinterested. Another said she wasn't very friendly.

"Who?" an incredulous Tina asked.

"It doesn't matter who," Sabrina said. "This is just the way it has to be"

"Why?" Tina demanded.

Sabrina had had it.

"I'm not going to argue with you, Crystal," she said, invoking the name the service had given Tina four months earlier. "This is it. You're no longer affiliated with Elite Desires."

Tina said nothing. She simply hung up.

Sabrina never heard from her again.

CHAPTER
16

Whether Tina worked as an escort after she left Elite Desires and before she hooked up with L.A. Dreams and Calendar Girls is unclear. But what is clear is that by the end of May 1995, Tina had found herself a job answering phones for a service whose office was located in the same building from which Debbie Lawson and Donna Mehdi ran their businesses. One evening in late May, Tina, who obviously knew what kind of operation the sisters were running, stopped by and introduced herself.

Born and raised in Flint, Debbie, then 33, and Donna, then 39, had lived in and around southeastern Detroit their entire adult lives.

Donna, who'd previously been employed as a clerical worker, a factory meat-cutter, and the manager of a construction site cleanup crew, opened L.A. Dreams in August 1994. Debbie, once a waitress and then a home healthcare worker, followed her older sister into the business, opening Calendar Girls a few weeks later.

The sisters bore little physical resemblance. Debbie, though heavy-set, was the more fashionable of the two. She wore cat-eye glasses and had her hair cut shag-like, bangs moussed in the front for height. Donna possessed an average build. Her light brown hair was short. Her glass frames were squarish and wire-rimmed.

"Are you by any chance hiring?" Tina asked the day she popped in the sisters' office.

"We could be," Donna replied.

"It's been real slow at the agency I work for now," Tina explained. "I'm not getting a lot of appointments."

Tina told Debbie and Donna she was a student at Oakland and that she waited tables at the Chop House. She also mentioned the research project she hoped to begin in the fall.

"Do you think any of the women who work for you would be willing to fill out a questionnaire?"

"Gee, I don't know," Debbie said. "It's possible, as long as they remained anonymous."

Tina did little to hide her excitement about the prospect of having found additional subjects for her project. It was also clear she was enthusiastic about the possibility of signing on with Debbie and Donna. Still, she stressed to the sisters that school was her top priority. Her availability would depend on her schedule there. She did say, though, that she'd most likely be free Thursdays, Fridays, and Saturdays.

That was fine, Debbie and Donna assured Tina. They had no problem with the women who worked for them making their own schedules. Tina jotted down her pager number and left it with the pair. They, in turn, promised to be in touch.

Debbie and Donna initially disagreed about Tina's potential as an escort.

"She's cute," Debbie said.

"Yeah, but . . . ," Donna replied, her words trailing off.

"But what?"

"She's real conservative."

"She does dress like a schoolteacher," Debbie seconded.

The two women laughed. But any reservations they might have had about Tina's wardrobe or about whether or not she was cut out for the business didn't keep Donna from paging Tina the very next day.

As Donna would later recall, a client had called and said he was interested in making an appointment with a "plain Jane." Tina, she immediately thought. She wasn't exactly plain. But she wasn't a model-type either.

Over the next two and a half months, through early August, Tina went on roughly a dozen appointments for L.A. Dreams and more than twice that many for Calendar Girls. Never once, the sisters later said, did they receive a single complaint.

During these months, Debbie and Donna slowly got to know Tina a little better. One day, Donna asked Tina what had brought her to the business in the first place.

"Do you really want the truth?" Tina asked.

"Yeah."

"Todd."

"Todd?" Donna asked quizzically. She knew Tina was referring to her live-in boyfriend of close to a year.

"Yeah, Todd. He had an affair."

"You're kidding me."

"No, I'm not," stressed Tina. "He had an affair. This is my way of paying him back. Best of all, he doesn't even realize it."

Donna didn't doubt for a minute that Tina was telling the truth. It had become clear Tina not only worked around her own schedule, but around Todd's as well.

Although technically each owned their own businesses, Debbie and Donna sometimes took turns manning each other's phones. It was around 5 P.M., August 11, when a call came in on the L.A. Dreams line. Donna had stepped out of the office, so Debbie picked up. The man on the other end, she'd later recall, had a very distinctive voice. He talked slowly and paused between words. Debbie knew immediately she'd never spoken to him before.

"In the escort business," she once said, "you don't know faces. You know voices."

From a Caller ID machine connected to the phone, Debbie could tell the man was calling from a party store in Southfield. He told her he was on leave from Fort Knox and that he wanted to make an appointment with an escort. Debbie quoted him the service's going rate: $170 an hour—$100 of which the escort kept for herself—payable either in cash or by credit card.

"What type of escort are you looking for?" she asked.

"A blonde."

Debbie described three or four different women, clicking off their heights, weights, measurements, and personality types.

"They all sound fine," he said.

"Where would you like one of them to meet you?" Debbie inquired.

He wanted the escort to come to his home.

"No problem," Debbie said. "Can I have the telephone number there?"

Debbie and Donna didn't like to take chances. Whenever a client asked to have an escort meet him at a private residence, for example, they required he provide the phone number of the house or apartment. The sisters then used a 1-900 name-finder firm to check whether the caller did, in fact, have a telephone in his name at that address.

"I don't have a phone," the caller said.

"That's a slight problem," Debbie explained. "As a rule, we don't service anybody at a private residence where there's no phone. We have to be able to confirm you're who and where you say you are.

"But," she added, "we do have a couple of women on staff who have mobile phones. I can check with them to see if they'd feel comfortable going to a location without a phone."

Of the escorts whose descriptions Debbie had read, only Tina and one other had cellular phones. Debbie repeated their descriptions. The man chose Tina.

Debbie took down the caller's address and told him someone would probably be over in a short while. She paged Tina. When Tina called back, Debbie told her about the special circumstances.

"You up for it?" she asked.

"Sure," Tina said. "No problem."

"Are you sure?"

Debbie and Donna were protective of the women who worked for them. They regularly reminded them that if they ever went on a call where they didn't feel safe, they should leave immediately.

Tina, who was still using the name Crystal, assured Debbie

that she felt perfectly comfortable going to the man's house. After all, she'd have her mobile phone with her.

Tina arrived at the man's home about an hour later, checked his driver's license to confirm he was who he said he was, then called Debbie to let her know that she had collected her fee and would be staying.

An hour later, Tina called Debbie from inside the house to let her know she was about to leave. She called again a few minutes later, this time to say she was safely outside. Tina didn't share any details of what had transpired. She said only that the customer "seemed like a pretty nice guy."

Two days later, at roughly 3 P.M., the same client called L.A. Dreams a second time. This time, Donna answered the phone. The man identified himself and said he wanted to make an appointment with the same escort he'd seen on the eleventh. Tina, however, had yet to call in that day to let Debbie and Donna know whether or not she was available to work.

"I'm sorry," Donna said. "She's not available right now. But we have another very lovely escort. Her name is Ashley. She's also a blonde and she has the same personality as the woman you saw. She's very energetic and very easy to get along with."

"I'd still like to see the woman I saw before," the man said.

"I understand that. The thing is she's not available right now," Donna replied, trying to pacify the caller.

"Do you expect she'll be available later?" he asked.

"She could be," Donna said. "I just don't know yet."

Although Tina was clearly his first choice, the client booked an appointment with Ashley. He then made an odd request.

"Please don't tell Crystal I'm seeing another woman," he begged. Donna agreed not to say anything.

It was around 7 P.M. when Ashley met the man in the parking lot of the Blue Bird Motel in Southfield.

"Do you want something to drink?" he asked her once they were inside the room he'd rented.

"That'd be nice," Ashley said. The man grabbed some change, ran down to a vending machine near the motel's office, and returned several minutes later with a can of soda in hand.

Ashley asked the man for her $170 fee, which he paid in cash. For awhile, they simply sat on the bed and talked.

"How long have you been working as an escort?" the man wanted to know.

"About six months. What kind of work do you do?" She was trying to deflect the conversation away from her.

He was in the military, he said. He'd been married, but his wife was dead. They'd had two children, but they didn't live with him. They lived with his late wife's mother.

"Why are you doing this?" he asked Ashley.

"I have two kids, too," she told him. "This is how I support them. I'm also using the money I make to pay for school. I'm going to quit as soon as I finish. Or when I meet someone who wants to take care of me and my kids."

"Any guy you meet is always going to be thinking in the back of his mind about what you do. He'll keep throwing it in your face," the customer told her, somewhat coldly. "I'd probably feel that way."

"I'd never get personally involved with someone I met through the service," Ashley explained.

He seemed tense. Ashley asked if he wanted a back rub. He said he did. Eventually the two had sex.

As Ashley was preparing to leave, he started talking about "Crystal" and how nice she was.

"But now I'm confused," he confessed, "because I love both of you. I told your boss I only wanted to see one girl. But she wasn't available tonight, so I made an appointment with you. I guess now I'll have to see her one day and you the next."

Ashley smiled.

"Can you give me a ride home?" he asked.

"Sure," she agreed.

As she pulled up in front of his home, the man asked Ashley if he could have her pager number.

"Sorry," she said. "I don't give that out."

Minutes after Ashley called Donna to say the appointment was over, the man called L.A. Dreams again, this time from a pay phone.

"Don't get me wrong," he said. "Ashley was nice. And she's cute. But if that other escort comes on, I would still like to see her."

"That's fine," Donna replied. "But she still hasn't called in."

"Well, when you talk to her, tell her I'd like to see her. It doesn't matter what time it is. Here's my pager number."

At around 7 P.M., Tina finally called.

"I'm available tonight," she told Donna, sounding like her usual chipper self.

"Good," said Donna. "The guy you saw on Friday wants to see you again."

"Oh really?" Tina responded. "Great."

Before Donna could page the man, he called back again. She told him Tina was available. He asked that she meet him for an hour. He was back at the Blue Bird.

After, as they say in the escort business, "servicing" her client for an hour, Tina called Donna and said he wanted her to stay for another hour.

An hour after that, Tina phoned in again. This time she said she was leaving the motel. Donna barely had time to hang up the phone before it rang again. It was the same man. He went on and on about how much he liked Tina.

The following day, on August 14, the man called L.A. Dreams yet again. He told Donna he wanted to take Tina to see the alternative band the Cranberries at Pine Knob, an outdoor amphitheater outside of Detroit.

"How much would that cost?" he asked.

Donna told him it would depend on the amount of time he wanted to spend with her. But if it was more than one or two hours, he'd be charged a discounted rate: $170 for the first hour; $100 for each additional hour after that.

During that same phone call, the man mentioned that he'd

bought Tina a ring. He planned to give it to her before he returned to Fort Knox on August 29.

"That's really nice of you," Donna said.

It wasn't unusual for customers to buy pricey gifts for escorts they saw on a regular basis: expensive lingerie, $100-plus bottles of perfume, leather coats.

"Why did you do that?" she asked.

"Because I think she's such a nice person."

Donna told the man that before she could book the appointment, she'd have to check to make sure Tina was available August 16, the day of the concert. She said she might have an answer by the end of the day. Several hours later Tina called Debbie.

"I'm not going to be available for a while," she said, sighing.

Tina said she'd wrecked her car. She added she was thinking about getting a new one. Once she did, she'd be ready to come back to work.

During the conversation, Debbie mentioned the call Donna had received about the Cranberries concert. Tina suggested they try to convince the man to take another escort. Debbie decided she'd go.

"It was a free concert," she later recalled thinking. "And I'd be getting paid, too."

The man called back later that day. Debbie, using the pseudonym Brooke, explained that Tina was unavailable, but that she was willing to go with him. She told him, however, that she "would not do what the other girls had done." That was fine. He really just wanted someone to go to the concert with. They agreed he'd call back the morning of the show to finalize their plans. He never did.

Five days later, on August 19, Donna answered a call that came in on the L.A. Dreams line. The caller used a name Donna did not recognize. But from his voice, she could tell it was the same man who'd been seeing Tina. This time, he asked if any brunettes were available. Donna described several escorts. He chose one named Marilyn and asked to have her meet him at the Econo-Lodge motel in Southfield.

Donna thought it strange, him pretending to be someone else. But it didn't necessarily mean he was dangerous. A lot of the service's customers used aliases. He was probably embarrassed about not having called back about the concert, she figured.

When Donna called Marilyn, a no-nonsense professional who was drop-dead gorgeous but very businesslike, she wanted to know whether the man had used the service before. Donna said he had. He'd seen both Tina and Ashley, she told her.

"But he's using a different name this time," Donna added. Marilyn agreed to take the appointment. When she got to the motel shortly before 11 P.M., she noticed her client seemed especially fidgety.

"Are you nervous?" she asked. The man admitted yes, he was a little anxious.

Marilyn suggested they talk for a while. He began telling her about his life in the military. Then he asked her about herself.

"Are you from Michigan?" he wanted to know.

"No," she said. "I'm from California."

He told Marilyn he had been living in Michigan for two years but that he was from the South. He hoped to return there some day.

After an hour was up, Marilyn left the motel. Minutes later, she checked in with Donna, who asked how the appointment had gone. It was fine, Marilyn reported. They'd spent most of the time talking about his Army career.

After his date with Marilyn, the man stopped calling. By Friday, August 25, Donna had long since stopped wondering whether he'd phone again.

Then came the first call from Todd. Because the phone was hooked up to a caller ID machine, Donna knew after one ring that the person at the other end was named Todd Nurnberger. She knew exactly who he was.

Donna pretended at first not to know anyone named Tina Biggar because she was trying to protect Tina, she later explained. On more than one occasion, an escort's boyfriend or husband had learned what she was doing. Not surprisingly, the men had flipped, making threats over the phone. As a result, Donna always played dumb whenever she got calls from her escorts' significant others.

"We're not in a business where you kiss and tell," she later noted.

Donna had no idea why Todd would be calling the service. She suspected, though, that it might have something to do with the fact that he and Tina were moving into separate apartments. Maybe they'd had a fight and Tina had moved in the middle of the night, Donna thought to herself. Now Todd was trying to find her.

After hanging up the phone, Donna realized that neither she nor Debbie had heard from Tina in eleven days, not since the fourteenth, when she called to tell them about her accident. Maybe it'd be a good idea to page Tina, Donna thought. She did, several times over the next few hours. But Tina never called back. Later that night, the sisters received their first call from Bill.

From Friday night through Sunday afternoon, Debbie and Donna tried repeatedly—without any luck—to reach Tina. They, too, were becoming worried. Tina had always been good about checking in whenever they'd page her.

Both Debbie and Donna were at Donna's house in Dearborn when Donna's daughter Shelly returned from her meeting with Bill and Todd. She told them she'd maintained to Bill that the only possible way she might know Tina was through her job at the hospital lab.

Shelly handed Donna the list of names Bill had given her.

"Mom, do you recognize any of these names?" she asked.

Donna eyed the list, then let out a sudden gasp.

Near the end of the list was the name Ken Tranchida. That was the man who'd seen Tina three times—the man who'd bought her a ring. Donna's eyes moved to the name below Tranchida's. She gasped a second time.

"Mickey Bentley!" she exclaimed. "That's the name Ken Tranchida used when he made the appointment with Marilyn.

Donna began to fear the worst. Why would Ken use an

alias, she thought to herself, unless he had something to hide.

"Oh my God, Debbie," Donna cried, throwing her hands over her face. "Ken has done something with Tina."

"What do we do?" she asked her mother, who also was present.

"You do the right thing," she told her daughters. "You call that girl's father and you tell him you recognize those two names."

The sisters looked at each other. They knew their mother was right.

"We felt kind of responsible because she'd met Ken through us," a teary-eyed Debbie would later say. "We couldn't sit on the sidelines."

The sisters also knew Bill had been talking to the police. If they came clean with him, they could end up being arrested themselves. But they knew they really had no choice. They owed it to Tina, they agreed, to tell Bill everything they knew.

CHAPTER
17

Who was the man with the ring? The man who'd trumpeted his illustrious Army career? The man who'd promised to buy Tina a car? A drifter and an ex-con named Kenneth Ray Tranchida, whose entire existence was built around lies.

The second of six children, Ken was born November 18, 1953, in Detroit, shortly after the end of the Korean War. His mother, Phyllis Skinner, worked at a local department store as a "marker girl," pricing merchandise. Short and dark-haired with little education and two wheelchair-bound siblings, Phyllis had twin ambitions as a young woman: a family of her own and a way out of her confining home life, goals she pursued relentlessly, largely through a series of disastrous romantic choices.

At age 20, Phyllis gave birth out of wedlock to her first child: Paul, Ken's older half brother. Two years later, she became pregnant with Ken. This time, her family insisted she marry the father-to-be, a local ne'er-do-well who ran the streets, drank, and frequented prostitutes. He abandoned Phyllis when Ken was less than a year old. She moved back in with her parents and, less than a year later, was pregnant a third time. The father was Joseph "Joe" Tranchida, a neighbor who lived two doors away and who was nine years her senior. Her mother objected to the barrel-chested former merchant marine, who had once baby-sat for Phyllis. Nevertheless, the couple married.

Joe would always think of himself as Phyllis's savior. "Ken's father never had a thing to do with him," Joe remembered. "I went to court to adopt that boy and his father never said word one."

Paul and Ken were adults before they learned the truth about their biological roots. It was a relative nonevent for Paul. To him, Joe would always be the only father that mattered. But it turned out to be a severe blow to Ken, whose unstable psyche was already starting to unravel.

Joe and Phyllis settled in a one-story bungalow several blocks from where they'd both grown up in Southfield, then a growing northwest suburb of Detroit. Joe got a job at Chrysler. Phyllis quit the store and stayed home with the children, who began to arrive quite regularly: four in six years, two girls, and then two boys.

When Joe got laid off from Chrysler in the 1960s, he found work as a high school custodian and bus driver. As if to prove his in-laws wrong, he increased his profile in the community, ushering at the Catholic church he and the children attended, and by serving as an auxiliary Southfield policeman.

If there was evidence Joe resented raising Paul and Ken—a charge he vehemently denies—it was the way he drove the boys harder than he did the rest of the children. According to Paul, the pair had to adhere to a strict schedule of chores and a narrow code of behavior. If they got out of line, they were subject to one of Joe's bellowing tongue-lashings, or, more often than not, a whipping with whatever instrument he found handy. But not until they undressed from the waist down and leaned over a bed, exposing their bare buttocks.

A hard early life aged Phyllis prematurely. In her thirties, she lost all of her teeth and never got replacements. She stopped smiling after that. The cause may have been genetic. Ken also lost his teeth in his early twenties. But unlike his mother, he was fitted for a false set.

Ken would look back on his childhood as tortured, remembering his stepfather as a cruel tyrant who never accepted him. According to Ken, Joe would laugh at the sight of him trembling in anticipation of a whipping.

Joe, meanwhile, denies he ever hit the boys at all and Paul and some of Ken's other siblings say Joe never singled out Ken. They say all the Tranchida children incurred Joe's wrath at some point during their childhood. In that era, corporal punishment was commonplace in workingclass families and Paul never thought of his childhood as being remarkably different from those of his friends.

"We got it when we had it coming," Paul recalled.

To him, Joe and Phyllis were decent, hardworking people who did the best they could to raise six children.

The gap in the ways the brothers perceive their early years is typical of how Ken and Paul viewed the world. Ken always looked for sympathy. Paul was the more emotionally mature, even-tempered of the two.

In the case for nature over nurture, the siblings were one for the books. In the first two decades of their lives, Ken and Paul shared everything but biological fathers: the same workingclass upbringing, the same adopted father in Joe. They went to the same public schools, hung out with some of the same friends. Both joined ROTC in high school and the military after they graduated. They even looked uncannily similar, sharing Phyllis's dark, curly, thick hair and prominent chin.

Yet by the time both were in their forties, they stood worlds apart. Paul was a hardworking business owner, with a wife, four children he loved, and the respect of most people who knew him. Ken was a nickel-and-dime criminal and con artist who'd bounced in and out of prison ten times since the age of 27. He'd never been jailed for hurting anyone, though. His most serious offense was breaking and entering an empty building.

Still, Ken couldn't seem to hold onto a job, applying himself only to sabotaging each new chance he got. He'd work somewhere for a few months, then get caught lying or stealing from his employer, at which time he'd disappear, usually without facing his accuser or collecting his last paycheck.

As Ken saw it, "I felt like I could do more, like I was too good for those jobs."

Still, with each new job came the chance for Ken to reinvent himself, an opportunity he'd rarely pass over. He used aliases and spun farfetched stories about his family and romantic history for coworkers and customers he met on jobs.

The one theme that consistently ran through Ken's bizarre tales was death, usually manipulated in such a way as to cast him in a sympathetic light.

Wives, children, girlfriends—somebody was always dying off in Ken's macabre little fantasies.

There was one pivotal loss in Ken's life. But, again, it was one he shared with Paul: Phyllis died of complications from diabetes at age 42. Ken was 21.

"Get the fuck out of here," Ken remembers his youngest half brother Daniel screaming at him at the funeral. "You're the reason she's dead."

No one else seems to have heard the argument between the two men.

Joe says Ken may have had a guilty conscience. The year before her death, when Phyllis was terribly ill, Ken had stolen some money she kept for household expenses. He had argued with her about it while she was still weak from a hospital visit—a charge Ken denies. Infuriated, Joe kicked him out of the house.

After high school, Ken had a short stint in the Army that failed miserably. He earned a sharpshooter's badge in basic training for his skills with an M-16 rifle. But he called home complaining that "everybody smoked pot" and that the military was full of troublemakers and misfits.

Feeling homesick and out of place in the service, he went AWOL for a couple of months, turning up on his parents' doorstep, Joe remembers. Ken says it never happened.

Whatever the truth, Ken was honorably discharged in January 1973, less than a year after he joined, for "not meeting medical fitness standards at time of enlistment."

Ken had slit his left wrist. Waiting behind in the barracks

one evening until most of the other men in his unit had gone to dinner, Ken used an Army-issue knife to slice two horizontal lines across the veins of his wrists. He then walked into his sergeant's office, where he calmly held up his bleeding arm to display his handiwork. Ken spent two weeks in the hospital under observation. In the end, he got what he wanted: a way out of the Army.

Ironically, Ken's favorite scams in the years following always involved his being in the military with some fancy title: sergeant, corporal. Ken would later say he always fantasized, in fact, about being "a general, someone with power."

Suicide attempts also became commonplace in his life. More than a dozen times in his twenties, Ken made pathetic, ineffective attempts to kill himself, his way of getting the attention and pity he seemed to thrive on.

After being discharged, Ken returned to the Detroit area, where he drifted through a series of dead-end service jobs: dishwasher, busboy, car wash attendant, gas station jockey. He moved in and out of his stepfather's house, where things had deteriorated rapidly after Phyllis's death.

Looking to fill space in his wife's absence, Joe Tranchida had taken in five foster children, a burden he was in no shape to handle, he said. He was named Southfield's "Citizen of the Year" for the seemingly selfless gesture. He still has the plaque he received proudly displayed on his wall.

But life inside the Tranchida house was anything but exemplary. Depressed and overwhelmed, Joseph left most of the child-rearing chores to the older children, who were still grieving the loss of their own mother. The motherless brood spun out of control. Joe came home one day from work to find one child threatening another with a butcher knife. The foster children were removed by child welfare officials, but not before one of the teenagers became pregnant by Ken's second-youngest half brother. The two teens married and had a baby girl. Born with a cleft palate, the infant died of starvation when she was less than a year old. The cause of death was gross neglect. The only crib the child had ever known had been a bureau drawer in a cheap motel. The baby also had been hospitalized once before her death for "failure to thrive," or not gaining weight. Doctors warned her parents they would press charges if she was brought in again in such pitiful shape. When she was, the physicians made good on their threat. The couple was convicted of involuntary manslaughter and spent time in prison for the baby's death.

Oddly, Ken would later tell several acquaintances that his daughter had been born with a cleft palate and had died as an infant. But in Ken's version of the tale no one was to blame. The baby, he said, had died of crib death.

Ken did have one real shot at marriage and kids. In the mid-1970s, he met a woman named Theresa Simmons. A desk clerk at a hotel where Ken worked doing laundry, Theresa was tough and experienced. They hadn't been dating long when Theresa got pregnant. Her parents weren't pleased with the prospect of having Ken as a son-in-law, but they were Catholic. They believed the two should wed.

Theresa had a miscarriage before the wedding. But it went off as planned, a large family affair at a high-profile suburban Detroit parish, Shrine of the Little Flower in Royal Oak.

Ken deceived his new bride from the start. He told her he was a state policeman, doing undercover work. To maintain the charade, he kept his new wife away from his family and anyone else who could have blown his cover. The newlyweds moved to Harbor Springs, a small resort town near Traverse City. Each night when he was supposed to be working, Ken would head for downtown Traverse City and walk the streets.

Sometimes he would come home, other times not.

"He used to stay away for days," Theresa remembered. When he did come home, sex wasn't something he was particularly interested in, she recalled. "He was never very good at it," she said. "He just didn't seem to care."

On a camping trip, Paul and his wife, Peggy, happened to run into Ken and Theresa. Alone with Peggy, Theresa confessed things weren't going smoothly for the newlyweds. Ken had yet to bring home a paycheck from his state police job, Theresa told her. They were having trouble making ends meet. Peggy said nothing, even though she knew there was no chance in hell that Ken was working as a police officer. He'd stolen from so many people he knew, including his dying mother, according to relatives. Ken has always denied stealing from his dying mother.

Paul and Peggy felt sorry for Theresa, but didn't get involved. It was only a matter of time, they figured, before Theresa figured out what was going on. Still, they discussed Ken's latest charade all during the drive home, agreeing the marriage wouldn't last long.

It didn't. Theresa found out about the scam and blew up at Ken. In an attempt to pacify her, Ken bought his wife new furniture and a Volkswagen Scirocco, writing over $8,000 in checks, despite the fact that he actually had about $200 in his account at the time. He was arrested several weeks later. Theresa had the marriage annulled while Ken was in prison.

Paroled after about thirty days, Ken sponged off family members, first his siblings, then the aunts and uncles who would help.

He took advantage of the fractured relationship between his mother's and father's sides of the family, crisscrossing from one set of relatives to the next, confident they wouldn't consult each other about his behavior. It was a safe bet.

When Ken wasn't freeloading off relatives, he was bouncing in and out of prison or halfway houses for misdemeanors ranging from passing stolen checks to stealing credit card numbers—crimes he often committed against family members.

Each time Ken got out of a prison, he'd return to Southfield, broke and looking for a place to stay. One winter, he parked his car in the driveway of his maternal Aunt Helen's house and slept in it. At the time, Helen was living in the Skinner family's former homestead, where Ken and Paul had spent the first years of their lives. (Joe's parents lived just two houses down.)

Helen's house was among a row of older homes facing Nine Mile Road, a major east-west thoroughfare in suburban Detroit. Set far back from the road, the tiny bungalows could have passed for forest cottages, forgotten by time and spared from the sprawling residential and office developments surrounding them. The Skinners and Tranchidas shared a common backyard: a thickly wooded, fenceless lot that ran almost to their back doors.

As children, Ken and Paul had spent countless hours playing in the isolated patch, memorizing every tree, as they ran back and forth between their grandparents' houses. As an adult, Ken often returned to the wooded enclave, even after his grandmother had died and strangers had moved into her house. It became a haven in times of trouble.

The winter he slept in his car, Ken worked as a Santa Claus bell ringer for the Salvation Army during the Christmas season.

He met and befriended another Salvation Army worker, Jerry Holbert, a burly, tattooed gas station tow truck operator who wasn't bothered by Ken's past, or at least what he knew of it. In truth, not much fazed Jerry, who wore his curly red hair in a ponytail and favored too-small T-shirts that exposed large expanses of overflowing girth. Not much for ceremony, Jerry took most people at face value. Ken was no exception.

"Ken didn't have but one friend in the world, and that was me," Jerry would later say. "That was his biggest problem. When the holidays rolled around, he usually spent them with me and my family. None of his folks would talk to him."

The Ken that Jerry knew was a gentle, soft-spoken guy with a few blind spots. Women were the biggest one. Ken fell in love too fast, Jerry thought. Divorced himself, Jerry could understand how any guy might be a little crazy when it came to women. Still, Ken had the qualities Jerry thought counted. For one, he got along with kids. Jerry had observed Ken playing for hours with Jerry's two children. And Ken never lied to him, not that Jerry knew anyway.

When Ken wasn't working, he sometimes begged for food from people who lived in his old neighborhood or from the priests at St. Michael's, the Tranchida family parish. Churches were another favorite haunt of Ken's, especially in times of distress. He sought out priests and nuns throughout his life, usually after committing a crime, looking to the church for the pity and forgiveness that eluded him elsewhere.

"He made everyone feel sorry for him," Joe Tranchida said. "He was a great con man."

As his actions became more outrageous, Ken's demeanor, oddly, grew more introspective. He'd always been somewhat shy, even in high school. But in his twenties, he'd become almost unbearably so. When he did speak it was in a halting, quiet voice that lent him an air of insecurity and aided him immeasurably in carrying out many of his scams. Accustomed to being greeted with disbelief, he began prefacing many of his sentences with the word "honestly," dragging it out in a whiny, nasal Midwestern drawl.

Two elderly women Ken had roomed with for several months during the mid-1980s were perfect pigeons for Ken's brand of deception, which usually involved securing life's basic necessities—food, a place to stay, transportation—without having to work. One day, the women called Paul looking for Ken. One of the only Tranchidas listed in the Detroit-area telephone books, Paul was accustomed to getting calls about Ken's many transgressions.

One of the women, a frail 80-year-old, explained that Ken had been living with her for several months but had disappeared without notice. She wanted to give him his mail, which included a passport application. Paul warned the woman never to let Ken into her house again. "He's a criminal and a con artist," he told her. But the woman refused to believe him. "Ken is the sweetest, shyest, most helpful young man in the world. How can you say such cruel things about your own brother?" she scolded Paul.

One paternal uncle who took Ken in learned the hard way that his nephew couldn't be trusted. Ken stole the elderly man's credit card and charged $900 on it to pay for a one-way airplane ticket. He wanted to fly a British woman, Patricia Dawson, who he'd met through a mail-order bride service, and her infant son to Detroit in early 1991. At the time, Ken was using his Mickey Bentley alias and living at the E.Z. Rest Motel in Southfield, where he worked as night clerk.

The day Dawson arrived from England, Ken, seeking money to impress his mail-order bride, walked away with $691 in receipts from the motel. The motel owner reported him to the police.

Ken returned to jail, his tenth prison stay in as many years. He was labeled a fourth-time habitual offender, a designation that under Michigan sentencing laws gave corrections officials the right to throw away the key if he ever got in serious trouble again. If Ken committed a serious felony—one punishable by five or more years in jail—he could spend the rest of his life in prison with no chance for parole.

Ken was nickel-and-diming his way to a lifetime behind bars.

In a victim's impact statement—a form that allows crime victims in Michigan to seek retribution from their offender—the motel's owner said she didn't want Ken to pay her back. He'd probably just "steal it from someone else," she told the corrections investigator. She also noted that she thought Ken had "mental problems. . . . He puts on a facade of jovial kindness, but this does not reflect his true personality."

Ken's "true personality" didn't shine through either in what became one of his favorite pastimes while in jail: writing to European women who advertised in mail-order bride catalogues to try to persuade them to come to the U.S.

"At one time, I was writing to seventeen different women," Ken would brag later, explaining that he had "different kinds of relationships" on paper with all of them. Ken's letters were full of lies, bloated claims about his wealth and background. They were easy falsehoods to perpetuate by mail, and they gave him a sense of connection and intimacy— bonds he could never forge in face-to-face dealings with women.

Not long after he landed in prison for the motel thefts, Ken initiated a pen-pal love affair with a woman from Coventry, England, named Sandra Brown.

"I'm going to take care of you and your children," Ken

wrote to the mother of three. Behind bars, without prospects, it was hardly a promise Ken could keep.

Ken was paroled in November 1993 for good behavior. But less than a year later, in January 1994, he was sent back to prison for violating the terms of his parole.

Throughout it all, Ken kept in touch with Brown by telephone and mail. At some point, their letters and telephone calls became sexually explicit, so much so that Brown would later describe herself as having been "intimate" with Ken even though they'd never met.

Brown and Ken may have steamed up telephone lines with their romantic conversations, but Ken never told Brown about his criminal record or his inability to hang onto even the most menial job. Instead, he filled her head with promises—a house, a car, all the things he was going to do for her and her children.

Not content just to sucker in unsuspecting European women, Ken got French police and the FBI involved in one of his cons. While in jail, he wrote French authorities asking them to help him locate his two children. Their English mother had died, he explained, and the children, a boy and a girl, had been taken to France by friends. Could they help him find the pair and bring them back to the U.S.?

Taking the matter seriously, the French police wrote the Detroit office of the FBI, asking the Bureau to flesh out the story. They also requested that photographs of the Tranchida children and their birth certificates be sent to U.S. Embassy officials in France.

Ken, of course, could provide neither. He couldn't even remember when his two children were supposed to have been born.

"There are a number of inconsistencies about his past life," concluded the FBI agent who closed the investigation after interviewing Ken in prison, "including the number of wives . . . and the number of children."

The inquiry ended just as Ken had hoped: with everyone wondering if he was telling the truth or not. Of course, he wasn't. He didn't have any children. But no one could prove it.

Ken hated being confronted with one of his lies, an incredible irony since he lied constantly, his stories growing more ridiculous and implausible as the years went by.

Getting caught in a lie made Ken sick and afraid—the same emotions he must have felt as a child facing a belt-wielding Joe—but at the same time, it was strangely empowering, exposing a violent side he kept hidden behind his veneer of insecurity.

Paul saw Ken's violent-when-cornered side when Ken stole a watch from him and got caught. It was a clumsy theft, one that made little sense. It happened in the late 1970s, before Ken had racked up any prison time and the half brothers' relationship was still somewhat civil. Ken was working on Paul's house when the watch turned up missing. When Paul caught Ken trying to return the timepiece, he asked him about it. The two ended up brawling on Paul's front lawn. Ken physically threatened Joe once as well, after Joe confronted him about the money he stole from his mother while she was sick.

"Ken could lie all day long," Paul commented years later. "He just couldn't take getting caught."

In psychiatric jargon, according to a doctor who examined him in 1991 after he was labeled an habitual offender, Ken, at age 38, was "maladaptive and dysfunctional."

The psychiatrist also noted:

Although claiming steady employment, this apparently seems somewhat haphazard with intermittent jobs primarily of a manual nature . . . with the resident bouncing to the next job. Family circumstances have apparently been difficult, resident having committed some of his property crimes against family members. . . . The resident had indicated making some 15 suicide attempts and having been treated at various mental health hospitals. . . .

Paul had a more blunt assessment of his half brother: "Ken is full of bullshit. He's a 'Feel sorry for me' kind of guy." Paul, in fact, was one of the few people early on who saw through Ken's machinations. The stolen watch and Ken's lies about being in police work would turn out to be only the tiniest fault lines in Ken's credibility, compared to the Grand Canyon of lies Paul would catch Ken in over the years.

Each of Ken's falsehoods was designed either to elicit sympathy or to boost his sagging self-image: Ken was dying of AIDS. Ken had graduated from the University of Hawaii. Ken was the father of twins with a Texas woman who had been killed in a car accident. Ken had a sister who was killed in a car accident. Ken's British wife had been a soldier in the Persian Gulf War and was killed in combat.

All lies.

By the time Ken was 40 years old, he'd concocted so many versions of his own life story that even he may not have been able to separate truth from fantasy.

But prison officials couldn't keep him in jail for being delusional. As far as the system was concerned, Ken Tranchida was, by most accounts, a model prisoner whose only offenses had been trivial monetary crimes. With jail overcrowding and dangerous criminals running free, someone like Ken—mild-mannered, contrite, and soft-spoken while behind bars—proved a good risk for parole.

On August 4, 1994, Ken was released early for good behavior. Free again, Ken had yet a new preoccupation in addition to death and fantasy, one he articulated very clearly to his friend Jerry Holbert, and to anyone else who would listen, something he'd dreamt of all those long, lonely nights in jail: he wanted to fall in love and get married. Five months after he was released he even bought a ring for his lucky bride-to-be.

In thirteen months of freedom, Ken would meet two women who he thought would help him realize that dream. One was a mother of three from Farmington Hills, who would eventually file a stalking complaint against him.

The other was Tina Biggar.

CHAPTER
18

K en was leaning inside Marta Showalter's van window to flirt with her when he heard Marta's 12-year-old daughter, Emily, complain about having to do a school report on a subject that began with the letter "E." It was sometime in late March 1995.

A 35-year-old single mother with three children, Marta wasn't exactly swept off her feet by Ken, but then she wasn't looking to be. She had long ago abandoned the fantasy of meeting Prince Charming. She was just hoping to find someone other than the "jerks" who usually asked her out, cheesy opportunists who balked at the idea of committing to someone with children or who expected sex in return for helping around the house.

Ken was working at the Marathon station near Marta's home in Farmington Hills. She knew him only by his first name—and by his fawning attentions. Every time she pulled into the station, he'd drop what he was doing to put air in her tire or fill her gas tank.

That was "men's work," he told her.

With the extra service came an accelerated familiarity and clumsy flirtatious banter on his part, advances Marta always politely deflected, dismissing it as harmless small talk from a shy, lonely guy.

"You should give me your number," he would demand, only half-teasingly.

"Now, you know I can't do that," she'd respond.

It got to be almost a game between them.

The same March day that Emily complained about the report, however, Marta explained to Ken that she had suggested engineering, but that Emily had given the idea a thumbs-down.

"Bor-ing," she'd told her mom.

"How about England?" Ken piped in, seizing an opening. "My wife was from England and I have a scrapbook that would probably help Emily a lot. It's got a lot of stuff in it. I'd be happy to bring it by your house."

"No, I don't think—" Marta started to say, when Emily interrupted with a chorus of "Please, Mom, please." Marta relented. She gave Ken her address and directions to her house. He seemed so eager to help. And there was something about his voice, so sweet and awkward, Marta remembered thinking.

"His voice was really insecure," she'd later remember. "There was something struggling about it. He was like this lost puppy looking for a home."

Marta and her children were eating when Ken came by that night. They invited him to join them for supper, an informal affair. He'd brought the scrapbook, although it wouldn't turn out to be very helpful for Emily's report, containing just clippings from British newspapers, postcards, and a photograph of a woman in a halter top in a setting Marta couldn't identify.

"That was my wife," Ken had told Marta sadly, pointing to the photo. She had been a soldier in the British Army and was killed by friendly fire during the Persian Gulf war, Ken explained. His two children were in England with their grandmother, he added. Even though there were no pictures of the children, Marta didn't doubt Ken. Still, it bothered her that he wasn't raising them himself. She thought that was irresponsible and told him so.

"You should be with them," she told him.

Ken shrugged her off, mumbling some excuse. What a sad little life this guy has, she thought.

The dinner invitation was obviously the entree into Marta's

life Ken had been looking for. From that night on, he was at
her house constantly. Throughout March and April, he
showed up at her door unannounced at least three times a
week, often early in the morning, ready to tackle some project
that required heavy lifting.

Unemployed and struggling to keep up with repairs on her
aging three-bedroom bungalow, Marta was glad to oblige.
Ken uprooted a row of old bushes. Together, they turned over
a large section of sod in her backyard and hauled in tons of
dirt to make a garden. He hauled a several-hundred-pound
broken heatilator out of her fireplace.

"He was incredibly strong," Marta would remember later.
"He wouldn't let me help with the heavy stuff. He'd say
things like 'Woman, you know it makes more sense for a
man to do this,' in this low, macho voice." She took it as
Ken's corny way of teasing her.

Marta thought of Ken as a lonely guy without a lot of
friends or family who simply wanted to be around people.
They never dated. Ken didn't make any sexual advances toward her. She wouldn't have been interested anyway. Ken
didn't appeal to her in that way. At five-foot-eleven, she was
three inches taller than Ken. And he lacked bottom teeth.
Emily had noticed it one day and mentioned it to her mother.

Also, Ken's curly, brown hair was cut strangely, Marta
thought: close on top, with a long, thin section that hung
down his back.

"It looked scraggly," she recalled. "I offered to cut it for
him, but he said he liked it that way."

Ken also wore mismatched faux-jewel earrings—one
green, one blue.

"With Ken, things were always colorful: his clothes, the
earrings," Marta would later recall.

Marta offered to pay Ken for helping out, but he wouldn't
take her money. She was a little uneasy accepting so much
free labor from a man she wasn't interested in romantically.
But at the same time, she felt she'd made her intentions, or
lack thereof, perfectly clear. Ken would sometimes hint he
thought their relationship was more than platonic by address-

ing her in awkward romantic ways, calling her things like "babycakes." But those remarks were infrequent enough for Marta to dismiss.

In late April and early May, Ken's visits became even more erratic. On several occasions, Marta came home from temporary secretarial jobs to find he'd been hanging around her backyard all day, moving things around in her garage or puttering with the garden or lawn.

"You were here when I wasn't?" a peeved Marta observed one day. "I don't like that, Ken."

Ken mumbled an apology. Marta's reprimand, however, neither dulled Ken's ardor nor did it curtail his comings and goings in her absence.

Several weeks later, she again came home to find he'd been at the house without her there.

"Your door was unlocked," he informed her. "You shouldn't leave it that way. You never know who's around."

Around the same time, Ken began leaving broken-stemmed roses—obviously plucked from some convenient garden—on the dashboard inside her car. He'd usually leave a note, too.

"Hope you enjoy the flowers (Roses). Miss You!! Please call. Love, Ken," read one such missive.

Marta hardly ever called Ken. And love wasn't an appropriate sentiment for him to express toward her, she thought. Still, it was kind of sweet. How could she get mad at a guy for leaving roses?

Ken would later say about the relationship that he "wanted more but it wasn't there." It was no big deal, in his mind, he remembered.

If that was the case, he never made it apparent to Marta. By Mother's Day, Ken's constant attentions had begun to grate. Out of the blue, Ken presented Marta with a ring: a blue sapphire surrounded by diamonds.

"It's beautiful," Marta told him. "But a ring means commitment, a relationship. We're not like that, Ken."

"Just wear it for a few days," he begged. "It doesn't have to mean anything. I just want you to have it."

Against her better judgment, Marta agreed. Three days later, she gave the ring back.

"I can't take this, Ken," she told him. She was mad at herself and a little embarrassed for having accepted it in the first place.

One morning, not long after the ring incident, Marta got up at 5:30 A.M. to find Ken at her side door.

"What are you doing here this early?" she asked, annoyed with him. Again, she got a sheepish response from Ken. He was awake, he explained. He'd just wanted to leave a note.

Ken began pressing to take her to the Cranberries concert at Pine Knob. After Marta said no, he attempted to change her mind by giving her a compact disc by the rock band. She stood firm. She didn't want to go out with him. She didn't even like the Cranberries.

"I thought he'd let it drop," she said, "but he just kept after me."

Ken didn't seem to understand any of the conventions of friendship or dating, or else he simply chose to ignore them, Marta observed. Self-absorbed and lonely, Ken had magnified their relationship far beyond what actually existed between them. Her feelings toward him were unimportant.

Ken's stories about death also began to multiply. One day, while Marta was at the gas station, he made a grave announcement: his 8-year-old daughter, who was living in England, had been killed in a car accident.

"So if it seems like I'm kind of out of it today, that's why," he told Marta. "I was up half the night. I wanted to call you, but I didn't want to wake you up. If I'm up again late tonight, can I call?"

Marta said no. She didn't want Ken calling her in the middle of the night. But she was baffled by the maze of Ken's reasoning. His daughter was dead and he was using that as an opportunity to ask if he could telephone her? How could he even think of such a thing at a time like this?

Marta expected Ken to leave immediately for the funeral. Instead, he came by her house several days later, where he laughed and joked with Emily as if nothing were wrong.

"Aren't you going to England?" Marta pressed him, out of earshot of her kids.

In the past, whenever she'd questioned Ken about his children, he'd always changed the subject, but Marta didn't let him slide this time.

"You should be in England, Ken," she insisted. "Your son's still there. He lost his mother, now his sister. He needs you."

Ken blew up.

"You don't know anything about my life," he shouted at her. "You don't know what I've been through."

Marta backed down. But Ken had managed to erase the last bit of credibility he had with her. He'd been too casual about his daughter's death. It didn't make sense.

Around the same time, Ken's car came up missing. He'd been in a car accident, he told Marta. His rusted 1980 Chrysler Cordoba had been totaled. Someone had run a red light. His stomach had been injured slightly in the accident. A puncture wound, he told her. He held his stomach to show her where it was hurt. But that was nothing compared to the people who hit him, he added.

"They were taken away in body bags," he said. Disbelieving, Marta asked to see his stomach, but he wouldn't show her the injury.

Marta began avoiding Ken from that day on. She refused to take his calls and began making up excuses not to see him. His obsession with death was too bizarre for her. She was a trusting soul—naive some of her friends and family would say—but Ken had stretched the limits of even her gullibility.

Growing increasingly uneasy around Ken, Marta began asking him point-blank not to call or come over anymore. After she'd make such a request, Ken would inevitably wait a few days and then show up at her door, asking if she was mad at him and begging to let him visit. Feeling sorry for him, Marta would relent, allowing him to slide back into the routine of visiting two or three times a week.

On June 24, something happened to convince Marta that she needed to cut all ties with Ken. The two of them were driving to a pet store to buy ferrets that Ken had promised to give Marta's children. Newly legalized, the tiny, furry creatures were all the rage. Ken had gotten Marta's children excited by saying they could "keep two" for him.

Apropos of nothing, Ken brought up the injury from the car accident. The reason he hadn't shown her his stomach, he explained, was because he was disfigured with horrible scars. When he was a child, he told her, his stepfather had tied him to a bed and tortured him with a razor blade.

Joe, Paul, and other family members say the story is a total fabrication, another of Ken's ham-handed plays for sympathy. Ken had never been in a car accident either. His car had been impounded May 23 by police in Royal Oak, after he was pulled over for having a stolen license plate. Police then discovered his driver's license had expired.

The razor blade story was all Marta needed to hear. Now Ken's strange tales involved sadism. Marta—kind-hearted, gullible, easygoing Marta—finally exploded.

"I don't want the ferrets," she screamed at him. "They're just an excuse to visit me more, and I don't want anything to do with you. I've told you that a million times."

"When have I ever asked you for anything?" he yelled back at her, half-angry, half-whining. "All I've ever done is work around your house, try to help. I've never asked for anything."

Marta couldn't help but blurt out her real thoughts about him.

"All this stuff about death and torture—you're a freakin' weirdo, Ken. I don't want to be anywhere near you," she yelled.

Ken got quiet. Neither of them said a word as Marta drove Ken to the house on Shiawassee Street in Southfield where he was renting a room. Marta felt bad for having lost her temper. Her words had been unkind; Ken was so sensitive. Still, she really did not want him around anymore. And it didn't seem like there was any other way to get through to him.

"Stay away from me," she told Ken as she dropped him off.

Marta didn't want Ken around her children anymore. Nor did she want him hanging around her house when she wasn't there. It gave her the creeps. She called the Farmington Hills Police and asked about filing a stalking complaint against Ken. She planned to wave it in his face if he tried slinking back to her house.

Ken didn't come over again. But he did keep calling. The first time, Marta told him about the stalking complaint and hung up. After that, she let her answering machine pick up. Once, when her father was visiting and Ken called, she handed the telephone to her dad, hoping he could scare him off.

"My daughter has asked you nicely to leave her alone," Marta's father told Ken. "She has a stalking complaint against you. If you don't stop calling, we're going to contact the police."

That seemed to do the trick. The calls started to taper off in July and stopped altogether by early August. Apparently Ken had found other diversions. Meanwhile, Marta's stalking complaint landed on the desk of Farmington Hills Police Detective Ronald Shankin, who called Marta to ask what she wanted to do about it. Ken was leaving her alone, she told the detective. She'd let it drop. Shankin noted the particulars of the case, along with Ken's and Marta's names in his personal report log. He marked the case "I" for inactive or closed. Then he forgot about it.

Two months later, Ron Shankin would search frantically to find the hasty notation. By then, another father and daughter would find their lives horribly entwined with Ken Tranchida's.

CHAPTER

19

Tuesday, August 29, dawned as the day of reckoning for Ken Tranchida—at least in Ron Shankin's mind. Finally, he was going to get some answers from Ken. About the car, about seeing Tina last week, about everything.

Shankin knocked on the front door of the Shiawassee house. He and the detective with him, Al Soderlund, carefully stepped back and to either side of the door, keeping an eye on the window nearest them. They had no idea what to expect. Ken or someone else might be inside the house and armed. They wanted to be ready.

The precautions weren't necessary. An elderly woman in a faded nightgown came to the door and introduced herself as Gloria Johnson, Ken's landlady. Ken wasn't home, she told the two officers, eyeing them suspiciously.

"What you do want with him?" Her voice, was cagey, unfriendly.

We just want to ask him a few questions, they told her.

What Shankin really wanted was to go inside the house. Badly. But Gloria made no overtures along those lines, and instead had parked herself in a chair on the crumbling cement porch.

Shankin had to settle for peering through the screen door, which was useless. He couldn't make out a thing inside the home's dark interior.

Ken had been up and gone by 7 A.M. that morning, Gloria

told them. He worked at some car wash. She didn't know the name, but she gave them the cross streets. She'd seen him the day before. Ken had spent most of the day shopping with her, her daughter, and her two grandchildren.

"Were you at a Kmart shopping center?" Shankin asked Gloria.

"Yes. Why?"

"How well do you know Ken?" Shankin asked, sidestepping her question.

"Well enough. He's a good boy. He pays the rent on time. What do you want with him?"

"Do you know of any girlfriends he might have, Mrs. Johnson, anyone who might have come to the house?"

Shankin showed her a photograph of Tina.

"Has this woman ever visited Ken here?"

Gloria said someone who looked roughly like the woman in the photo—she was a blonde, anyway, with shoulder-length hair—had been at her house with Ken the previous weekend. At least she thought it was last weekend, she couldn't be sure. She'd had six strokes, she explained. Or maybe it was seven. Her memory wasn't that good.

Actually, the young woman had come to see Ken several times in the past couple of weeks, she then remembered. She stayed an hour or so each time she visited. Gloria didn't know much about her. She and Ken usually went into his room. She hadn't seen her in about a week or so, though. Maybe it was two weeks. She couldn't be sure. Again, she reminded them, she'd had several strokes.

"We're looking for this woman," Shankin explained patiently. "Her name is Tina Biggar. She's missing. Her family is worried about her."

"What does any of this have to do with Ken?" Gloria wanted to know.

"We're not sure," Shankin said. "We just want to talk to him.

"Can we take a look in Ken's room?" he added casually.

He was at the older woman's mercy. If she agreed, they could go in. If not, they'd need a search warrant. He didn't have evidence to convince a judge to sign such a search warrant.

"No, I don't want you poking around his stuff," she answered testily. "Those are Kenny's private things, and I wouldn't let the police or anyone else in there."

They were batting zero. No Ken. No access to his room. What if Tina was in there, alive or dead? Shankin, though, couldn't think of any reason Tina would want to hide out in this house. And even if Gloria's memory was slightly fuzzy, surely if she'd smelled a dead body she would have alerted somebody. Her mental faculties weren't that unsound. They were sound enough to want to protect Ken from the police.

Back at the station, Shankin picked up yet another thread, calling back "Sabrina" at Elite Desires. By this point, he was in no mood for her lies about the service providing Linda Evangelista–types for rich guys.

"Cut the crap, lady," he told her. Very un-boy-scout-like behavior, he knew. But he needed to get somewhere. Nice wasn't working.

"I know what you do and I know it isn't just companionship or models that you are providing men with. Frankly, I don't care. This isn't a vice investigation. We want to find a woman named Tina Biggar and you obviously had extended contact with her earlier this year."

It worked. Sabrina confessed her name was actually Carol Esposito. She was responsible for hiring and, when necessary, firing the service's escorts. Yes, she'd known Tina.

"She came to us looking for work as an escort sometime around last November and we hired her," Esposito admitted. "But we had to fire her in March. She was always late for appointments. Sometimes she didn't show up at all."

"You haven't heard from her since then?" Shankin asked.

"Not a word," Esposito replied.

As he hung up the phone, Shankin realized he had a whole new ball game on his hands. He'd been looking for a college student. Now he was looking for a woman who'd been working as a prostitute.

This revelation didn't make Shankin any less determined

to find Tina. But it did make the investigation a hundred times more slippery. Shankin had been focusing on just four men: Todd, Ken, Luke Jackson, and Peter Nelson. Who knew how many more people, customers or otherwise, Tina had crossed paths with who might have wanted to hurt her?

Shankin reviewed what he knew about Tina's career as an escort. She'd worked for Elite Desires for roughly four months, from late 1994 to early 1995. Bill, meanwhile, had spoken of other escort services, L.A. Dreams and Calendar Girls. Were those Tina's next stop after Elite Desires?

A telephone call to Donna Mehdi confirmed it. Tina had been working for L.A. Dreams and Calendar Girls since May 26, Donna told him. She was much more up-front about Tina's work as an escort than Esposito had been.

And with good reason.

Tina had met Ken Tranchida through her escort service.

Just when Shankin's head was swirling with thoughts of Ken and Tina, another country was heard from: Germany. Peter Nelson was calling the detective from overseas.

It was through Elite Desires that Tina met Nelson, the Indiana man Todd had quizzed her about in July.

Nelson was a regular Elite Desires client, sometimes booking as many as six appointments—with different escorts—during a single weekend. But he was eventually placed on Elite Desires' "Do Not Service" list after some of the escorts complained he was pressuring them for their pager numbers—he wanted to see them without going through the service—and their real names.

Tina, who first serviced Nelson in November 1994, did agree to see him on her own. They met about a half-dozen times over the next five months or so. They also talked on the phone several times a month as well. At some point in their relationship, she stopped charging him for sex.

Some of Tina's friends knew she was seeing a man named Peter. But Tina lied to them about how she'd met him. She couldn't tell Aimee she'd met him at the Chop House, as she'd told Todd. Instead, she said they'd met one night at a local bar while she was waiting for a friend who never showed up. Nelson, she said, was in town on business and also by himself.

Aimee would later say Tina's explanation puzzled her.

"It didn't sound like Tina," she said. "She'd never sit alone at a bar, even if she was expecting to meet someone. She'd just as soon wait in her car.

"But then I thought, 'Well, maybe that is how she met him. Maybe the guy just swept her off her feet.' "

Tina eventually professed to Aimee that she was "head over heels" in love with Nelson. She'd even said once that she wanted to spend the rest of her life with him.

She also told officemate and fellow researcher Danielle Lentine about Nelson. She'd said she was in love with him and that she'd marry him if he asked. But with Lentine, she went back to her original story about how they met, explaining she'd waited on him at the Chop House.

Peter Nelson was open with the detective on the phone, surprising, Shankin thought, given the way he'd met Tina. He had no idea where Tina might be now. The last time he'd seen her was in July.

"Is she with you there in Germany?" Shankin asked. "Just tell us if she is, Peter. Her family needs to know."

"No, honest, I don't know where she is. She's not here."

Nelson sounded earnest.

Still, Shankin hung up the phone perplexed, not sure whether Nelson could be believed. If Tina was in Germany with him, he'd have no way of knowing. It'd be a bitch trying to track her down overseas. This guy had money. If she was worried about paying her bills and she wanted to get away from Todd, an affluent businessman might be just the ticket.

Had Tina violated one of the cardinal rules of prostitution and fallen in love with a John? Had the same thing happened with Ken? If so, it was a sure sign Tina wasn't cut out for the business.

When Bill phoned Shankin at the end of the day to compare notes, Shankin told him about the calls to Elite Desires and

L.A. Dreams. It was clear Bill already knew Tina had been working as an escort.

"He didn't say, 'My daughter was a prostitute,' and I didn't say it to him either," Shankin recalled later. "I didn't need to. At that point it was apparent to both of us. The duffel bag, the study, the escort services . . . He knew and I knew. There was no need to say it."

But if Bill was crushed by the discovery of his daughter's double life and his worries about her safety, he rarely showed it. Other than the blow-up about Tina's status as a voluntary missing, Bill's demeanor toward Shankin and the other detectives in the bureau had been unfailingly polite and helpful, to the point of sometimes being more solicitous of their feelings and frustrations than his own. They looked tired. Had they eaten? Had they gotten enough sleep?

Somebody needed to be asking Bill those questions, Shankin thought. In between running down leads, Shankin had heard Bill on the phone with Connie, calming her fears, and with people at the Coast Guard air station, tending to his command duties.

After Bill's outburst Monday, Sergeant Doug Anderson had cleared Shankin's caseload so he could work on Tina's case full-time. Other detectives in the bureau were assigned to back him up: Soderlund, who had already pitched in at Johnson's house, and detectives Patrick Comini and Robert Tiderington.

Bill was in and out of the detective bureau so many times every day he'd become almost a fixture: the big guy with the puffy red eyes.

Some detectives had heard or seen Bill's occasional outbursts of frustration. Yet, they all regarded Bill with respect, realizing that they'd act exactly the same way if it were their daughter missing.

Bill's plight had especially touched then-Lieutenant-Sergeant Martin "Marty" Bledsoe, who was the top guy in the investigative section, over Anderson. Bledsoe, a big bear of a man, had built by hand a cottage on an island in Lake

Michigan in the Upper Mackinaw Straits. Bill's search-and-rescue duties extended to that area from time to time. And, like Bill, Bledsoe was interested in flying. He'd been moved by the sight of Bill, his large shoulders slumped in despair as he sat in the chair next to Shankin's desk. He looked about as far from hope as a man could be. He'd also seen Bill do a one-eighty, swinging back with upbeat energy.

"He was on this roller coaster," Bledsoe remembered later. "One minute he was saying, 'We've got to find her, I know she's still alive,' like he'd just gotten this shot of energy. The next minute it was, 'We've got to find her body, I know she's dead,' as if he'd given in to all his worst fears."

On Wednesday morning, Shankin hit the road again. He and Soderlund headed back to Gloria Johnson's. She didn't have a telephone, so there was no use trying to track Ken down that way. Instead, the two detectives were hoping to get lucky. Maybe Gloria would let them in this time. Or perhaps Ken would show up. Eventually they were going to nail this guy. It was only a matter of time.

Gloria was still wearing the same faded nightgown when the two detectives knocked on her door. But she didn't seem quite as defensive as she'd been the day before. Instead, she seemed genuinely worried about Ken.

"I haven't seen him since he took off yesterday morning," she told the two detectives. "I don't know where he slept last night."

"Why not let us into his room, Gloria?" Shankin tried again, his voice gentle. "We're worried about Kenny, too. But we can't help him without information. His room might be a place to start."

"Okay," she relented. "But don't take anything. Those are his things."

She led them to a locked door on the first floor of the house and produced a key from inside her pocket. She fiddled with the lock for a few seconds. The door swung open to reveal a tiny, messy bedroom scattered with shoes, clothing, and papers. A thin bare mattress was supported by a flimsy red frame.

"Is this the way Ken usually sleeps, without sheets or covers or anything?" Shankin asked Gloria.

"That's not even the mattress he usually uses," Gloria said. "He just brought that in here last week some time. He dragged it down from upstairs. It was an extra I had. He said he got sick on his old mattress. I don't know what he did with it."

The mattress was grubby, but there were no specific stains Shankin could pick out. But then Ken hadn't been using it for that long. Shankin scanned the room for blood, body tissue, any signs of a struggle. Nothing was amiss. There were some Army jackets and other clothing hanging neatly in the closet. Pressed and straightened, they looked out of place amidst the mess of the rest of the room.

Where was Ken's old mattress? Shankin wondered. Had he really gotten sick on it? Why hadn't he simply washed it off? Maybe because whatever had been on it wouldn't wash off.

Gloria waited until the two officers were done looking around the room and followed them outside. Shankin asked about Ken's movements the previous week, from Monday through Wednesday—specifically from the day of the botched car sale to the time Todd last saw Tina.

Gloria explained she wasn't very good with days or dates—the stroke thing, again. But one evening last week, Ken had come home with a small dark car. She'd thought it was a little strange because Ken didn't have a car, but she hadn't spoken to him about it.

"That's his business," she said. "I don't go puttin' my nose into my tenant's business where it doesn't belong."

Ken left with the car later that night, about 11 P.M., Gloria added. He returned about a half hour later, but on foot. The car was gone. And he wasn't wearing a shirt. She remembered that specifically. Ken didn't usually go without a shirt. He'd been wearing one when he left. She didn't remember what kind. She also thought it odd that Ken had stayed out that late.

"He's usually home in bed by 10 or 10:30 every night," she said.

Gloria couldn't remember "Kenny," as she called him, arguing with anybody at the house. Or seeing the blond woman around the day Ken had the car. He was alone when she saw him with the car and when he'd returned on foot.

Shankin and Soderlund left their business cards with Johnson, asking her to call as soon as she heard from or saw Ken.

Back on the road, they agreed it might have been Tina's car Ken had been driving. Gloria had said it was a dark-colored vehicle. It was a long shot, but maybe she thought of silver as a dark color. Anyway, Gloria's memory wasn't the most reliable.

The two detectives cruised the parking lots of some local motels Donna Mehdi had said she thought were Ken's haunts, looking for Tina's Honda. Nothing.

Shankin had tracked down the car wash where Gloria said Ken worked: Classic Car Wash on Telegraph. That was their next stop.

Again, Ken hadn't strayed far from home. The motels, the car wash—all were along the same five-mile strip of Telegraph Road, a major north-south thoroughfare that runs though Detroit and Southfield north to the area's most exclusive suburbs. But Ken seemed to stick to the five-mile stretch located in Southfield, his hometown.

Ken's manager at the car wash, David Pund, said he hadn't seen Ken in a week. But that wasn't unusual.

"He works for a couple of months, then he doesn't show up for a couple of weeks, and then he's back working again," Pund said. "I'm used to him taking off."

Pund explained that he put up with Ken's erratic schedule because Ken worked hard when he was there, earning about $100 a week in tips, in addition to his weekly hourly wages, which totaled about $125.

The only thing out of the ordinary to happen with Ken in the past couple of weeks was that he'd shown up for work one day wearing a new pair of glasses. Ken said he'd fallen on his bike and wrecked the old pair, which had thick, black frames. The new pair had gold wire rims.

Pund added that Ken sometimes ate at a nearby twenty-four-hour hamburger joint. A waitress working the counter there easily identified Ken from a mug shot. She said he'd been coming in for breakfast for the past few months. She'd also seen him on his bicycle across the street at the 7-Eleven and at the Marathon station, where she thought he might have worked at one time.

Ken was a regular, the counter person at the 7-Eleven told the detectives. In fact, one of their clerks, a young woman named Kim Dreyer, knew Ken personally. The young man gave them Dreyer's telephone number and address.

Dreyer, a pretty, petite blonde with an upturned nose, said Ken was a hard customer to forget.

"He kept hitting on me," she told the investigators. Dryer explained she'd met Ken when he worked at the Marathon gas station across the street from the store, earlier that year. He came into the 7-Eleven at least once a day, usually to buy a Three Musketeers candy bar and to flirt with her.

When it became clear she wouldn't go out with him, Ken came up with a number of "deals" designed to hold her attention.

In May, he told her he was going to sell her his car. She'd been complaining hers was on the fritz. He said his was in great condition and a "steal" at only $500. But several weeks later, he told her he'd been in an accident and the car wasn't drivable anymore. (This was about the same time Ken told Marta he'd been in an accident, when his car had actually been impounded for stolen plates. It's not clear if Ken ever legally owned the car. He never retrieved it from the impound lot.)

In early July, Ken told Dreyer he would give her two ferrets. He had stressed how expensive they were—several hundred dollars—but that she could have them for free. He wanted her to come over to his apartment to pick them up. She didn't have a cage or food, so she never made the trip.

And just this past Sunday, August 27, Ken had come by

the store again with yet another of his bargains. He wanted to sell her another car: a small, gray-green compact. She didn't get a close look at it. But he said it was a great deal for only $500. She was interested, but she wouldn't have any money for a couple of weeks. She said she'd page him when she did.

Dreyer still had the pager number Ken had given her. The detectives decided to try the paging routine with Ken again. It had worked once before. Dreyer dialed the number, then punched in her home telephone number.

After twenty minutes, the detectives decided to throw in the towel. Ken obviously wasn't answering his pager. They'd have to try to collar him some other way. They left Dreyer with instructions to call them immediately if Ken showed up for a candy bar—or anything else.

The owner of the Marathon station where Ken had worked earlier that year said he hadn't seen Ken for a couple of months. But he did remember picking him up for work on occasion at a nearby house. He gave them directions. He also remembered that Ken had a good friend named Jerry Holbert who lived in a local trailer park, the Flamingo, and who worked as a wrecker driver at another area gas station, Benner's Amoco.

The Benner's manager gave the detectives Jerry's telephone number. The sun setting, Shankin and Soderlund resolved to try to find either Holbert or Ken the next day.

Shankin brooded for a moment as he drove back to the station. Ken's world was this tight little circle, the same convenience store, the same breakfast joint, one or two close friends. Why was he so damn hard to track down?

Even though it was late in the evening, Shankin called Jerry when he got back to the station. He vowed it would be his last call that night. He and Soderlund had been at it for more than twelve hours.

Ken wasn't with him, Holbert said, and he didn't know of any other friends Ken had except some woman named "Marta, Marta Show-something."

"Marta Showalter?" Shankin asked. He didn't know where

in his brain that name had come from. It just kind of sprung to his lips.

"Yeah, I think that's it," Jerry said. "Showalter, that sounds right."

Showalter. Where had Shankin heard the name Marta Showalter before? Showalter was a very distinctive name. If he'd come across it at work, it was in his daily report log. He noted everything in there.

True to form, Shankin found the note he'd made in the log in June in response to Showalter's complaint: "R/P [reporting person] states that Ken Tranchida had been stalking her. Stalking has stopped. Doesn't wish to file formal complaint."

Perhaps Ken's stalking of Marta had stopped. But how about Tina? He'd bet anything that once Ken had hooked up with Tina, he'd been impossible to shake.

CHAPTER

20

Shankin showed up at Jerry Holbert's early the next morning—without warning. He didn't want Holbert taking off on him.

He needn't have worried. Holbert, who had been sleeping, rolled out of bed and pulled on a pair of sweats and a ripped T-shirt to greet the investigator.

He'd been up all night working at the gas station, he explained. He grabbed a Pepsi—breakfast—and offered Shankin one. The detective declined. Too fattening. Obviously something the 300-plus-pound Holbert didn't worry too much about.

What Jerry may have lacked in nutritional self-discipline, he made up for in openness, however. Good-natured and without a trace of nervousness, he happily told the detective everything he knew about Ken, with little or no prodding.

Ken and he had been good friends for seven years, Jerry told Shankin. They'd met at the Salvation Army, "the church," Jerry called it. He didn't know of a single other friend that Ken had. Or any family members who would still talk to him, for that matter. He felt sorry for Ken. He knew he'd spent time in prison, but everyone deserved a chance to get straight, he thought, hold down a job, have a roof over his head.

After Ken got out of jail the last time, Jerry arranged for him to room with Gloria. Gloria was Jerry's former mother-in-law. It was a little complicated, with her being his ex-mother-in-law and all, but Jerry was still on somewhat good terms with Gloria. He helped her with work around her house. Hell, Jerry helped just about anybody who asked him.

Jerry didn't know Tina. But he did know that Ken liked women. A lot. He fell in love real fast, and when he did, he would do almost anything to win a woman's affection. Ken really wanted to settle down and get married.

Like that girlfriend he'd told Shankin about the day before on the phone, Marta. Ken would have "done anything for her. He did, just about. He mowed her lawn, worked on her garden. . . ."

Jerry didn't know why it didn't work out between Ken and Marta. They got into some fight about ferrets or something, he thought. After Marta, Jerry had fixed Ken up with a friend of his. She said he was "a complete gentleman," but nothing came of it.

Jerry said he usually talked to Ken once a day or so. On Monday, the twenty-first, he'd gotten a page from Ken, but hadn't returned it. Tuesday, the twenty-second, however, Ken had paged him "like thirty times." Sleeping or busy, Jerry never got back to Ken.

Ken finally called him from a car phone around 4:30 that afternoon. He remembered wondering "where in the hell Kenny had gotten a car phone." Ken told him he wanted him to come over to Gloria's that night. He didn't say why.

Jerry agreed, showing up at around 7 P.M. But Ken wasn't there. Ken called him around 9:30 P.M., but Jerry was busy at the station. He told Ken to call him back. Ken never called back, but started paging him again after midnight, and then again, the next day, Wednesday, beginning in the morning and ending around 2 P.M.

He had no idea where Ken was staying if he wasn't still at Gloria's.

"He hasn't been here," he stressed.

Ken had been a little different since his last prison stay, "more uptight," Jerry explained. "He used to be pretty easy-going.

But now when he gets mad about something now, he just flies off the handle.''

"Excuse me for a second," Shankin interrupted Jerry. His pager was going off. He recognized Bill Biggar's mobile telephone number. "Do you mind if I use your phone?"

Bill answered on the first ring.

"Ron, I just got a call from the escort service," a breathless Bill told Shankin. "Ken called asking for a date with a redhead. They traced the number from caller ID. He's at the Plum Hollow Bowling Alley in Southfield."

It was the break Shankin had been waiting for. Bill gave him the cross streets and directions to the bowling alley.

"I've got to go, Jerry. We've found Ken."

"Don't hurt him," Jerry called to Shankin as he ran from the trailer and hopped into his car, an unmarked black Chevy Lumina.

Shankin flew to the address Bill had given him, about a four-mile drive. He knew he was in Southfield. A different city. Out of his jurisdiction. But his adrenaline was pumping. He had the warrant from Royal Oak. He had the stalking information. Ken had stood him up for the interview Tuesday. He had enough to keep him. Southfield or not, Ken was coming back to the station with him to answer some questions about Tina.

He saw a bicycle leaning near one of the bowling alley's doors. Ken's, he figured. He used another entrance. It took a second or two for his eyes to adjust to the darkness once inside, but he quickly saw that there were several groups of senior citizens bowling.

A guy who looked just like Ken—at least from what Shankin could see from his profile and the back of his head—sat talking on a pay phone opposite the door Shankin had come in. The detective quietly approached a manager behind the counter, introducing himself as a police officer and asking to use the phone. At least thirty feet away, Ken never turned around, obviously engrossed in whatever conversation he was having.

Shankin called Southfield police. It wasn't going to be their arrest, but they needed to know what was going on. He told the dispatcher who answered about the outstanding warrant from Royal Oak and that Ken was wanted for questioning on a missing persons case in Farmington Hills. Then he asked them to send a backup car to meet him at the east door of the building. That was the door nearest Ken. If Ken decided to bolt, he'd either run into Southfield Police or he'd have to go through him.

Five minutes passed. No Southfield. Ken didn't move from his perch near the pay phone. Shankin's heart was pumping. Where were they? He wanted this guy, but he didn't want to do this alone. Nor did he want the Southfield Police bitching later that they hadn't been notified of an arrest in their city. Ken started staring at the door and bouncing his leg up and down. He was getting antsy, too.

Ken got up to leave. Shankin pounced. There was no way in hell this guy was going to walk out of there. Ken was in the entranceway, when Shankin caught up with him.

"Hi, Kenny, how're you doing?"

Ken stopped dead in his tracks, spun around, his hands up in the air. He took one look at Shankin and turned back around, assuming the prisoner stance, legs spread, arms behind his back. It was obviously a position he'd been in a few times.

"I know, you've got me," he said, his voice resigned, even.

"I've been trying to talk to you, Ken," Shankin told him as he handcuffed him. "Where you been staying?" His tone was friendly. They were cop and prisoner, but Shankin didn't want to start right in on him playing the heavy. He wanted to get to know him a little better.

Actually, he wanted to get to know him a lot better.

"With friends," Ken replied, his voice cool, noncommittal. Shankin ushered him out the door, hoping like hell Southfield would show up soon. Ken's bike was still leaning against the building.

"Is this your bike, Ken?" Shankin asked. "We'll throw it in the back of the car. Southfield Police will be here any minute. They'll take it. You're going to go back to the Farmington Hills station to answer a few questions.''

''I don't know what you want with me,'' Ken replied, his voice sputtering in that grating half-whine Shankin remembered from their telephone conversation.

Shankin lost it. They'd been playing cat-and-mouse for three days and he didn't know what they wanted with him. Bullshit.

''You're fucking lying, Ken. You know damn well why we want to talk to you.'' Shankin pulled the handcuffs tighter.

''Does the name Tina Biggar ring a bell?''

CHAPTER
21

The interview room the Farmington Hills Police use for prisoners is little more than a whitewashed cell with a telephone, a small table, and several beat-up brown metal chairs. The only adornment, a four-foot metal bar welded to the wall, has handcuffs dangling from it, a reminder to jail guests that if they even think about causing trouble, police can make their stay a little more uncomfortable.

Shankin didn't think handcuffs were necessary for Ken. Compliant to the point of servility while being loaded into the back of a Southfield patrol car and later processed by cadets at the Farmington Hills jail, Ken now sat opposite Shankin, slumped in one of the brown chairs. Unshaven and unkempt, he wore blue jeans and a dirty T-shirt. Shankin almost felt sorry for the guy. With his thick glasses and his "poor me" demeanor, Ken looked so, well . . . pathetic was the only word Shankin could use to describe him later.

Shankin called the Royal Oak Police to let them know he was holding one of their prisoners. But he suggested they "take their time" in coming to get him. Later was better than sooner.

Shankin's boss, Sergeant Doug Anderson, sat in on the interview. But it was Shankin who did most of the talking. They started with the nonthreatening stuff, asking Ken about his background. He told them he was alienated from his parents and most of his half brothers and half sisters, punctuating his quiet, two- and three-word replies with "yes, sir," and "no, sir."

When they asked him about his military record, Ken brought up the suicide attempt, holding up his left wrist so they could inspect the tiny white scar. Shankin asked him why he'd done it.

"Life sucks," Ken said, his stuttery whine quickly turning hard. "It sucked then and it sucks now."

He talked about working at the car wash and for a landscaping service. He didn't seem in any hurry to bring up the subject of Tina. Neither was Shankin. The detective wanted to gauge the change in Ken when Tina's name did surface.

Running out of softball questions, Shankin finally invited Ken to tell him about his relationship with Tina. His voice was even, nonthreatening. He didn't want Ken to feel cornered.

Ken said they'd met through an escort service. The first time they got together, he explained, she had picked him up at his room on Shiawassee and taken him to the Bluebird Motel, where they had sex. He paid her $170.

After that, he called the service two or three more times asking for her. About a week after they met, they became friends. She told him her real name was Tina, not Crystal. They started hanging around together without calling the service. He said he owed her about $1,000 for the times they had sex without using the service.

Soon, they became inseparable. He'd travel to school with her and hang around the student union while she was in class. They'd lunch together and shop. The week of the eighteenth, he'd helped her paint the apartment that she was planning to move into in Ferndale.

To hear Ken tell it, the money he owed Tina was an insignificant formality. Tina wanted to be with him because she cared about him, not the money.

When Tina began looking for a new car, they'd gone to Anderson Honda together to pick one out. He admitted he didn't have the money, but it was Tina's idea, he said, to pretend the money would be wired from abroad.

Tina graduated from Kodiak High School in Kodiak, Alaska in 1990. (*Beverly Raburn*)

Following in her father's footsteps, Tina enrolled in South Dakota State University's Army ROTC program as a freshman, where she joined the Plains Riflemen, the corps' drill team.

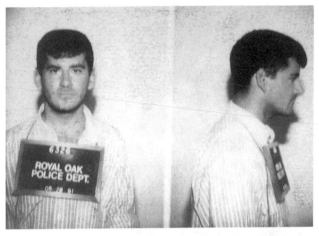

1991 police mug shot of Ken Tranchida. (*Dennis Boyer*)

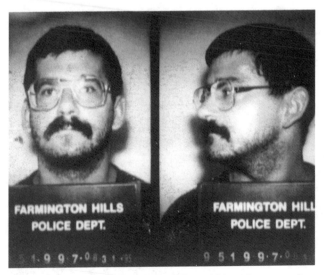

1995 police mug shot of Ken Tranchida. (*Courtesy of Farmington Hills Police Department*)

Tina and Ken rendezvoused at the Blue Bird Motel in Southfield. (*Author's Collection*)

Ken Tranchida dumped Tina's body in the woods behind a Southfield home formerly owned by his aunt. (*Author's Collection*)

Todd Nurnberger, Aimee Vermeersch and Bill Biggar spoke at a candlelight vigil for Tina. The event took place at Oakland University four days after Tina's body was discovered. (*Author's Collection*)

Tina is buried in Elkton, South Dakota, where her parents grew up, beside her brother, Matthew, and her maternal grandmother. (*Author's Collection*)

Farmington Hills police detectives (left to right)
Al Soderlund, Ron Shankin, Patrick Comini and
Robert Tiderington searched tirelessly for Tina.

Southfield police (left to right) Officer Ken Rochon,
Detective Sgt. Michael Cischke and Officer Bill Pylkus
inherited Tina's case from neighboring Farmington Hills.

Sisters Debbie Lawson (left) and Donna Mehdi hired Tina as an escort in May 1995. (*John P. Zich*)

Tina (right) and Rochester Chop House manager Aimee Vermeersch were co-workers and confidantes.

Tina and Ken Tranchida met several times at the
Southfield home where Ken rented a room.
(*Author's Collection*)

A 10-man Coast Guard honor guard greeted mourners
outside the Acme, Michigan, church where Tina's funeral
was held. (*Dale Young*)

Ken Tranchida, still bandaged at his arraignment, sliced his wrists as police closed in. (*Charlie Tines*)

Shankin stopped him. "Why would Tina want to do that, Ken? That doesn't make any sense. She really wanted that car."

In a twinkle, Ken reversed himself. "Well, I kind of thought of it, but she went along. Honest."

Shankin pressed him. "Why would she do that, Ken? It wouldn't make any sense for her to lie about money for the car. She needed that car. She was counting on it. Tina is a smart young woman. She knows she can't lie about thousands of dollars."

Ken wouldn't budge. In his version of events—at least the one he would give to Shankin during this meeting—Tina knew about the bogus loan and had gone along with it.

Shankin left the topic alone. He wanted more details about the last days Ken had spent with Tina.

On the twenty-second, Ken recounted, Tina had picked him up at his house and they drove to Oakland University. While she went to her office, he watched television at the student union. It was their usual routine. At 2 P.M., they met back at her car. After that, they went shopping and had dinner.

Ken then borrowed her car for a few hours to take care of some personal business. When he was done, he paged her two or three times. She finally called him back later in the evening. She wanted him to drop the car off at her apartment, which he did, meeting her, as she'd instructed, at the front gate of the Muirwood complex. She drove him home. But right after she got back to her apartment, she paged him.

"She just left you, Ken, and she paged you?" Shankin wanted to know.

"Yeah," Ken said, "she just, you know, wanted to say hi."

"You're telling me she paged you at 11:30 at night just to say hello?"

"Yeah. That was, something, you know, that she, we, used to do." Ken was looking off to the side, a shy smile on his face.

For a guy with no bottom teeth who'd spent more time in prison over the past decade than he had out, Ken certainly had an awfully high opinion of himself, Shankin thought. He painted a picture of his relationship with Tina as a loving couple in the first blush of love. In this script, she wasn't a hooker and he wasn't a John engaged in sex-for-hire. In Ken's mind, Tina genuinely cared for him.

On Wednesday, the twenty-third, Ken said Tina was supposed to pick him up between 7 and 8 A.M. She never showed.

"I paged her, like, twenty times," he said. "She never called me back."

That was his first story. When Shankin continued to press him, Ken finally blurted out, "I do know where she is, but I-I-I can't say. I called her apartment once when Todd was there and she yelled at me. I don't want Tina ever to get mad at me again. If I tell you where she is, she'll get mad."

Ken was whining again, his little-boy-lost routine.

Shankin took an envelope out of his pocket and dumped a set of keys on the table in front of Ken.

"Why were you carrying Tina's keys when you were arrested?"

Todd, who'd been waiting with Bill in the detective bureau, had identified the keys as Tina's. He was certain they were hers because of the key ring. They'd bought it together while whitewater rafting that summer.

Ken's expression went flat and icy as he studied Shankin, a look that seemed to say, "You think you've got me. Well, don't bet on it." In an instant, he invented an explanation.

"She had a new set of keys made for me."

Shankin groaned. "Give me a break, Ken. These keys aren't new. They've obviously been used hundreds of times. And it's Tina's key ring."

"Honestly, she had them made for me, and she gave me this ring," Ken stuttered. Then, as though it were an afterthought, Ken tacked on a whole new twist to his story. Tina had made the keys, he said, so he could "hold" her car for her while she was out of town. They were supposed to speak again Friday, September 1, the very next day. Tina would tell him then when she was coming back.

He and Tina had an elaborate paging routine, he explained. When she called, she would enter four twos in his pager. He would page her back with a telephone number where he could be reached. She would then page him back again with a number where she could be reached.

Ken's intricate web of lies was starting to give Shankin a pounding headache. He had as many stories as the detective had time. To think he'd almost pitied this guy.

The detective took another stab at getting to the truth.

"Tina has a family, Ken. A mother, a father, a sister, brothers. They all want to know where she is. They love her. They're worried about her. Tell me, where is she, Ken?"

Shankin leaned forward, resting his chin in his hand, his face inches from Ken's.

"I don't care about the police, or her family, or anybody," Ken said, looking away. "I just care about Tina. I don't want anything to ruin our friendship. She said she would never talk to me again if I told where she was, and I don't want that to happen."

"What have you done with Tina, Ken? Have you harmed her?"

"No," Ken answered, squarely meeting Shankin's gaze.

"I-I-I love her too much," he whined, tripping over the word. He didn't want to make her mad, that was all. There was nothing worse than Tina being mad at him, he said, and he knew firsthand how angry she could get from the time he'd called the apartment.

Sure, and I bet she was also plenty mad when she found out that you weren't coming through with that car loan, Shankin thought. But he said nothing.

"What did you do with your old mattress, Ken?" Shankin demanded. "Gloria said you told her you got sick on it and she never saw it again after that."

Ken repeated the story he'd told Gloria Johnson. He'd gotten sick and had taken it outside to air. Someone had stolen it from the backyard.

After three hours of interrogation, Ken was no closer to revealing Tina's whereabouts than he was when they'd first brought him in. Shankin was running out of questions to ask, and Ken wasn't rushing to fill the silence.

At 5:30 P.M., Sergeant Anderson, who'd been sitting quietly, left, but Shankin wasn't willing to let Ken go.

"What did you do with Tina's car?" he asked again. Ken said he knew, but he wasn't telling. He was "holding it" for Tina. She would be angry if he told them where it was.

"Why didn't you show up for the first interview with me?" Shankin wanted to know.

Ken said he knew he'd be arrested on the outstanding warrant. He didn't want to spend time in the Royal Oak jail again. He'd gotten beaten up there once.

Finally, a weak spot. Royal Oak. Shankin explained to Ken that Royal Oak police officers were on their way as they spoke. If he cooperated, however, and told them where Tina's car was, perhaps he could arrange for Ken to spend the night in Farmington Hills and be bonded out on the Royal Oak warrant the next day for $250.

Ken didn't believe him. They would never bond him out, he said. "If I go to the Royal Oak jail, I'm going to have to spend the next twenty-eight years in jail."

He asked to be sent back to his cell. He'd had enough.

Throughout the interview, Todd and Bill had sat nervously in the detective bureau reception area, awaiting word. When they saw Shankin's face they knew it wasn't the news they'd been hoping for.

"He says he knows where she is, but he won't tell us."

Todd clapped his hands together, heaving a sigh of relief. "Thank God, she's alive," he said.

Bill's expression remained grim. "He's lying. He's done something to her."

Neither man wanted the detective to give up. Push him. Squeeze him. Do whatever it takes. Just find out where Tina is, they insisted to Shankin.

Shankin had another idea: Jerry. Ken trusted Jerry. Whatever had happened the previous week with Tina, Jerry had been the first person Ken had paged. Maybe Jerry could talk some sense into him.

The burly tow truck driver answered Shankin's page instantly. He said he'd be happy to try to get some information out of Ken.

"But I've got a few runs to take care of first. It might be an hour or so."

"Damn it, Jerry," Shankin told him. "I need you now."

Less than a half-hour later, Jerry was looking at Ken through the glass window that separates prisoners from their visitors at the Farmington Hills jail and talking to him via telephone.

Shankin stood outside the door, listening in.

"Don't be an asshole, Ken," Jerry counseled his friend, his voice thick with disgust. "Tell these people where she is."

Ken gave Jerry the same song and dance he'd given Shankin. Tina would be mad at him. He'd promised her he wouldn't tell.

"Damn it, you didn't hurt that girl, did you, Ken?"

No, Ken assured Jerry. She was fine. She was safe. He just couldn't tell anyone where she was. He'd "promised Tina" and he would never, ever break a promise to Tina.

"Then just tell them where her car is," Jerry screamed.

It worked. Jerry came out a minute later and told Shankin Ken would tell him where he could find Tina's car if Shankin would promise that Royal Oak would release Ken on the $250 bond.

That was easy enough. Shankin repeated what he'd told Ken earlier. His bond was $250. If he pays it, he walks. They couldn't hold him for anything else.

Actually, they could have. Under Michigan law, habitual offenders suspected of committing a crime can be held for up to forty-five days without being charged, a law Shankin and his superiors were either unaware of at the time or didn't consider applicable since, at the time, Ken was not officially suspected of causing Tina's disappearance. Ken also had missed a scheduled appointment with his parole officer on July 20. A warrant could have been issued for him for being a parole absconder had that information been confirmed, Farmington Hills police later said.

The Farmington Hills Police eventually took some heat for not keeping Ken in custody. But that day, Shankin simply played the cards he thought he'd been dealt. He couldn't hold Ken unless Ken confessed. And he wasn't going to kick the shit out of him to get him to do so. That might be the way some detectives operate, but it wasn't the way the Farmington Hills Police or Ron Shankin did business.

At least now they knew where Tina's car was. Ken admitted he'd left it in the parking lot of an apartment building near Gloria Johnson's house. He didn't know the name of the apartments, but he knew the general area and named some major streets near Gloria's.

After the Royal Oak Police led Ken away in handcuffs, Shankin, Bill, and Todd set out together to find the car. It was later, after 9 P.M., when they began cruising the parking lots in the area Ken had pinpointed.

"That's it," Todd called out, pointing to an older model Honda parked in a dark corner against a wall. Locked, with the windows rolled up, the car—at least from the outside—didn't look any different from when Todd and Bill had seen it last.

Flashlights in hand, they set out to inspect it more closely. Shankin knew they could be tampering with a crime scene. He asked Todd and Bill not to touch anything, as he gingerly opened the driver's door a crack. The overhead light came on, illuminating the Honda's interior.

Peering in, they saw fast-food containers in the back seat, some scrap paper, and coins and other personal items in the console between the front seats. It looked generally untidy, but nothing screamed out at them.

"Does anything look different?" Shankin asked Todd.

Nothing appeared to be out of place, Todd reported.

They went around to the trunk. All three men held their breath as Shankin turned the key. When the trunk light popped on, they exhaled. It contained Tina's snow boots, a coffee mug, a box with an old pair of brake shoes inside, and an oilcan. No Tina, thank God.

Shankin poked around the trunk with a flashlight. Nothing looked different in there either, Todd told him. Tina usually replaced her own oil. And she'd had her brakes fixed recently.

The trio also noticed that what they thought was coffee or hot chocolate had spilled out of the mug and congealed on the trunk's carpet. Shankin gingerly lifted a small corner of the carpet to expose the spare tire well. There was nothing out of the ordinary in there, either.

An obviously dejected Bill wandered off by himself. Shankin watched the military man as he stood alone, looking up into the warm night sky. It wasn't difficult to imagine what was going through his mind. They'd talked to the person last seen with Tina. Now they even had Tina's car, but still no Tina. At the same time, Ken seemed to be slipping away, along with the answers they so desperately needed.

Bill's reverie was short-lived. Tina was still missing and there was work to be done. The three men started knocking on doors at the apartment complex to ask if anyone had seen any activity around the car. No one had. It had simply appeared there one morning, several residents said. They assumed it belonged to another tenant. No one had given it a second thought.

Shankin arranged for Tina's car to be towed back to the station. Once there, he searched around the front seats and found some letters and poems Ken had written to Tina, Tina's credit cards, her blood donor card, and some scribbled lists of men's names and telephone numbers. He also took a coffee cup and an empty bottle of Arizona Iced Tea. He then put police tape around the whole car, sealing it as seized evidence.

Shankin made a copy of a poem Ken had written to Tina for Bill and Todd. After Bill read it, his mood seemed to darken perceptibly.

> *Dearest Tina,*
> *My heart is yours*
> *For you to keep*
> *Your love will lift*

> *Me off my feet*
> *You came to me*
> *Your love so willing*
> *I know it's worth*
> *All our waiting.*
> *Love,*
> *Ken*
> *XOXO*

Obsession, Bill thought. That's what this was about. Not a car loan. Not Tina's secret life. It was about the sick, twisted obsessions of a pathetic lonely man.

"Where's my daughter, Ron?" Bill asked Shankin.

The million-dollar question. Shankin wished the hell he could answer it.

CHAPTER
22

After having come clean with Bill about Tina's having worked for them as an escort the night Bill and Todd met with Shelly, Donna and Debbie didn't hold anything back.

"From that point on, we were totally honest with Bill," Donna would later say. "There was no lying, no keeping him in the dark."

Over the next several days, Donna and Debbie searched for Tina around the clock. Along with Bill and Todd, they followed up on tips about Ken's whereabouts and posted fliers with photos of both Tina and Ken. Ashley, Marilyn, and other escorts lent a hand, too, as did Shelly and Donna's other daughter, Shannon. Even Donna and Debbie's mother did what she could. Before long, the sisters were devoting so many hours to looking for Tina that they had to shut down their services.

"We'd leave the house at 9 A.M., get home at 7 P.M., sleep for a couple of hours, then go back out," Donna said.

The sisters took an immediate liking to Bill. They found it especially admirable that having discovered the truth about what his daughter had been doing didn't make him love her any less.

"It wasn't about what she was doing—that she was leading a double life," Debbie said. "He wanted his daughter found."

But what touched Debbie and Donna most was Bill's concern for their welfare.

"He kept saying he didn't want us to get hurt," Donna would later remember. "He even said at one point that he felt bad taking us away from our businesses."

Donna and Debbie found themselves feeling sympathetic toward Todd as well, even though they knew he'd cheated on Tina.

"Everybody makes mistakes," Debbie noted.

Like Bill and Todd, Debbie and Donna focused their efforts on tracking down Ken, but they often found themselves a step behind him. At one point, they stopped to talk to employees at a McDonald's near the house on Shiawassee. It turned out Ken had just been there himself.

Every so often, they'd have a glimmer of hope. At McDonald's, for instance, they learned that Ken had bought six hamburgers.

"We thought, 'Great. Some of them must be for Tina,' " Donna said. But then they'd find out he'd ordered them with onions. Tina, they happened to know, disliked onions. "So we knew they weren't for her."

The evening of Thursday, August 31, Debbie and Donna received a call from Todd.

"We've come up with a plan," he told the two sisters.

Todd explained that he and Bill were at the Farmington Hills police station. Ken was going to be transferred from there to the Royal Oak jail, where he could be bonded out for $250. He and Bill were convinced Ken was the only person who could tell them where Tina was, he told Debbie and Donna, but Ken was unlikely to open up to them.

"We think you should bail him out of jail, then try to get him to talk," Todd said.

The plan made perfect sense to the sisters. But then they came up with a twist of their own. They'd have Shannon come along. She could pretend to be Tina's younger sister, Julie. Seeing Julie, they thought, might trigger Ken's guilt.

"We thought we could break him," Donna later explained.

Late that night, Debbie and Donna and Shannon descended upon the Royal Oak jail with the $250 needed to bail out Ken. The sisters put up $100 each. Bill contributed the remaining $50. Bill and Todd arrived at the jail, too. According to the plan, they'd remain parked across the street while the women talked with Ken.

Unexpectedly, the group literally bumped into Jerry outside the jail. He, too, had come to bail Ken out. Debbie and Donna told him they'd already put up Ken's bail. They were waiting for him now so they could talk to him about Tina. Jerry agreed not to interfere.

After Ken emerged from jail, Shannon, a tall bleached-blonde who could pass for 18, approached him and introduced herself as Tina's sister, Julie.

Ken, staring at her in silence, began to shake.

"You look like her," he finally said. "But she's better looking than you are."

Though startled by Ken's bluntness, Shannon ignored the comment.

"Ken, I need to know where Tina is."

"I can't tell you," Ken responded. "If I do, Tina will get mad at me," reiterating what he'd told Shankin earlier. "And I don't want her to ever be mad at me or to yell at me again. Besides, I told her I wouldn't tell anyone."

Ken soon began rambling.

"I've taken Tina away from all of this. She's much happier."

Ken then started blathering on about how much he loved Tina.

"I'm worried I'm getting in the way of her work," he said.

Shannon was getting nowhere. Maybe flattering him would help her earn his trust, she thought.

"I can see why my sister likes you so much," she tried.

Ken ate it up. A beautiful young woman was paying attention to him. And he didn't even have to pay.

He'd last seen Tina on Tuesday, the twenty-second, Ken told Shannon. He'd gone with her to the Oakland campus, where she needed to drop off some papers. He then went home and had gone to sleep. In the morning, he awoke to find Tina's car in the driveway of the house where he rented a room. The doors were unlocked and the keys were inside.

Tina had gone out of town, but had called him several times since she'd left, Ken claimed. He told them about his and Tina's paging routine.

Ken soon began to chafe under the barrage of questions. At one point, he blamed Tina for his troubles, according to Shannon's later testimony.

"I'm pretty mad at her," he said. "She's the reason I'm in this mess."

He then issued a threat that frightened even Shannon, who'd been confident from the start that she could handle this creepy ex-con.

"If I could see Tina right now, I'd bend her over my knee," he weirdly asserted. "I'd choke her, hang her. You know what I mean. I'd like to bend her over my knee."

Hang her? Shannon thought. What a perverted thing to say.

"Ken, where's Tina?" Shannon pleaded again.

He finally cracked.

"She's in Dayton, Ohio," he claimed. "With a client. I've called her there at a number I have back at my room."

"Drive over there with me," Shannon demanded. Before Ken had a chance to answer, Jerry interceded.

"Ken can ride with me," he offered.

Jerry and Ken headed for the house on Shiawassee in Jerry's car. Donna and Debbie and Shannon followed. Bill and Todd brought up the rear, staying far back enough not to be detected.

The caravan parked in front of the house. Ken went inside and emerged several minutes later with a slip of paper containing a phone number with an out-of-town area code Shannon didn't recognize. The women used a cellular phone to dial the number. A recording at the other end told them the number was out of service.

When they confronted Ken with this fact, he retracted what he'd said earlier. Now he was claiming he'd never contacted her at the number.

Debbie had had enough. No longer able to restrain herself, she exploded at Ken.

"Ken, you're lying," she yelled. "You're lying to us. We need to know where this girl is."

Shannon asked Ken if they could go inside the house and talk. Ken agreed. For three hours, he and Shannon sat in the kitchen going back and forth, playing a mental game of tennis.

"I got nothing from him but a bunch of lies," she later told the police.

Debbie and Donna, meanwhile, had struck up a conversation with Gloria Johnson, who was home when the group arrived at the house.

We think Ken has something to do with Tina's disappearance, they confided to the elderly woman. Gloria said she'd see if she could make Ken talk.

Playing off what she knew was Ken's fear of returning to jail, Gloria went to the kitchen and asked him about the missing mattress, the same one Shankin had quizzed her about. Ken didn't appreciate Gloria's tone.

"I told you I got a scratch on my hand and went to the hospital to get a tetanus shot," he shouted at his landlady. "The shot made me sick and I got sick on the mattress. So I took it outside to air it out."

"Then why isn't it out there?" Gloria wanted to know.

"Because I took it to the cleaners."

Debbie's and Donna's hearts sank. Ken had probably gotten rid of the mattress because it provided a clue to Tina's fate.

Later that night, the sisters and Shannon combed the neighborhood, searching garbage sites and Dumpsters for any trace of the mattress. They came up empty-handed.

At around six in the morning, the trio returned to Gloria's house. Ken was gone. So was Jerry. Exhausted, they called it quits for the night. They'd get some sleep, they agreed, then start over again later in the day.

For Shannon, later in the day meant 9:30 A.M. Before she'd left Gloria's the night before, Ken told her if she'd go with him to a pay phone in the morning, he'd page Tina and she could speak to her then.

"I don't owe anybody but you an explanation," said Ken, still believing he was talking to Tina's sister.

Shannon arrived at Gloria's house at the appointed time. Again, Ken had vanished.

CHAPTER
23

Father Maynard Tetreault was taking apart a lawnmower, its parts spread wide across the apron of the garage of Duns Scotus College Seminary in Southfield. It was just before 4 P.M. when he caught sight of a visitor he didn't recognize as one of the runners or walkers whose exercise routines regularly took them inside the seminary's wooded boundaries.

It was Monday, September 4: Labor Day. It had been clear and sunny that week, the kind of perfect, 80-degree weather Michiganians welcome in the fall months, knowing all too well the kind of stark weather shifts that overnight can turn the Great Lakes state into a bone-chilling bog.

Classes hadn't been held at Duns Scotus for more than a decade; the last public Mass was said there in 1992. But Father Tetreault and a handful of other priests still made their home within the friary's imposing red-brick walls, there to maintain it until it could be sold to another church or to a real estate developer.

Good neighbors, the priests during the summer mowed about a third of the friary's 106 acres, expansive rolling fields they generously opened up to schools for soccer games and to the city of Southfield for its annual summer Gold Cup Polo Match. Area residents regard the closed friary almost as they would a park. Children sometimes come on bikes to toss around footballs. Golfers bring their clubs to practice their swings, thwacking drives deep into the seminary's fairway-like fields. College students from nearby Lawrence Technological University steal into remote corners at night to drink beer, unseen by anyone at the church and seminary, nearly a half-mile away.

The short, dark-haired, olive-skinned stranger who approached Father Tetreault that Monday afternoon wasn't a student or someone in search of exercise, however. Of indeterminate age, with glasses and dark curly hair, he carried himself almost hunched over, a man whose body parts somehow didn't fit together.

The stranger had the bulky upper torso of a weightlifter: thick, muscular shoulders and a bulging back. But his legs, visible beyond his blue shorts, were almost stubby. Sweaty and unshaven, he held a Mountain Dew bottle in one hand, taking a deep swig from it now and then. His other hand was shoved deep into one of his pockets. He approached the cleric directly, apparently eager to talk.

"I grew up around here," he told the priest, voice slow and halting, working each word around his tongue before spitting it out. "I used to watch the fathers mow the grass then, too."

"Well, as you can see, not much has changed," Father Tetreault responded, making small talk with the stranger. To the priest, he didn't appear to be a very prosperous fellow. He's probably a vagrant in need of money, Father Tetreault thought. Then it clicked. The boyfriend of the missing college student.

The previous week, a man had stopped by the rectory office, politely introducing himself as Bill Biggar. A tall, sandy-haired gentleman with close-cropped hair and a mustache, Biggar had told Father Tetreault that his daughter, Tina, had been missing for a week. Her family and friends were worried sick that something horrible had happened to her. Their best hope for finding her was to track down a man who knew where she was. Someone she'd been dating, he said. But he was missing, too.

"He grew up around Duns Scotus and people have seen

him around here," Biggar had said. "If you spot him, can you call the number on the flier?" Biggar handed Father Tetreault two photocopied sheets, one picturing Tina, another of the man who knew where she was.

The young woman's photo showed a pretty, apple-cheeked blonde with a broad, toothy smile and high cheekbones. The photocopy of the man was hard to make out. It was a poor copy. But he looked darker, older.

"Is it possible that sometime in the past week, someone who needed help—someone who was hurt, maybe—might have rung the the rectory bell and not gotten an answer?" Biggar had asked the priest before turning to leave.

He was imagining a father's worst nightmare: his daughter, out there somewhere, perhaps stumbling through the seminary's thickly wooded forests in need of help, only to reach the sanctuary of the church, where her cries went unanswered. But it showed he was holding onto hope. His daughter was alive in that scenario.

The priest could offer little comfort.

"There's just a few of us here," he explained. "We're not always in the office."

Biggar thanked him again, asking the priest to call if he spotted either his missing daughter or the man who knew about her.

Father Tetreault hadn't been startled by Biggar's inquiry. People came to Duns Scotus surprisingly often in search of missing people, and they weren't always off the mark. Confused motorists wander off nearby freeways and onto the Duns Scotus grounds. Alzheimer's patients stroll away from local nursing homes and end up there. Even silent, the friary's fifteen-story bell tower, visible from a distance, seemed a beacon for lost souls.

With the man from the flier standing in front of him, however, Father Tetreault was nervous. He knew the man's reappearance would create a stir, not a happy thought.

The Franciscans wanted desperately to sell the friary, and at least a dozen real estate deals had fallen through over the past nine years. Some people had begun to think the place was jinxed.

Father Tetreault didn't welcome any controversy, especially any Gothic nonsense of the sort that mothballed seminaries seemed to inspire, even when a missing person isn't involved.

But he had been struck by Bill Biggar's heartsick plea. The priest excused himself, leaving the stranger standing in the same spot near the garage as he disappeared inside the seminary office. He dug out one of the fliers, studying the face for a moment.

"Kenneth Tranchida is on the grounds of Duns Scotus," he told the answering machine that took his call.

Jerry Holbert was fighting mad. Three days ago his buddy Ken had disappeared from Jerry's trailer, taking with him a handful of quarters from a liquor bottle Jerry kept filled with change for his kids. He hadn't heard a word from Ken since. It wasn't the money that upset him. It was the earful he'd gotten from Ron Shankin after Ken took off.

Where was Ken Tranchida?

And more importantly, where was Tina Biggar?

He wished he knew. What the hell had Ken gotten him into?

Jerry was working at Benner's Amoco in Farmington Hills, one of the two guys taking care of the busy gas station during the long Labor Day weekend. Because of his size—six-foot-three, 325 pounds—and his slow, easy manner of speech, some people mistook Jerry for lazy. That was far from the truth. In addition to the job at the gas station, he looked after fifty rental properties, took care of his ex-mother-in-law's house, and volunteered at the Salvation Army. He hardly slept, actually. Addicted to television, he stayed up late into the night glued to the tube, drinking Pepsi. Too many good movies on in the early A.M. hours to waste sleeping, he reasoned.

He'd met Ken at the Salvation Army in 1988. Nice guy. A little lonely. Strange when it came to women. But, hell,

what guy wasn't a little crazy when it came to women? Jerry
had had his own troubles with his ex-wife. And Ken was
always there for him. True, Ken had gotten into trouble and
landed in the slammer a few times in the years Jerry had
known him, but basically that was because he didn't have a
soul in the world he could trust other than him, Jerry figured.
And Ken never lied to him, not that he knew of anyway.

Until now. And it really stunk, because Jerry liked Bill
Biggar. He felt sorry for him. He'd gotten to know him over
the last couple of days, since the night they bailed Ken out
of jail. Not that they had a lot in common. Bill was a Coast
Guard commander in Traverse City in northern Michigan. A
stand-up guy, he came off every inch a military man. Jerry,
on the other hand, was just Jerry. Hair down to his shoulders,
stomach big enough to hide his feet. Good-hearted, he'd give
his last dime to a stranger on the street if the person needed
it. Family members told him he was too soft-hearted, especially when it came to Ken. But he was no Bill Biggar. Bill
was clean-cut, straight. Serious. A real All-American type.
Jerry swore like a sailor, but nothing else about him was
military material.

When Bill called at 4 P.M. that afternoon to tell him that a
priest had seen Ken at Duns Scotus, he squeezed his bulky
frame behind the wheel of his station's wrecker and sped over
to the seminary. Ken had a lot of questions to answer, and
Jerry had no qualms about beating the answers out of him if
he had to.

It made sense that Ken went to Duns Scotus, Jerry thought
on the short drive to the seminary. He remembered Ken telling him he used to go there when he was a kid to walk and
clear his head. Ken liked to talk to priests, too. They made
him feel better about himself. No wonder, Jerry thought, with
the crazy family life Ken had.

Because the bushes had grown up so high around the rusted
sign at the gate, Jerry almost missed the turn into the seminary. But as soon as he hit the drive, he spotted Ken standing
by the garage. With Bill. And Todd. And some of the women

from the escort service that Tina had worked for.

Here come the fireworks now, Jerry thought, seeing the welcoming committee that had gathered in Ken's honor. But Jerry had every intention of getting the first licks at Ken. He aimed the six-ton wrecker at his friend, stopping just inches from him. Bill and Todd jumped out of the way. Ken just stood there. He knew Jerry wouldn't hit him, he'd later say.

"What have you done with Tina, Kenny?" Jerry hollered, hopping out of the truck and flying toward Ken. "I oughta beat the shit out of you for lying to these people. Tell Bill where his daughter is, you lying motherfucker."

Jerry was really wound up. He outweighed Ken by more than a hundred pounds. He could have hurt him badly if he wanted to. He pushed Ken in the chest, sending him stumbling backwards. He shoved him again. He was hoping Ken would take a swing at him, so he could knock him out cold. It would serve the bastard right, thought Jerry.

But Bill Biggar stepped between the two men, his voice as cool and even as the oncoming evening breeze ruffling the evergreen boughs overhead.

"Don't hurt him, Jerry," Bill said. "I need him."

Southfield police officers Ray Taylor and Keith Birberick were having an early dinner at Kerby's Coney Island when they got the call to go to Duns Scotus. The two patrolmen had just started their afternoon shift. Birberick, a training supervisor, was riding along with Taylor, a rookie. Birberick had wanted to shovel down a few Coney Islands—a Detroit version of the Brooklyn hot dog—before hitting the streets. Taylor had already eaten at home. He was nursing a root beer, watching Birberick wolf down his dog.

"There's a suspicious person on the grounds at the seminary," the dispatch sergeant said when Taylor answered a radio page, calling the desk from a pay phone in the restaurant. "It's got something to do with that missing girl, Tina Biggars," the sergeant added, erroneously tacking on an 's' to Tina's last name as many people did. The two patrol officers had heard about the missing woman in roll call that day. College kid from Oakland University. Real pretty girl, the officers agreed. The case, though, belonged to Farmington Hills.

Taylor had been to Duns Scotus before. Perfect place to bury a body, he thought. Birberick, on the other hand, wasn't thinking about bodies. The lanky patrol supervisor was worried about his sinuses, which reacted violently to evergreen and grass—both in abundance at the seminary. I won't be able to breathe for a week, he moaned to himself.

Birberick decided he'd let Taylor take the lead. That was protocol in training sessions with rookies. He'd stand back, maybe talk to the priests who'd retreated to the rectory after contacting Bill. Birberick would also call the desk, tell them what they had out there. But when the two officers pulled into the seminary drive, it was clear they would both have their hands full.

Seven men and women were gathered in a tight knot near the garage, all shouting questions at a curly haired guy in blue shorts who was obviously in distress. Sweating, folding and unfolding his arms, stabbing the toe of his sneaker into the ground, rocking back and forth, eyes darting everywhere—he was doing everything but running away, the thing he probably most wanted to do. But that wasn't an option. The group had closed the circle around him.

The officers introduced themselves. Bill Biggar seemed to be the appointed spokesman for the group. He assured the officers there would be no trouble. They just wanted to talk to Ken about Tina, his missing daughter.

Taylor could see that Bill Biggar clearly needed to vent. He seemed in control, though. Not like that wrecker driver, Jerry. He was hot under the collar. They had to hustle him off to the side to cool him down. Todd seemed to make Ken really nervous, too.

"Are you going to kill me?" Ken asked Todd.

"No," Todd assured him. "I just want Tina back."

Taylor didn't think there was any harm in letting Bill Biggar have a shot at Ken. The officers moved off to the side, listening, trying to identify all the players and to piece together the circumstances that had brought this mismatched crew together. It wasn't easy. This story had a lot of curves and they'd obviously arrived somewhere in the middle.

From snatches of conversation they picked up, they learned one of the women was Tina's younger sister, Julie (in truth, it was Shannon), and that another younger woman was named Shelly. There was an older woman, whose name was Donna, and a strikingly attractive woman named Marilyn. And then, besides Bill and Jerry, there was a man named Todd. He was claiming to be Tina's boyfriend, even though the officers had gathered from the conversation that Ken had also been dating Tina. This made no sense at all to Taylor. From the flier he'd seen at roll call, Tina was a looker. This guy Ken was obviously a loser. Why would she give him a second thought?

Birberick saw the potential for a train wreck. He stepped back over to the patrol car to call for backup, a supervisor on the scene and for an unmarked car—someone to follow Ken after this was all over.

Southfield police officer Ken Rochon, riding alone that night, answered the backup call. His first order of business was to telephone the Farmington Hills Police to let them know they had found Ken, a courtesy call. Suburban Detroit police agencies are careful not to step on each other's toes. Investigations that originate elsewhere are sacrosanct, which is pretty much the norm for law enforcement agencies the world over. Shankin paged him back.

"We have Ken Tranchida here," Rochon told him. "Bill Biggar's talking to him and Ken keeps changing his story. He looks nervous as hell. What do you want us to do with him?"

"Did he tell you where Tina is?" Shankin asked Rochon.

"No, but he sounds guilty as hell. If you want us to take him—"

Shankin cut him off. "We've done that already. Royal Oak bonded him out. I don't have a warrant on him, so I can't hold him. Unless you guys have something, or unless he confesses, there's nothing we can do."

Thanks, but no thanks, Rochon thought as he hung up the mobile telephone.

Bill, meanwhile, continued to question Ken.

"Just tell me where she is, Ken. Tell me where my daughter is. Is she out there somewhere?" he asked, gesturing to the woods beyond the seminary's open fields.

Ken kept repeating the same story, with slight variations, each designed to cover the last lie he'd been caught in. Some of what he said was nonsense. But for the most part, Ken sounded like a lovesick teenager, not a 41-year-old man. He kept saying how much he loved Tina and how he would never hurt her. None of it added up. And it wasn't only what he said, but the way he said it: he mumbled; he stuttered; his voice was monotone. And then every once in a while, he'd take another sip from his Mountain Dew.

"She's in Ohio, in Dayton, on business," he said. "I dropped her off at the airport. She was going to meet a client. She needed the money to pay her bills. She put $10,000 down on a car and she was going to Ohio so she could pay off the car. I've told you all this before. I'm supposed to pick her up at the airport after this weekend—"

"Today's Monday," Shannon said, interrupting him. "The weekend's over, Ken. You're lying. She's not in Ohio. Where is she really, Ken? What have you done with her?"

Ken shifted gears. "After the holiday. I'm supposed to pick her up tomorrow. I can call her. I'm supposed to call her."

"We've tried the number you said was hers, Ken," Shelly interjected. "It was disconnected. And I called American Airlines. She was never on an American flight."

"She must have taken a different airline," Ken mumbled. Cornered again, he simply offered up another story.

Shelly tried a different tack. "The poem you left in Tina's car. What did it mean?"

"I wanted to know the other side of her life," Ken replied. For a moment, his speech seemed to come from a place inside him where each word wasn't weighed.

"I feel so good around Tina. She's so special to me. I love her so much. I feel so bad about it all—"

Shelly cut him off. "What do you mean by 'it all,' Ken?"

The wall went back up. "Her problems," he stuttered. "Everything that was bothering her—that is bothering her." He caught himself.

"We love her more than you do, Ken," Shelly replied. "We could have helped her, but now I don't think we can because I think you killed her."

Ken put his hands over his ears. "Don't talk to me like that," he half-yelled, half-moaned.

Bill picked up where Shelly left off.

"I know my daughter, Ken. You said you were going to buy her a car. But you never had any money to buy her a car. When she found out, she got mad and you hurt her. What did you do with her?"

"I would never hurt Tina. I loved Tina. I still love her," he said, again catching himself referring to Tina in the past tense. "I'm supposed to call her. That's how we do it. I call her and she calls me back.

"Then call her now," Shannon demanded, thrusting a mobile telephone into Ken's hands. Shaking, he dialed a long-distance number.

"Now, she's supposed to call me back," he said. "That's how we do it. I call her on her beeper and she calls me back.

"I can't say for sure that she will," Ken added, hedging his bet. "But she's supposed to."

The telephone was silent.

The Southfield officers could see that Bill was in control of this investigation and they admired him for it. They wouldn't have let this guy off the hook either, had it been one of their daughters missing. Still, they didn't intend to let this go on all night. They'd been called there as peace officers and were on the scene to see that Bill and Tina's friends didn't harm Ken. But the group seemed to be growing more and more frustrated as Ken became more evasive, his answers increasingly implausible as the questioning went on. Already they'd been there an hour and they didn't seem to be getting anywhere.

Whenever Bill or anyone else refuted one of Ken's stories,

he'd simply concoct another. But this had to end at some point. They were cops, not baby-sitters.

In what seemed like a last-ditch effort, Bill tried to appeal to Ken's sympathies.

"Please, Ken," Bill implored, his voice near breaking. "The hardest part is not knowing if she's dead or alive."

Ken finally put an end to it.

"I think I'm going to be sick," he said, doubling over and clutching his stomach.

Rochon led Ken over to the grass, where he fell to his knees and began vomiting. First clear liquid, and then torrents of blood, bright red, spilled out of Ken's insides.

"Are you all right?" Rochon asked Ken.

"I'm okay, I just have an ulcer," Ken replied, wiping his mouth on his T-shirt, his chest still heaving.

The police had seen enough.

"Okay, guys, Ken's had it for the night," Rochon said. "It's time to move on, folks."

Then, as if nothing out of the ordinary had transpired, Ken asked Rochon for a ride to a gas station a few miles away.

"I'm not taking you anywhere, Ken," Rochon replied, his voice cold. Just 30 years old, Rochon's hair was cropped close and he usually had a friendly, informal manner that disarmed both coworkers and suspects. But he was convinced Ken was lying. He had done everything just short of confessing: contradicting himself, talking about Tina in the past tense, vomiting blood.

Whatever he'd done to Tina Biggar, it must have been pretty gruesome, Rochon thought. In his four years on the force, he'd never seen anybody so nervous that they vomited blood.

"I know you did something with Tina," Rochon told Ken. "It's only a matter of time before we find out what." Rochon knew the case was out of his jurisdiction. There would be hell to pay if he got caught stomping on another department's investigation. Still, Rochon fancied himself something of a cowboy. In his book, you did whatever it took to nail the bad guy, even if it meant stretching the rules sometimes.

Ken asked if he could leave. Rochon reluctantly agreed. He didn't have a choice. The women left in one car, Bill and Todd in two others, and Jerry in the wrecker. Ken ambled through the gate and headed west down Nine Mile Road. A Southfield police officer trailed behind him in an unmarked car.

Southfield undercover police officer Bill Pylkus had been heading home from a volunteer stint guarding donations for a Labor Day telethon when he heard the patrol run to Duns Scotus over the police radio in his truck. A burly sweetheart of a cop whose life revolved around police work and his dog, studio-made portraits of whom he kept in his wallet, Pylkus was off-duty that day. But he was a sucker for any kind of police action. He swung over to the monastery, hooking up with Rochon just as Ken was leaving Duns Scotus on foot.

"We're going to tail this guy," Rochon told Pylkus, explaining Ken's involvement with Tina.

The women from L.A. Dreams had taken Rochon aside while Bill was questioning Ken, confiding that they were from an escort service and that Tina had been working with them. They also confessed that "Julie" was actually Shannon, Donna's daughter. Rochon laid out the whole convoluted scenario for Pylkus.

"It's Farmington Hills' case, but it's probably going to land in our lap," Rochon added. "She may be dead. And this Ken guy lives in Southfield. He's guilty as hell. He's got a record about a mile long and he was spitting up blood here."

"The Ken you're talking about is Kenneth Tranchida?" Pylkus asked excitedly. "I know him. I went to high school with him. Let me swing past and make sure it's the same guy."

Pylkus snuck a glance at Ken walking down the road, passing him slowly in his truck. He looked a little older, a little more haggard than the shy ROTC member Pylkus remembered from Southfield High. But, then again, Pylkus had changed, too. Years had passed since he was the clean-cut president of Southfield High's class of 1972.

Having worked undercover for more than five years, Pylkus now had hair down to his shoulders and a shaggy beard that matched. He looked like a druggie or a biker, which was basically the idea. Ken had changed, too, but there was no mistaking his curly, dark hair. It was definitely Pylkus's old classmate.

Pylkus headed home, reminding himself to talk to the guys in the detective bureau about the case the next day. Rochon had probably been right. Southfield would get it. They always got the spillovers: drug killings from Detroit, bodies and stolen cars from other suburbs. With more than 300 acres of parks and underdeveloped land, Southfield was a prime dumping ground.

Pylkus also made a mental note to pull out his high school yearbook. Ken Tranchida, that quiet little ROTC nerd, with a prostitute? And a prostitute who was a college student, no less. Who would have figured?

Meanwhile, Rochon and another undercover police officer had followed Ken to a gas station, where Ken used a pay phone. Several minutes later, a black 1989 Cadillac pulled up and Ken got in.

Rochon tailed the Cadillac to the Farmington Hills border. He knew better than to go farther. "Damn it," he swore under his breath, pounding his fist on the steering wheel. Then he remembered some people who could cross city lines. Private citizens who were very interested in this case. He pulled out his mobile phone.

CHAPTER
24

"So why'd you kill that girl, Ken?"

Ken was staring at the television set in the living room of Jerry Holbert's house trailer. Jerry was hosting his regular Monday night poker game. One of the players, Jerry's brother-in-law, David, was halfway paying attention to a losing hand in a five-card stud game, halfway needling Ken in the next room.

"So why did you kill her?" David pressed Ken again.

Ken turned and stared at him, giving him an icy look. But he didn't say a word.

Guffaws erupted around the poker table.

Jerry had borrowed a friend's Cadillac to retrieve Ken from a gas station near Duns Scotus after Ken's vomiting episode.

Jerry was still pissed at him, but, hell, he'd told himself, the guy had nowhere else to sleep. Gloria Johnson didn't want him around anymore. She'd told Jerry that. And Ken had begged him on the telephone to come get him. At least he's with me. I can keep an eye on him, Jerry figured.

The first thing Jerry did when he got back to the trailer was insist that Ken take a shower and put on some clean clothes. "You smell rough," he told Ken.

With Ken settled in, Jerry went ahead with plans for his regular Monday night card game, ordering a couple of pizzas. The players were all Jerry's relatives. Most knew Ken, having seen him at family functions before—one of Jerry's strays.

Good-hearted Jerry, he'd take in anyone. While Ken was in the shower, Jerry filled them in about the police questioning Ken about Tina's disappearance.

"I don't know where she is, and he's not saying," Jerry told the poker players. "I just wish to hell the cops would leave me alone."

David had just been razzing Ken with the remark about killing Tina. He didn't really think Ken had done anything to hurt her, but he left him alone after the nasty look Ken had shot his way. Whatever, David figured. This was Ken's mess. He wasn't getting mixed up in it.

Actually, they'd all stopped paying attention to Ken after that, turning their focus instead to poker. There was money at stake. Mesmerized by the television set, Ken didn't seem to notice.

But outside the trailer, there was a great deal of interest in what Ken was doing. Following up on a tip from Rochon— he'd paged them to let them know that Ken had crossed into Farmington Hills from Southfield and that he could no longer tail him—the searchers who'd converged at Duns Scotus had followed Ken to Jerry's. They knew Jerry's place was Ken's likely destination. The Cadillac parked outside the trailer confirmed it.

Ken had told the group gathered at Duns Scotus that Tina was supposed to call him the next morning at 10 A.M., after, of course, their now-familiar paging routine. To ensure that Ken lived up to his half of the bargain, they blocked every entrance to the trailer park.

Shelly and Marilyn had also convinced the owner of the trailer next to Jerry's to allow them to come in. Once inside, they eavesdropped through the thin walls on Ken and the poker players. They heard the crack David had made about killing Tina—hardly a laughing matter, as far as they were concerned.

Bill remained parked outside for several hours until he couldn't stand it any longer. He knocked on the door.

"Hey, Jerry," he said, greeting the wrecker driver as he opened the door, his tone breezy. He saw Ken sitting in the living room, his hair still wet from the shower. "I thought Ken might be hungry, after getting sick and all. I just thought he might want to get something to eat."

"You're going to bring him back here, right?" asked Jerry, still protective of Ken. Bill had been even-handed and polite, but who knew when he might snap, Jerry thought. And as far as he was concerned, there was no concrete proof that Ken had done anything to Tina. Ken kept telling him he hadn't. And Jerry wanted badly to believe his friend.

Bill assured him that he would return Ken to him, which seemed to satisfy Jerry. After all, he liked Bill, too. That's what made this whole damn thing so confusing. Jerry was starting to feel trapped between the two men.

Ken was quiet as he and Bill drove to a Denny's restaurant near the trailer. It was about 1 A.M. The older man watched Ken wolf down his food like an animal, saying very little.

"Where is she, Ken?" Bill asked about halfway through Ken's meal.

"Ohio," Ken said, wiping his face on a napkin. "Dayton."

"Can you call her?"

Ken went through another halting explanation of the paging routine. They usually did this on Tuesdays and Fridays, he explained. He hadn't done it last Friday, however, because he'd been in jail. That was the day Shankin had picked him up. And now the Farmington Hills Police had his pager. They'd taken it from him when they arrested him. Because of that, he wasn't sure he would be able to make the call the following day either. He seemed genuinely disappointed.

"What if we went and got your pager from Farmington Hills?" Bill asked. "Could I be there tomorrow when you did it?"

Ken had no problem with that. He even threw Bill another scrap to pin his hopes on.

"If that doesn't work out, I'll take you to Tina or I'll tell you where she is," he added.

Bill asked Ken to tell him again when he'd last seen Tina, pressing him for specifics: why she'd left, what she'd been wearing, any luggage she might have taken with her, any times he might have talked to her after that.

Ken repeated the story about dropping Tina off at Detroit Metropolitan Airport so that she could catch a flight to Ohio. It had been about 9 A.M. on Wednesday, the twenty-third, he said. She didn't have any luggage with her, just her book bag.

She was trying to ''get away from some guy she'd met in Alaska,'' Ken told him. She'd been wearing a tan top and green shorts and carrying a tan and black backpack. They'd talked two days after she left, on August 25. She'd said everything was fine, but she hadn't told him when she'd be back.

''What did you do with Tina's phone?'' Bill demanded.

Ken said she'd taken it with her. Same with her laptop computer.

''What happened to your old mattress, Ken?''

He'd gotten sick on it, Ken said, as he had so many times before.

Bill wanted to believe Ken was telling the truth. And because Ken could be so specific about the tiniest details, it was tempting to be taken in. The missing book bag. The green shorts she'd been wearing. The information about Luke Jackson, the Coast Guardsman Tina had dated in Kodiak. Tina apparently had confided in Ken just enough to allow him to portray their friendship as a close one.

Still, Ken's memory had enough lapses and his story changed a few degrees each time to obscure the important details, such as what flight she was on, what airline she had used, and where she was staying.

If Ken was lying and had done something to harm Tina, why would he tell Bill he'd take him to her or tell him where she was? Surely, no one could be that manipulative, that unfeeling—that evil.

Still, Bill, as always, remained the model of restraint during dinner, even as he peppered the conversation with questions, two hours of pushing, cajoling, even begging. ''Ken, please, tell me where my daughter is,'' Bill tried again and again.

Bill wasn't alone with Ken at the restaurant. Donna and Debbie had called Rochon to tell him that Bill was going to

.en out to dinner and that they were worried about the commander. Although he'd finished his shift, Rochon decided to stake out the restaurant. It still wasn't his investigation. And the restaurant wasn't in Southfield. But he was on his own time. He could stand by just to make sure there wasn't any trouble.

When Bill got back to Jerry's trailer with Ken, he told Debbie and Donna, who were still parked outside, to go home. It was late.

"I'm going to spend the night in the trailer with Ken."

"Bill, are you crazy?" Donna said, frightened. "It's not safe. You don't know what he's capable of."

Bill was resolute.

"I'm not going to let him take off again. He said he was going to call her tomorrow, and I'm going to be here to make sure he does."

Bill filled Jerry in on what Ken had said and Jerry invited him to stay. It was plain to Jerry that Bill was determined to keep Ken in his sights, even if it meant sleeping in his car all night. He didn't want Bill to have to do that. He'd already been through enough.

Bill stretched out on one of the two couches in Jerry's living room, while Jerry lay down on the other. Ken, who hadn't had the luxury of a roof over his head for a few days, slept in Jerry's bed.

Ken quickly drifted off to sleep. Bill, however, stayed awake all night, listening, staring into the darkness. Ken wouldn't slip away on his watch.

At about 8 A.M. the next morning, Ken woke up. Though eager to get going, Bill gave Ken a half-hour or so to get his bearings.

"Ron Shankin's in by now, Ken," Bill finally said. "We can go over to Farmington Hills and get your pager." Bill's voice was firm. He was in charge now, directing Ken, making it clear he wouldn't have room to renege on the promise he'd made the night before.

Once at the station, Shankin, Bill, and Ken went into a conference room in the detective bureau, where Bill explained what Ken had promised. Shankin didn't have a lot of faith that the paging routine would pay off, but he handed Ken's pager over to Bill. It was obviously important to him. Ken wanted his bicycle, too. As if he were dealing with a small child, Bill promised Ken he could get it later, after they'd talked to Tina.

A creature of habit, Ken felt most comfortable in the five-square-mile radius around Gloria's and Jerry's houses in Southfield and Farmington Hills. So Bill drove him to a pay telephone across from the Flamingo Trailer Court. Ken had told him he and Tina had used that pay telephone before for their paging ritual. She might recognize that number.

Ken started dialing the pay telephone, studiously punching in a telephone number and then a series of "twos." Nothing. The same response they'd gotten at Duns Scotus.

"She's probably mad at me because I didn't page her last Friday," Ken muttered.

For more than an hour, Bill, struggling to keep his temper in check, sat in his car watching as Ken punched in the same numbers.

"Ken, you said last night that if this paging thing didn't work out, you were going to tell me where she was. You said you would take me to her. This obviously isn't working. Where is she, Ken? You promised."

"She's at the Hilton Hotel in Dayton," Ken sputtered.

"How do you know that?"

"When she paged me last week, on the twenty-fifth, I thought I recognized the area code from Ohio. So I called this friend of mine in Dayton, Chris, Chris Campbell, and I, uh, asked him to see if she was calling from a telephone near the Hilton."

"And this Chris person checked it out for you?"

"Yeah," Ken seemed to be warming to the tale now—the more convoluted, the better. "He went over there and it was a phone booth right next to the Hilton."

Bill used his car phone to call directory information for the Dayton area code.

"There is no Hilton Hotel in Dayton," the operator informed him. Bill walked over to Ken, who was still at the telephone booth, his frustration level ratcheting skyward with every step.

Somehow, through it all, he'd been able to keep his cool around Ken, drawing on every inch of his strength as Ken lied to and manipulated everyone around him, again and again.

"Information says there is no Hilton in Dayton, Ken," Bill told him.

Ken simply came up with another excuse.

"Well, that's what my friend Chris told me—"

Bill cut him off. "Let's call your friend Chris in Dayton."

Ken didn't hesitate, the words easily tumbling out. "Sure. I don't remember the number, but you can call information."

Bill did. There were about a hundred Chris Campbells listed in the Dayton directory, the operator informed him. Of course, Ken couldn't remember where his friend lived or what his middle initial was.

The Coast Guard commander's wall of militaristic reserve finally came tumbling down.

"This isn't checking out, Ken," he said, his voice resonating with anger. "You're lying and you know it. If you were telling the truth, you'd be able to call this Chris Campbell. He would be able to confirm your story."

Even the most dedicated pathological liar might have called it quits at that point. But Ken just kept on going. It was his game, after all. One he had started and one only he could end. And he wasn't ready yet. Not while there was still room to squirm.

He *could* call Chris, Ken insisted. He had his telephone number in the safe in his room. Bill called him on it. "OK, let's go get it."

En route to Gloria's house, Bill telephoned Jerry and Ken's Uncle Pete. He knew Gloria wouldn't let Ken in without Jerry. And Pete was the one family member who still believed Ken had some good in him. Between the two of them, maybe they could get an ounce of honesty out of him.

Pete and Jerry were happy to help. Jerry arrived first, but wasn't able to open Gloria's door.

Ken went around to the side of the house and crawled into a window. He then let Jerry and Bill in from inside.

A minute or two later, Gloria's next-door neighbor pulled into her driveway. Seeing the front door open, she pounded furiously on the screen door.

"Gloria doesn't want anybody in her house," she told Bill when he came outside. "Whoever's in there, get them out— now—or I'm calling the police."

Bill explained that Jerry, Gloria's former son-in-law, was in the house with them, but the woman wouldn't hear of it.

"She doesn't want anybody in her house. Period. Not even Jerry."

Bill didn't want to upset Gloria. The poor old woman had been through hell with Ken. He'd been able to take a quick look around Ken's bedroom, though, noting a mattress, some plastic buckets, a cooler, and an air-conditioning unit on the floor. But his eyes were drawn mainly to a large heavy safe next to the mattress.

With Gloria's neighbor insisting that they leave, there wasn't much else he could do now. They would have to wait until Gloria came home. Bill, Jerry, and Ken were still on Gloria's front porch when Pete pulled up.

Ken's uncle quickly worked up a full head of steam, talking about what a good person Ken was and how he just needed a little help in order to "reform" himself. His nephew would never hurt anybody, he assured Bill. Ken sat there basking in the attention, obviously pleased with his uncle's sadly misplaced trust.

It was more than Bill could stomach. He hadn't slept in twenty-four hours and he'd spent most of that time listening to Ken's ridiculous lies about where his daughter was. He'd had more than enough. He left Ken, Jerry, and Uncle Pete still sitting on Gloria's porch. He'd had it with Ken's charades. Importantly, he had a new focus, anyway: he wanted inside Ken's safe.

CHAPTER
25

After the bizarre scene with Ken at Duns Scotus, the search for Tina became a multitentacled monster, its grasp stretching in a dozen different directions.

And if this creature had any head at all, it was Bill.

Not satisfied with Farmington Hills' efforts, Bill had figuratively, if not literally, called in the infantry, reaching out to every law enforcement agency he could corral, from the FBI to the Michigan State Police to Michigan's Attorney General.

Shankin wasn't sitting still either.

It had rankled him to see Ken free on bond, breezing in with Bill for the pager and going about his business as he pleased, when everything out of his mouth about Tina's disappearance had been a lie.

Shankin called the Oakland County Prosecutor's Office to ask if there was any possible way he could hold or even charge him.

Summing up the complicated case as best he could to an assistant prosecutor, he explained Ken's twisted maze of lies, starting with Tina's supposed trip to Ohio to Ken's having her keys in his pocket when he'd been arrested.

It wasn't enough, Shankin was told. They couldn't charge Ken with just the evidence Shankin had. And they couldn't hold him without charging him.

Politics were partly to blame.

Then-Oakland County Prosecutor Richard Thompson, na-

tionally known as the public sparring partner of assisted suicide physician Dr. Jack Kevorkian, had gotten elected by
trumpeting his near-perfect conviction statistics. Thompson
didn't believe in plea bargains, even for little old ladies who
walked away with 35-cent combs from Kmart. Consequently,
a case had to be airtight before Thompson was willing to
pursue it. If Oakland County police agencies wanted to bring
charges, they'd better well stick. Anything that fell short
could damage Thompson's statistical record, which, in turn,
could hurt his chances for reelection. (A year later, Thompson
was out of a job anyway, ousted by voters who took a dim
view of his repeated attempts to convict Kevorkian for violating state laws on assisted suicide.)

But even Shankin had to admit there was little to go on in
Tina's case. There was no physical evidence that Ken had
done anything to harm Tina, or for that matter, any proof that
Tina had been harmed at all. The answer was the one he'd
expected: Unless he confessed, they couldn't hold Ken.

That confirmed, Shankin redoubled his efforts to nail down
something more concrete. He had to have more than just a
hunch that Ken was guilty. That meant eliminating other suspects, including any men she might have met through her
escort activities. Shankin had found several pieces of scrap
paper in Tina's car. Listed on them were the names of some
men, along with their telephone numbers. When he started
calling the numbers, it became clear many of them were
"freelance" customers of Tina's—men she'd first met
through the escort service but who she then saw by making
direct arrangements.

The normalcy of her customers' lives astounded the young
detective. Most were articulate, obviously educated profes-
sionals. Some had families, wives. Shankin didn't blow their
covers as he reached them at their places of business and in
some cases, their homes. But he shook his head in disbelief
as one after another recounted their pay-for-sex arrangements
with Tina, or "Crystal," as they all knew her.

"I took her to dinner," one man recalled as casually as if

he'd been remembering a dental checkup. "We went to a motel after. We just had oral sex."

"I got a blow job. It was just a one-time thing," another recounted. "I haven't seen her since, honest."

And yet another: "We went out, but we didn't have sex."

When Shankin pressed him, he admitted, "Yeah, okay, she gave me a blow job, but I don't know her."

Shankin wasn't a prude. But hadn't these guys ever heard about AIDS? Then again, he reasoned, maybe a condom gave them the same measure of comfort it had given Tina.

But even a condom couldn't protect Tina from the wrong John, like Ken. Or possibly one of these guys.

Most of them checked out, although Bill had come across one name repeatedly on Tina's telephone bill that was cause for concern: a doctor whose medical license had been suspended and who was under investigation for murdering his wife. Bill had even gone looking for the man trying to learn more, but had no luck. He was nowhere to be found.

Luke Jackson was still on Shankin's short list as well. Jackson, it turned out, had several run-ins with the law after his relationship with Tina had ended. On May 28, 1990, he was charged with Driving While Intoxicated. Jackson initially pled not guilty to the charge, but later changed his plea to no contest. He was sentenced to seventy-two hours in jail, ordered to enroll in an alcohol education program, and fined $250. Also, his driver's license was revoked for 90 days.

He served the jail time in late October. But less than three weeks later, he was in trouble again. On November 12, Jackson was arrested and charged with two counts of fourth-degree assault and one count of disorderly conduct. According to court documents, an "intoxicated and combative" Jackson was observed brawling with a fellow enlisted man in the barracks hallway. He bit and struck a Coast Guardsman who attempted to intercede, and made "bodily harm and/or death" threats to an MP who responded to the disturbance.

All three charges were dismissed by early December. Jackson, however, had yet to meet the terms of his drunk driving sentence. Chances are he never intended to. On January 22, 1991, a Kodiak peace officer notified the court that he'd been unable to deliver papers ordering Jackson to appear at a March 12 hearing about his failure to complete the alcohol education program.

"Jackson is no longer Coast Guard and has departed Alaska," he wrote on a "return of writ unserved" form. Jackson also failed to pay the $250 fine. It was referred to the state attorney general's office.

Using his Coast Guard connections, Bill had been able to track Jackson to an apartment building in Fort Lauderdale. Shankin called the police in that city and asked them to check out the address. They were happy to comply, but the results were disappointing: the apartment was empty. Jackson had lived there some months back, neighbors reported, but he'd moved out and hadn't left a forwarding address.

While Shankin was working the telephones, he got a call from a Detroit-area FBI agent named John Ouellett. One of the women associated with L.A. Dreams, Debbie Lawson, had called an FBI agent she knew in Ohio about Tina's disappearance. That agent, in turn, called Ouellett, asking for his help. Ouellett called Shankin and offered to give Farmington Hills a hand.

Ouellett was polite and considerate, but Shankin couldn't help but think the L.A. Dreams people must have complained about him. It wasn't hard to imagine what they'd said: Some young detective from a local department isn't doing anything to find Tina. He even had the main suspect in custody and he let him go!

But he didn't spurn the outstretched hand of the feds. The more help the better, he figured. Besides, the FBI had the kind of interstate powers that would come in handy if Jackson's trail got hot. Or if Tina's former client, Indianapolis businessman Peter Nelson, turned out to be involved somehow in her disappearance.

Shankin was on the verge of having to bow out himself. Starting the very next day, the sixth, he was going to be off the case for several weeks. Several crucial weeks, he knew. But he had no choice.

For more than six months, he'd been planning to attend a weeklong interviewing program, run by the state police. And after that, he was scheduled to go on vacation. He knew Bill wouldn't be pleased when he found out that a new detective would be handling Tina's case. But his bosses had ruled on the subject: Go to school, you need the training. "We'll take care of the Biggar case," they assured him.

Shankin was ordered to hand off Tina's disappearance to Robert Tiderington. A slim 38-year-old detective with the blond good looks of a country singer, Tiderington, before joining the Farmington Hills force, had racked up nine years of experience as a patrolman and undercover officer for the Detroit Police.

"I don't have to worry about you not doing anything with this case," Shankin teased "Tids," as he called him, while briefing him on Tina's disappearance. He also warned him about Tina's determined father. "Bill will ride your ass just like he did mine," he told his colleague.

Bill didn't disappoint. He was at Tiderington's desk the next day, wanting to know if the detective had talked to the FBI. They'd already interviewed him and the women from L.A. Dreams, Bill informed the detective. Bill also told him he was certain Ken was responsible for Tina's disappearance and told him about Ken's behavior at Duns Scotus.

The Southfield Police were convinced Ken was guilty, Bill said. Soon, he added, the FBI would be, too.

The FBI had taken a genuine interest in Ken. When Ouellett called Tiderington later that day, he had new information about Ken. While Ken was in a prison on the western side of the state in 1992, he'd sought to get the FBI involved in an international custody matter. Ken had told an FBI agent in Kalamazoo that he had two small children in France and that he was trying to track them down.

Nothing had ever come of it, but during the course of his investigation the agent had developed a rapport with Ken. The agent planned to drive in from Kalamazoo that week to interview Ken. They'd already called Ken at Jerry's trailer to schedule an appointment with him for that Friday, September 8.

Did they really think Ken would show up or that he was going to tell them anything? Tiderington thought as he hung up the telephone. Right. Ken had failed to show for his appointment with Shankin, and when Shankin finally did track him down, he spent an entire afternoon trying to get Ken to spill his guts with no results. But if the feds thought they could nail Ken, God bless 'em, Tiderington thought. Who was he to argue?

The feds, however, weren't the only ones who wanted a shot at Ken. Ken's Uncle Pete and Jerry had left Ken at Gloria's. Seeing this, Gloria's neighbor made good on her promise and called the police.

Southfield's Pylkus was several miles from Gloria's house, working undercover, when he heard a radio run to 27013 Shiawassee.

"Landlady says unwanted person, former tenant named Ken Tranchida, is at her house," the dispatcher reported.

Pylkus headed over to Gloria's to back up the marked patrol car that was being sent. He also wanted to check out what was going on with Ken. This might be his only chance.

Ken was in the front yard, and Gloria and her neighbor were sitting on the front porch. Two uniformed Southfield Police officers who had arrived on the scene were mediating the dispute. The upshot was that Ken wanted to get something from his room but Gloria wouldn't let him in.

"The police have been to my door a half-dozen times since you left," Gloria yelled at Ken. "I don't want you around here anymore."

Gloria implored one of the police officers: "Please, make him go. I've had six strokes. I'm not healthy. I can't take this."

"I just want my things," Ken said meekly, his voice in its pathetic mode.

"You're not going in unless they go in with you," Gloria said, glowering at him.

Pylkus, who'd been standing back, chose at that point to wander across the grass over to Ken.

"Hey, what's going on?" he asked Ken innocently.

"I used to live here, but now she won't let me in to get my things."

"Hey, you look familiar. I know I've met you before. What's your name?"

"Ken Tranchida," Ken mumbled.

"Ken Tranchida, it's Bill Pylkus," Pylkus said, using his best long-lost-friend voice and grabbing Ken's hand and shaking it vigorously. "Southfield High, Class of '72? Class president? Remember me?"

Ken looked disoriented. He couldn't figure out why his former classmate, now a long-haired biker type, had chosen this moment to show up on his landlady's doorstep.

But Pylkus didn't miss a beat.

"I'm a cop now. I'm undercover. That's why I'm dressed like this," Pylkus said, gesturing to his blue jeans and T-shirt. "What are you up to?"

Ken told him he just wanted to get some of his things from his room. By this time, the uniformed officers had convinced Gloria to let Ken in, but only if the police accompanied him.

But Ken wasn't anxious to do anything in front of the police. He took one quick look around and grabbed a key from a pile of belongings in his room.

As he was coming out, Pylkus asked Ken if he could see the key. He'd seen Ken stuff it in his pocket.

Ken patted his pockets. "I don't know what I did with it," he offered lamely. "I just had it. I must've lost it."

Pylkus kept up the long-lost-friend routine as he patted Ken down, asking him lightly what this whole thing was about anyway.

The key had miraculously disappeared.

"So, Ken, what have you been doing with yourself since high school? What's up?"

Pylkus hadn't forgotten about Ken's arm's-length rap sheet.

But he was hoping Ken would warm to the buddy act.

It worked. Ken told him about his job at the car wash.

"It's not a really good job, not like yours or anything," Ken said, somewhat embarrassed. "I mean, you're the success story. You're a cop."

"Ken, it's not what you do, it's how you do it. If you're the best car wash attendant there is, that's all that matters." Pylkus was really sucking up now. But Ken was eagerly lapping it up, as he always did when any attention came his way.

"So what's this all about?" Pylkus asked again.

"They think I know something about this girl Tina who's missing," Ken said, sulking. "They think something bad has happened to her."

"Did something bad happen to her?" Pylkus asked innocently. Ken ignored the question.

"No, she's in Ohio, but I-I-I need to talk to somebody," Ken told Pylkus. Ken's words always caught in his throat. But when he became nervous, the interval between words became almost interminable. "There's a lot-lot-lot of stuff bothering me." He was almost at the point of tears, Pylkus noticed.

"Hey, Ken, I'll tell you what. Here's my card. Call me tomorrow and we'll get together and talk about old times and we'll also talk about what's on your mind. We can have dinner."

"I don't have a car. I don't have any money," Ken replied.

"No problem," Pylkus said. "I'll pick you up and it'll be my treat. It doesn't have to be any place fancy. Just a couple hamburgers or something."

"You'd do that for me?" Ken asked incredulously. Either some of the shy high school student remained in Ken, or he was playing the pity angle yet again for all it was worth. Pylkus couldn't tell which.

"Sure, we're both Blue Jays, aren't we?" Pylkus said, invoking the nickname of Southfield High School's sports teams.

After Ken left, Pylkus called Farmington Hills' Tiderington, telling him about his plans to have dinner with Ken the following evening. They both agreed that Pylkus should wear a body microphone to the meeting.

Elaborate preparations were made to record the meeting between the old high school classmates, with Pylkus borrowing a body transmitter from the Southfield detective bureau and practicing using the hidden equipment. When Ken didn't page Pylkus the next day, they tried to reach Ken on his pager.

"I kept waiting for him to page me back," Pylkus would recall later. "I thought it might work. You could tell he wanted to talk to somebody."

Not yet apparently. The page never came.

And on Friday, when Ken's other law enforcement pal, the FBI agent from Kalamazoo, showed up at Jerry's door for his appointment with Ken, Ken was nowhere to be found.

Aware that the game was almost up, Ken Tranchida again had vanished.

CHAPTER
26

When Bill heard that Ken had missed the appointment with the FBI, he was more determined than ever to find out what was inside the safe in Ken's room. With Ken gone, the safe might contain the only hope he had of finding his daughter.

Ken's room was still something of a mystery. When Bill had gone through it the first time with Ken standing there, he hadn't had the time or the permission to do the kind of digging he'd wanted to. Nor was he sure he would have recognized Tina's things if he had seen them.

But Bill was desperate to look inside the safe. So he and Todd decided to go back to Gloria's one more time and to take Jerry with them.

The hard part was convincing Gloria to let them inside.

"I don't want you going in there without his permission," she told the three when they showed up on her doorstep one morning. Jerry soft-soaped her. They were just looking for things that might lead them to Tina, he assured her. They wouldn't disturb anything. Finally, Gloria relented.

The tiny room was just as Bill had remembered it. The mattress. The safe. The floor strewn with paper and clothing. Todd immediately spotted some of Tina's belongings, things he'd noticed missing from the apartment.

"Those are Tina's roller blades, and her wrist guards," he called out excitedly. "And the brake wrench I gave her." He also found the battery to Tina's cellular telephone.

"That bastard," Todd said. "Tina didn't give him any of this. She probably had this stuff in her car."

After that, the three men turned the room upside down, looking for anything that might provide a clue to Tina's whereabouts: a scrap of paper with a telephone number, a weapon, blood, anything. But other than the possessions Todd had pointed out, they found precious little. A pair of woman's underwear looked vaguely familiar to Todd. But when he checked them closely, he was certain they weren't Tina's. Wrong size.

The trio's hopes soared when they found a key lying on top of the safe. But none of them could make it work in the safe's lock. Accustomed to working with unyielding metal objects at the gas station, Jerry wasn't the least bit daunted by the useless key.

"I can open this at the station with the air hammer," he said. "We just have to get it in the truck."

Todd and Bill said they would help. The three also agreed that they should all be present when the safe was opened. If by some horrific chance, Tina's body or parts of it or some other equally gruesome evidence were in the safe, they wanted the others to be around to verify what they had found and where. If, on the other hand, the safe was empty, they agreed they should get it back in Ken's room as quickly as possible, before the police discovered it was gone.

Removing the safe proved easier said than done. It was only about eighty pounds. Still, its two-foot-square frame was bulky and Todd needed Jerry's help to lift it and load it into the wrecker.

Bill clearly knew that what he was doing was unethical, if not downright illegal. He could be risking his career, the investigation, everything. But at that moment, nothing mattered except finding Tina. The safe was all they had. If it meant breaking a few rules, so be it. For all they knew, Tina's life hung in the balance.

Bill and Todd followed Jerry to Benner's Amoco.

Working quickly, Jerry and Todd connected the hammer to

an air hose and aimed it at the safe's heavy door. In a matter of minutes, the seal around the door collapsed and the door swung open.

Inside, they found two photographs of Tina, one taken at the Q Club, another at the 1994 Chop House Christmas party. Todd recognized them as photos Tina had kept in her car. There were also photographs of Ken posing with women who were obviously topless dancers. In one, an attractive brunette was sitting on his lap. There was a ring, a blue sapphire surrounded by diamonds, with a receipt dated December 1994. There were also a pair of Ken's glasses and some papers, among them, Ken's discharge from the Army and a medical bill from a local hospital. There was nothing bloody or disgusting, thank God, the men thought to themselves. Yet the safe also contained little that had been either helpful or telling. The ring, Bill and Todd figured, must have been the one Ken had told Donna he'd bought for Tina. But that just proved what everyone already knew: Ken was a liar. The receipt revealed that Ken had had it in his possession for more than a year when he met Tina.

The men returned the safe to Ken's room and put the ring and the papers back inside. But with the broken door hanging from one hinge, there was no hiding the fact that it had been tampered with.

Again, they were at a standstill. No Ken. No Tina.

Disheartened, Bill called Debbie Lawson.

"I don't think there's any hope," he told her. He sounded lower than Debbie had ever heard him in the weeks since the search had begun. "I'm going to go back to Traverse City."

"Don't give up, Bill," she said, trying to comfort him. "We won't. We'll keep looking every day. We'll work with Todd. There's got to be something out there that the police have missed."

The sisters had the time to spend looking for Tina. For all intents and purposes, they'd gone out of business.

"If we were in the office and the phone would ring and it was a regular client, we'd take the call," Donna explained.

"But most of the time we weren't there. We were out looking for Tina, and then for Ken."

"The business wasn't our top priority," Debbie would later add. "It was Tina."

Debbie and Donna spent nearly every ounce of energy they had trying to learn what had happened to their one-time employee.

As Donna put it, "We ate Tina. We slept Tina. We thought Tina. All we did was look for Tina."

Although neither Bill nor Debbie nor Donna knew it at the time, there were at least two pieces of physical evidence the police had missed, evidence that linked Ken to Tina's murder. Bill, Todd, and Jerry might have unwittingly destroyed one when they broke into the safe.

The second was locked inside a car parked behind the Farmington Hills police station, where it sat unnoticed for two weeks.

CHAPTER
27

It was only a matter of time before the media caught on to a news story as juicy as the disappearance of a beautiful local college student who had been studying prostitution. The dam broke on September 13, when the *Oakland Post*, Oakland University's student newspaper, ran a story after having spotted the "missing" posters that had been tacked up around campus by the people who were searching for Tina.

Todd, Bill, and Tina's friends carefully edited their remarks to the newspaper, scrupulously omitting any references to her involvement with the escort services.

"I think she got caught up in this so-called [prostitution] underground because of her studies," Tina's close friend Aimee Vermeersch told the paper.

Bill was even more obtuse.

"There's very few facts as far as it goes," Bill was quoted as saying. "The fact is that Tina turned up missing."

Relatively unguarded, though, was Tina's 17-year-old sister Julie, who revealed her deepest fears. "I keep thinking that she is dead or that she had been kidnapped. I keep thinking of *The Silence of the Lambs*. . . ."

The *Oakland Press*, a local daily, was the next to pick up the story. Two days later, Detroit's two major dailies finally got wind of it.

"Missing Student was Studying Prostitutes," blared a headline in the *Detroit News*.

Local television crews followed suit, and from September 15 on, reporters of every stripe trekked daily to the Farmington Hills Police Station for updates—Camp O. J., Tiderington and his colleagues jokingly called them, invoking the image of the media mob that had assembled outside the Los Angeles courthouse for the Simpson trial.

Bill was able to protect Tina's image to a point. But in the end, media coverage of her disappearance and death became an unstoppable juggernaut, rolling over even his best efforts to conceal the fact that his daughter had been working as a prostitute.

Bill would later condemn the press for their savage intrusion into Tina's private life, but it did serve *one* purpose: Law enforcement agencies suddenly became *very* motivated to find her.

The Farmington Hills Police Department, which had done everything in their power to track Tina down, began to devote even more of its limited resources to her case, assigning three detectives—Tiderington, Comini, and Soderlund—to work it full-time and arranging for round-the-clock surveillance teams to watch places where Ken might turn up.

The state police and the FBI redoubled their efforts as well. The Southfield Police, too, sent out detectives and undercover cops to track down Ken.

While other detectives followed up on new tips that had begun to pour in in response to the media explosion, Tiderington again went over everything Shankin had dug up.

Much of it was repetitive, but he was hoping to stumble on something, anything, that Shankin might have missed.

He went back to Phil Black, questioning him again about the car. Like Shankin, Tiderington also checked out the motels Ken frequented, among them, the Blue Bird and the E.Z. Rest.

At one point, Tiderington called Todd and asked him for the serial numbers to Tina's cellular telephone and computer. He then entered them into a computer database to see if they had turned up in a pawnshop or as stolen goods. If either were the case, they might be attached to a paper trail that would lead to Tina.

Every day, coming to and from work, Tiderington parked his car not too far from Tina's silver Honda, which had been sealed with yellow police tape and moved from the garage to a red-brick wall behind the Farmington Hills Police Station. And every day since he'd taken on the case, he looked at the Honda and reminded himself that he needed to take another look inside that car.

On September 14, at around 4 P.M., fourteen days after the car had been towed there, Tiderington finally freed up some time to do just that. It was the last task he planned to tackle before heading home after a long day.

Robert Plotzke, the department's evidence technician, drove the car into the garage. Plotzke would unseal and process it. That meant videotaping the exterior and interior and photographing everything inside the trunk. Realizing it was a process that might take a while, Tiderington went inside to get a soda.

In less than five minutes, a breathless Plotzke was at Tiderington's desk. "You better take a look at this," he told the detective.

After doing the required videotaping, Plotzke had opened the trunk. In the daylight—an advantage Shankin hadn't had—he could see brown and dark red dime-sized spots and flakes on many of the items. Blood. On the coffee mug. On Tina's boots. On her gloves. On a dish towel. Even on the brake shoes.

The two men looked at each other, their eyebrows raised. But neither spoke. When Plotzke tried to lift the trunk carpeting near the stained items, he discovered it was stuck to the bottom of the trunk. He broke the seal the congealed substance had made and pulled the carpet up high, much higher than Shankin had done two weeks earlier.

Spread out over about a two-foot square on the far right side, just under the black rubber seal of the trunk, was a pool of dried and congealed blood that had apparently soaked through the mat and collected below.

"Holy shit," Plotzke whistled.

Plotzke used a hemident test—a test done with a special chemical kit, distilled water, and Q-tips to determine whether the antigens found in blood are present—on some of the items to insure that he and Tiderington weren't completely out of their minds. Almost immediately, the test Q-tip turned a bright blue-green—positive for blood. The two men hustled into Doug Anderson's office.

"You gotta come look at this, Sarge," Tiderington told him. "There's blood in the trunk. A lot of it."

Plotzke began collecting and bagging the suspected bloody items, noting them as physical evidence on a property record that would be turned over, along with the newly discovered items, the next day to the Michigan State Police Forensic Laboratory: one pair brown and blue "Sport" boots, size 9; one Thermos mug, Oakland University logo; one pair of tan gloves; one box brake shoes; three glass bottles "Arizona Iced Tea"; one trunk carpet; one towel.

Plotzke also took three swabs of blood from the pool under the trunk carpet and pulled and bagged hair and fiber samples from the front and back seats of the car.

Tiderington, meanwhile, was on the phone, nailing down a search warrant for Ken's room. They didn't—and might never—have Tina's body. They also didn't know where Ken had killed her. As a result, it was crucial to collect as much physical evidence as possible: Ken's room was the logical place to start. It might as well have been Grand Central Station, with all the comings and goings before the police experts had a crack at it. But there was still a chance that all the evidence hadn't been trampled over.

The Southfield Police and Michigan State Police agreed to meet Tiderington and Anderson there the next day.

At 6:20 P.M. on September 16, a team of state police evidence technicians descended on Gloria's house. They noted the condition of Ken's bedroom in precise detail:

The east wall of the bedroom was comprised of boxes south of the doorway. A stand, supporting a safe, south of the boxes and several plastic containers in the southeast corner. Leaning against the south wall was a large mirror. Several more boxes were near the west wall, extending from the southwest corner, north. On the north wall, in the northwest corner was a closet. On the floor east of the closet was a fan and refrigerator. The bed was located in the middle of the floor, head to the south. It was comprised of a mattress and thin frame, both red in color. A pair of Everlast brand tennis shoes were found under the stand which supported the safe.

There were dark stains on the tennis shoes. The evidence technicians bagged them for testing, in case it was blood.

When they turned the rest of the house upside down, they found a stained mattress leaning against a wall in an upstairs bedroom. They cut two samples of cloth and foam rubber from the mattress and bagged them for evidence. Two long, blond hairs were caught on a screw of a heat duct on the second floor. They bagged those also.

Tiderington shimmied into a cramped crawl space under the house, once used for storing coal, shining a flashlight around the dirty, cobwebbed hole. It was empty.

When they left early that morning, after more than eight hours of going through Gloria's house, police took away only the sneakers, the hairs, two photographs of Ken and other women, and a bill from Botsford Hospital. It wasn't much, but it was more than they'd had two days before.

Their search rekindled by the discovery of the blood, the Southfield Police now went on an all-out manhunt for Ken, sending undercover police, including Pylkus, to canvass businesses along Telegraph Road.

Tiderington, meanwhile, said he had to hammer on Ken's parole officer to enter Ken into the computer as an absconder from parole and to issue a warrant for his arrest. It was something that could have been done any time after July 20, when Ken first missed the meeting with his parole officer. The warrant meant that if and when Ken was found, he could be arrested and held.

The time for cat-and-mouse games with Kenneth Tranchida had long passed.

CHAPTER
28

It was becoming increasingly unlikely that Tina would be found alive. And if Tiderington had any doubts, they were erased when he got back the results of the forensic tests from the evidence he'd collected in Tina's trunk on September 19. All the items tested positive for the presence of A and H antigens, consistent with Tina's type A-positive blood.

There had been no need to call Bill to confirm Tina's blood type. It was on Tina's blood donor card, which Shankin had found in her car along with her credit cards. In fact, Tiderington didn't say anything to Bill about the blood. All he told him was that they were running laboratory tests on some things they'd found in the car.

"It was just too much for a father to hear," Tiderington would later recall. "And we weren't 100 percent sure it was Tina's blood, either, although we had a pretty good idea."

Aware that many aspects of the case straddled at least two Oakland County communities, Farmington Hills invited Southfield detectives, the FBI, and the Michigan State Police to a meeting to discuss the case, a kind of brainstorming session. The detectives agreed to split up the work that still needed to be done. Southfield would continue trying to find Ken; Farmington Hills would track down leads on Tina; and the Michigan State Police and the FBI would lend a hand with technical and interviewing support.

The first order of business was having cadaver-sniffing

dogs scour Duns Scotus. The closed monastery was a favorite haunt for Ken, and with about 100 acres of woods and fields, it was an obvious place to bury a body.

A state police helicopter equipped with heat-sensing computers that can pinpoint recently moved earth by detecting changes in soil temperature flew over Duns Scotus, area parks, and the ravine that ran along the Rouge River, an urban river with hundreds of tiny tributaries that runs south through Oakland county, eventually emptying into the Detroit River.

Southfield's Pylkus was in touch with Tiderington almost every day, bringing him new information. He led Tiderington and Detective Al Soderlund to Ken's stepfather, Joe's, house, where a septic drain field had been dug not that long ago. Acquainted with Joe from his days as an auxiliary Southfield policeman, Pylkus greased the way for the Farmington Hills detectives and a team of Michigan State Police cadaver-sniffing dogs to check for bodies around the recently excavated site.

As the police were leaving, Soderlund questioned Joe. The older man said that in the past five years he had talked to his stepson no more than a half-dozen times. The last time had been in May or June, when he'd come over asking to dig up some lilac bushes for a woman he was seeing.

But, he told Soderlund, "Ken did call my sister Mary recently. And some other young woman did, too. Might have been the missing girl. It was something about Mother. She couldn't make it out. You might want to talk to her."

Joe's brother, Pete Tranchida, also talked to his nephew Ken quite frequently, Joe told the police. In fact, Pete had called him earlier in the week to say that Ken was applying for jobs at Burger King restaurants in Howell and Brighton, two cities more than 50 miles north of Detroit.

Joe also suggested that the police try Paul, Ken's half brother.

The police tried Pete first. No matter how much trouble Ken was in, Pete seemed to be a constant in his life. It made sense that he would turn to his uncle now.

Police staked out Pete's house, also in Oakland County, for

several days without seeing anything. If Ken was hiding there, he was holed up well. They decided to go in.

Pete gave them permission to search the house, but he wasn't happy about it, ranting and raving at the police as they combed the tiny three-bedroom home.

"They stormed my house like Nazis," he complained to the media.

Searching Pete's house netted a big fat zero. Soderlund made a mental note to check with Paul, as soon as possible. Perhaps he was the one relative who would help them hit pay dirt.

While everything may have been meshing at the foot-soldier level among the myriad of agencies involved in Tina's search, tensions simmered between the higher-ups at the two police departments.

The media frenzy hadn't helped. After news of the missed blood in the car leaked out, Farmington Hills was criticized in some quarters for its handling of the case. Farmington Hills Police Chief William Dwyer didn't appreciate the barbs, especially since some of the sharpest ones were coming from Southfield Police Chief Joe Thomas.

The final blow for Dwyer, a 32-year police veteran and a former head of narcotics enforcement for Detroit Police, was getting a call at home from one of his deputy chiefs telling him that a surveillance team that had been staking out the stretch of Telegraph Road which Ken frequented was told to "get the fuck out of Southfield" by some Southfield undercover cops.

That was all Dwyer needed to hear. He called Southfield's Thomas at home to read him the riot act. "What the hell is going on, Joe?" he demanded to know. "Your guys kick my guys out of Southfield. This is a bunch of shit. We just met with your detectives to smooth things over with this case. We agreed this is our case, and that you guys would help out."

Thomas, known for his fairness, agreed to check it out. But he didn't appreciate Dwyer's tone and he told him so.

Their exchange ended on a cool note.

Stinging from the insinuations that his department wasn't

doing all it could, Dwyer put the detectives on the case seven days a week, which would have been necessary anyway if they were to keep up with all of the tips that had begun to stream in.

One officer at Farmington Hills did nothing but answer the telephone all day, taking reports on Tina sightings: Tina was seen in Windsor, working as a street prostitute. She was spotted at a truck stop off I-75 in Ohio. She had been seen parked with Ken at Duns Scotus several weeks earlier.

Some of the tips seemed more legitimate than others. The Windsor tip, for one, the police and searchers decided, was worth checking out.

Just a mile across the Detroit River, Windsor, Ontario, isn't much more than a stone's throw from the Motor City, connected by both a bridge and an underwater tunnel.

Meanwhile, a psychic who sometimes works with local police departments on missing persons cases had told Aimee Vermeersch that "Biggar was being held by water and that she wasn't in Detroit any longer."

"I'd never talked to a psychic before," Aimee would later say, "but you hold on to anything."

To top it all off, Connie Biggar, a devout Catholic who'd been praying nonstop for her daughter's return, had told Aimee that in her prayers she kept seeing what looked to her to be some sort of Chinatown.

Windsor had a Chinatown.

A search party set out for Windsor's downtown business district Saturday, September 16. Aimee, Bill, Todd, and about a half-dozen other people were involved in the effort. Some knew Tina. Some didn't.

"Everybody's heart was racing," Aimee would later recall.

For sixteen hours, the group went from business to business on foot, getting what they thought were some pretty good leads.

Several people swore up and down that they'd seen Tina.

A salon stylist said he'd cut Tina's hair just a few days before. He described her as an American who lived "up north."

A waitress, after being shown a photo of Tina, said she, too, had seen her recently, but that her hair was shorter than it was in the picture.

In the end, none of the tips panned out.

Ken sightings, too, were on the rise. Most of them were hit-and-runs: Ken was seen walking along Telegraph; Ken had applied for a job at a steakhouse in Clarkston.

As part of Farmington Hills' effort to go over everything, once, twice, even three times, Soderlund, a tall, sandy-haired detective, called up Ken's name on CLEMIS again, just as Shankin had originally done. The Shiawassee address popped up, along with two others: Ken's stepfather, Joe's, and one at 21142 Nine Mile Road, less than a half-mile from Joe's.

Pylkus, meanwhile, had also gotten a tip about the Nine Mile Road address. While going door to door on Eight Mile Road, a car wash owner to whom he'd shown Ken's mug shot had become excited: "My house. My house," the Spanish-speaking man told Pylkus.

Once Pylkus calmed him down, the car wash owner explained that the man in the mug shot, Ken, had been to his house several weeks earlier. The car wash owner gave Pylkus his address on Nine Mile Road in Southfield. Like the one Soderlund had come up with, it was less than a half-mile from Joe Tranchida's house.

Pylkus called Soderlund, who compared it to the address that had come up for Ken on CLEMIS. It was two houses away on the same side of the street.

Soderlund promised himself he'd get to both houses the next day. As he was making plans along those lines, a man named Mark Hawthorne came into the station to report he'd seen Ken. For now, the houses on Nine Mile Road would have to wait.

Hawthorne said he'd struck up a friendship with Ken while Ken was on the run. But when he saw Ken's photograph in the newspaper, he decided he'd better go to the police.

Hawthorne first met Ken at a Farmington Hills elementary school park. Ken had been shirtless and had scratches on his chest, Hawthorne reported. He was sitting on a jungle gym going through a wallet. It was sometime during the week of August 21, Hawthorne thought. The two had struck up a conversation and Ken had told Hawthorne that he had been sleeping in Dumpsters. Hawthorne agreed to put Ken up at a motel in Farmington Hills.

According to Ken, Hawthorne gave him the impression that he was interested in Ken sexually and Ken played along, letting Hawthorne think he'd agree to sex in exchange for the room.

Ken claimed that when Hawthorne made sexual advances toward Ken at the hotel, Ken threatened to commit suicide, saying he would "drink peroxide."

Ken had apparently forgotten having sex with L.A. Dreams' Ashley and remarking, rather coldly, that no man would want to marry her when they found out what she did for a living.

Apparently taking money for sex wasn't okay for women, but it was perfectly all right for Ken to lead a man on, acting as if he expected payment in the form of a room.

Although Ken professed his undying love for every new woman he met, it was clear he didn't respect or even like women all that much. They were merely pawns for his many con games.

"They lie to you and you can lie back," was how he would later sum up his relationships with topless dancers and prostitutes, who from the time he was in his late thirties on were really the only women with whom he formed bonds.

The schoolyard where Hawthorne had first met Ken was the next place Soderlund searched. But doing so meant the detective would have to put off searching the two houses on Nine Mile Road. He again promised himself he'd get to them. Soon.

The state police brought in their cadaver-sniffing dogs and spent the day searching a several-acre wooded area around the elementary school. They turned up nothing.

Todd and Tina's apartment, overlooked in the investigation until that point, also held new interest. Since Todd wasn't the primary suspect, Shankin hadn't seen the need to go through the apartment. But the blood in the car had given new significance to every place Tina might have spent time with Ken.

Farmington Hills Detective Patrick Comini and evidence technicians went to the apartment September 18. Todd had already moved out; the apartment was empty. But bad news awaited them: after the apartment was vacated, the carpet had been cleaned and the apartment had been painted.

Like Ken's room, it wasn't in the best condition for ferreting out physical evidence from a weeks-old crime. But the technicians made do, betting on the outside chance that there might be some trace evidence.

They were able to make out several small one-to-two-inch-round stains that looked like blood on the carpet in the living and bedroom. They did hemident tests. The spot in the living room tested iffy, the Q-tip turned a light blue. But the bedroom test was more conclusive. The stain was blood. They didn't know, however, how new or old it was, or whether it was animal or human blood. Further tests would have to be done to determine these things. They cut out two small sections from both rooms and bagged them for forensic tests.

Acting on Joe Tranchida's suggestion, Soderlund and Comini went to visit Ken's half brother, Paul, who lived in Farmington, another Oakland County suburb. He had already talked to Ken's parole officer, so the two detectives knew Paul'd be cooperative.

As predicted, Paul was gracious and open with Soderlund and Comini the next day when they stopped by his house. He told them about being estranged from Ken for almost a decade because of his brother's long history of stealing from family members.

Still, Ken had called him out of the blue several weeks earlier, somewhere around August 23. The conversation lasted maybe twenty or thirty seconds, Paul remembered.

Ken asked Paul if he'd seen his Aunt Helen lately. Paul replied no. That, basically, was that. Since Paul had caller ID, he noted the name of the party whose telephone Ken had been using. It was a name he didn't recognize: Todd Nurnberger.

"I remember thinking, 'Who the hell is Ken scamming now?' " Paul told the detectives.

Paul explained that the aunt Ken had asked about once lived in the same house on Nine Mile where their grandparents had lived, 21142 Nine Mile Road. Helen had stayed on after their grandparents died, but several years ago she'd sold the house and moved out of state. It was two houses away from where their other set of grandparents had lived.

Paul had already given both addresses to Ken's parole officer when he'd called several weeks earlier looking for Ken, he explained to Soderlund and Comini.

Ken was nothing if not predictable, Paul added. He could be counted on to screw up and lie about it. Then he could usually be counted on to run to one of three places when he was in trouble: a wooded field in Southfield near Joe's house, the grounds of Duns Scotus, or to the two houses on Nine Mile.

"We know about the houses on Nine Mile, they've come up before," Soderlund told him.

Then why haven't you checked it out? Paul thought. But he said nothing. He knew better than most that Ken was the consummate game player. If these guys hadn't gotten around to checking out Aunt Helen's house, it was probably because Ken had led them on a dozen other wild-goose chases.

On the way back to the station, Soderlund and Comini agreed that early the next morning, come hell or high water, they were going to walk the grounds of the two houses on Nine Mile Road: Aunt Helen's and the one Pylkus had given them the tip on.

"Wear your hunting clothes," Soderlund told Comini. "I think there's some pretty thick brush back there."

Next to Ken's Aunt Helen's house was the Phi Kappa Epsilon house, an engineering fraternity tied to Lawrence Technological Institute. The seven young men living there over the summer had recently reshingled the fraternity house's aging roof. The new shingles were delivered in late August, and the brothers had to spend a weekend laboring on the roof. Still, they were proud of their handiwork. The only problem was that the smell of the shingles wouldn't go away. The fraternity house lacked air conditioning, and at night, a horrible odor wafted through the open windows. Despite the passage of weeks, the odor didn't lessen. In fact, it seemed to get worse. "It made you want to puke," remembered Jeremy York, a 22-year-old chemical engineering major. Finally, they became convinced that the smell wasn't coming from the shingles, but from an animal that must have died in the woods next to them. At one point, one of the fraternity brothers went over to the fence bordering the house's volleyball pit and poked a stick through, raking around a young walnut tree for whatever might be on the other lot that was responsible for the horrible smell. Bored, he gave up.

An engineering student, he knew that the area's sandy soil acted like a giant septic field, pulling down any liquids that might come from a decomposing animal. Small animals such as moles and woodchucks, prolific in the wooded patches that surrounded the fields, would carry off the rest. It wouldn't take long for the earth to reclaim whatever was over there.

CHAPTER
29

Comini and Soderlund, both deer hunters, were wearing clothing for stomping through the woods: flannel shirts, blue jeans, and boots.

It was a good thing. The house on Nine Mile at which they started that morning, the one Pylkus had said Ken had come to, was set on a quarter-acre plot thick with poison sumac, an overgrown apple orchard, and the chest-high compost heaps of at least three houses whose fence lines touched the property.

It was slow going, but they combed the field from front to back in about two hours. Moles had dug up much of the land not covered by brush, making it difficult to tell the difference between the animals' work and holes that might have been dug by a human. They'd have to bring the cadaver-dogs back for a more thorough going over.

The homeowner's son, Jorge Luna-Gen, answered the door when the detectives knocked. He remembered Ken well. Ken had visited his house on August 29, between 5 and 5:30 P.M. He recalled the date, because his sister had bought her school books that day. The time had stood out because he and his family had been eating dinner when Ken knocked on their door.

Ken had parked his bicycle in their driveway. He wanted to look around the backyard, he told them. His grandparents had lived there once and as a child he'd spent a lot of time in and around their house. After they gave him permission, Ken walked off into the brush, heading west, disappearing from view.

They didn't see him again that night, but his bicycle was gone the next morning. Jorge's sister thought she saw him again in their backyard, also heading west into a wooded stretch, around 9 P.M. He also suggested that they check with an older woman who lived next door. She'd complained recently that someone had removed the cement cap from an old water well on her property.

The heavy cement cap on the well was slightly askew when the two detectives checked, pushed off to the side just enough to slip a body inside the well. They pushed it all the way to the side and looked down. Fifteen feet of standing water, maybe more.

Comini took a long, rusty utility pole and pushed it around in the dark water. He couldn't touch the bottom, nor could he feel anything. They made a note to ask the state police divers to come out.

Divers. Dogs. They were starting to feel next to useless.

The second address, just two doors west, Ken's Aunt Helen's old house, was really more of a cottage than anything else. The grassy driveway had been allowed to grow wild, as had the entire rear of the property, which was full of sumac, goldenrod, and raspberry bushes.

The owner, an elderly man who'd bought the house from Ken's aunt two years earlier, actually lived around the corner, he told the detectives after meeting them at the door. He just used the small white cottage as a combination tool shed and retreat. He gave the two detectives permission to walk around the property. He'd be gone anyway. He was going to take the bus to get some groceries and run some errands.

Soderlund and Comini split the parcel up, walking strips end to end. If the Luna-Gen's property had been thick, the rear lot of this house was ten times so. Neglected for more than a decade, it had returned to a completely wild state. Poison sumac, which the two men carefully pushed aside, had sprung up everywhere. So had raspberry bushes, which left a thousand tiny thorns stuck to the two detectives' clothing.

After a half-hour of pushing through the dense brush, they gave up and headed back toward the car. "The fraternity boys next door probably would have smelled something if she was over here," Soderlund told Comini.

Comini walked ahead of him. As he neared the rear of the house, he spotted a pile of what he thought looked like old clothing. He called to Soderlund.

Comini knew when he got within ten feet of the pile that it was Tina's remains. It had to be. Her clothing, the shoes. The blond ponytail. Ken's ties to the house. A closer look confirmed it. In a few seconds, Soderlund was standing behind him.

The two men backed up, stepping lightly. They knew better than to touch anything. This was a crime scene. Soderlund went to his car to get his mobile phone.

"We have a body here," he told Sergeant Doug Anderson.

Soderlund looked at his watch. It was 2:47 P.M. A light wind and dark clouds were rolling in from the north. It looked like it might rain.

Tina's disappearance was now officially a homicide case.

The Michigan State Police crime lab evidence technicians who had been called to the house on Nine Mile Road worked slowly and methodically: measuring, diagramming, photographing and videotaping the decaying corpse from a dozen different angles. In all, they shot five rolls of film with thirty-six exposures each, including close-ups of the body from a dozen different angles, and close-ups of Tina's hands and feet.

They noted the precise location of the body as being on the east side of the yard, 39'2" from the northeast corner of the house and 6'2" from the chain fence.

She had been wearing denim shorts with a black leather belt, a Liz Claiborne pullover shirt, a dark bra, and black sandals. "Victim was also wearing a Fossil brand wristwatch with a leather band," they noted.

The horribly advanced decomposition of the body was also

described in precise, if impersonal, scientific detail: "The body was in an advanced state of decomposition, and also showed some damage to the left leg, which appeared to be due to gnawing by animals. No other apparent wounds or signs of recent trauma were seen. Little or no skin or flesh remained on the skull and the lower jaw was detached. Several teeth had fallen out of their sockets. A clump of hair with a black elastic hair band wrapped around it was lying next to the head."

The technicians gathered samples of fly pupae and larvae from the body, as well as soil samples from underneath the body and the fence.

In a matter of a half-hour, more than a dozen law enforcement officers from every agency that had been involved in the search for Tina swarmed over the once-tranquil field. A camera crew and reporters from a local television station were the first media outlet on the scene. They had arrived even before the Southfield Police or all of the evidence technicians had assembled.

It wasn't long before all of the area's television stations and every major newspaper in and around Detroit sent reporters and camera crews to the scene. Each tried to peer past the yellow police tape in an attempt to glean some idea of where Tina had been found and what condition her body was in. Tina's story had been front-page news and had led broadcasts for two weeks. This was the break in the case they'd all been waiting for. They were all over it like a cheap suit.

The two police chiefs, Dwyer of Farmington Hills and Thomas of Southfield, both gave television interviews, as did a Michigan state lieutenant, each of them putting their own spin on things, stressing the important role their respective agencies had played in the investigation. Of course, all the questions eventually turned to Ken Tranchida: Where was he? Did they have any idea about his whereabouts? Bravado dropped a level as the police fielded these inquiries. He was "out there," was about all they could say. They would find him, they assured reporters.

L.A. Dreams' Donna Mehdi was home when she got a call

around 5 P.M. from Ashley, the escort who had also been out with Ken. She was crying.

"Turn on your TV," she sobbed to Donna.

Donna didn't want to believe it. She called John Ouellett, the FBI agent who'd questioned both her and Debbie.

"Did they find Tina?" she asked.

"I can't tell you that," Ouellett said.

"Goddammit, we've gone this far," Donna reminded the agent. "Tell me."

"The truth? It's Tina."

Todd was at work at Parke-Davis the afternoon of the twenty-first. When he returned from lunch that day, there was a message on his voice mail from a local TV producer. But before he returned that call, he called Donna. He knew she and Debbie were still working the streets, trying to find anyone who might have information about Tina or Ken.

When she answered, he barely recognized her voice. She was hysterical.

"What's wrong?" asked Todd.

"It's on the news," cried Donna. "Haven't you seen it?"

"Seen what?" he replied. "I'm at work."

Donna told Todd the police had found the body of a young woman in the backyard of a house where Ken's aunt had once lived. Local TV stations were speculating it was Tina's. She also recapped her conversation with Ouellett.

A stunned Todd flew out of the office and headed for Southfield.

"I was doing close to 100 mph," he'd say later, describing his harrowing drive. "I was passing on the shoulder, flashing my lights, whatever it took to get around people."

Arriving on the scene, Todd jumped out of his car without even bothering to put it in park. When it started rolling, an officer on the scene grabbed his keys, got behind the wheel, and brought it to a stop.

He wanted to find Ouellett, who had told Donna he was on his way to Southfield. But within moments, he was surrounded by reporters and TV cameramen. A policeman rushed over and positioned himself between Todd and the hoard. Another then ushered Todd across the street. Seconds later, a detective from Southfield pulled up, screeching to a halt.

"Get in," he instructed.

Todd obeyed and was spirited off to Southfield police headquarters, where he remained for several hours. He had gotten no closer to where the body lay than the edge of the home's front yard. But he had no doubts in either his head or his heart that Tina had been found at last.

Aimee Vermeersch got the news that Tina's body had been found on her car phone. A local TV reporter who had been covering Tina's disappearance called for a comment.

She had been on her way to pick up her son at school. Immediately pulling over to the side of the road, she stopped her car and started to cry. She couldn't stop shaking, she remembered later.

Aimee dropped her son off at home and sped over to the Southfield home where Tina's body had been found. As soon as she arrived, she was greeted by a swarm of reporters, photographers, and TV cameramen.

"I've got to find Todd," she said, pushing through the crowd, tears streaming down her face. "I've got to find out what's going on."

Todd, she learned, already had been whisked off to Southfield police headquarters. Aimee headed back to her car. She'd catch up with him there. But before she left, Tiderington caught up with her.

"We're going to find him," he promised her.

So many people began coming and going from the scene where the body had been found that police had to secure almost a half-square-mile area around the house, reasoning it was better to cover too large of an expanse than the reverse. Even then, they had to chase away a television cameraman who tried an end-run, coming up through the rear of the property in an attempt to get film of the spot where the body had been found.

Amid this zoolike atmosphere, Tiderington tried desperately to reach Bill Biggar by telephone in Traverse City. Maddeningly, the Biggars' telephone had been busy for more than an hour.

When the detective finally did get through, Bill was livid. He'd already gotten the news from a Detroit television reporter.

"You could have at least called me first," he said, angry and distraught. Tiderington tried to explain that the line was busy, but he knew nothing he could say could assuage Bill's grief. His daughter, his first-born, was gone. The police hadn't been able to find her for weeks. And now they hadn't even been the first ones to inform him that her body had been found. No words could soothe. Tiderington knew better than to even try.

Soderlund, meanwhile, was trying to track down the owner of the property to get his permission to search inside of the house.

When the elderly man wandered back down Nine Mile Road, grocery bags in hand, he saw all the commotion around his house and began to cry. When Soderlund led him behind the yellow police cordon and told him about finding the body, it was more than the elderly gentleman could take.

Why is he so upset? Soderlund wondered. After chatting with the man for several minutes, it became clear to the detective that he was just sensitive. He couldn't stand the thought of a young woman being found dead on his land. He gave the officers permission to search the house.

Once inside, it became clear that neither he nor the house had been involved in Tina's death. It was, for all practical purposes, empty, containing only a cot, a radio, and a few tools.

Evidence technicians finally removed Tina's remains at 7:30 P.M., transporting them to the Oakland County Morgue. The county's forensic scientists officially cleared the scene at 8:10 P.M. By then, a cold, light rain had begun to fall.

CHAPTER
30

In the game of "Let's find Ken," Southfield was now officially it.

The discovery of Tina's body meant that the case would pass from Farmington Hills' hands to Southfield's. In a meeting at the Southfield Police Station, the Farmington Hills police happily passed off the two thick files the case had grown to to Southfield Police Sergeant Michael Cischke and Detective Mark Zacks.

Every officer on both forces who'd had anything to do with the investigation was instructed to "make paper," or to fill out report forms documenting in detail the work they'd done, from the very beginning to the time the body was found. They were now building a murder case against Ken that would have to stick in court.

By this point, there was no doubt in anyone's mind who'd dumped Tina's body in that field. It was Ken's aunt's former house. Sometime around the time of the murder, he'd called his half brother Paul looking for that very same aunt. He'd lied about everything concerning Tina's disappearance.

Some of the officers' reports benefited from being written *after* the body was found. Ken's vomiting at Duns Scotus was now "ominous." One Southfield police officer who was at Duns Scotus wrote she had a "gut feeling" that Ken had killed Tina after seeing the way he'd reacted to the questioning at the monastery.

She well may have. But then again, hindsight is always 20/20, Ron Shankin would later grumble. He'd done the best he could with a missing persons case. Now that they'd found a body, he sniffed, everyone was Sherlock Holmes.

The Southfield Police, for their part, had a litany of complaints about how Farmington Hills had handled the case: the missed blood, the detectives' failure to have Todd and Tina's apartment searched, and, above all else, the fact that Ken had been released. They were also peeved that a television news crew had arrived on the scene before they did. It was the ultimate insult, as far as they were concerned, that a news organization would hear about a dead body in Southfield before the police did. Cellular telephones, not the police radios that the media regularly monitor, had been used to spread the word about the body to the brass. Somebody inside Farmington Hills had tipped the reporter before informing them, they figured.

Cischke and Zacks had been only peripherally involved in the case before Tina's body was found, helping execute the warrants at Ken's room and aiding in the search for Ken.

They'd first heard about the case from Pylkus weeks earlier, when "Roach," as Pylkus was known, borrowed the body transmitter for the meeting with Ken that never took place.

"This thing is going to end up in our laps," Pylkus had warned Zacks. Sergeant Jane Murray, who had seen Ken vomit at Duns Scotus, had given Cischke an almost identical warning.

Their prophecies had come to pass. But it was no longer a "soft" missing persons matter. It was a cold, hard homicide. Someone had dumped Tina's body in a field where it had rotted and been pulled apart by animals. All signs pointed to Ken. They wanted him, and they wanted him bad. They were just a little angry that they had to hunt him down.

Farmington Hills had "blown it," Cischke would later say. "That car told the whole story."

Those were strong words coming from Cischke, a 42-year-old detective whose attire ran to tweeds and whose droopy mustache, kind face, and earnest, laid-back manner made him resemble a slightly distracted professor. The pipe he kept tucked in his back pocket completed the picture.

By nature, Cischke—"Zeb" his colleagues called him— was thoughtful, not critical. He was the first to admit that anyone could have missed the blood. It was a mistake. Shankin was only human.

Zacks, a Young Turk at age 30, brash and outspoken, was Cischke's polar opposite. They made a good pair. If Cischke was somewhat critical of how Farmington Hills had handled the case, Zacks was more blunt.

"We got *shit* from them," Zacks would recall later. "If Ken was the focus of the investigation, why'd they let him go? In my book, if someone is the focus of an investigation, you squeeze the hell out of him. You don't let him go."

Still, neither man was the type to sit around and brood about what they didn't have.

After the meeting at the station, Zacks and Southfield undercover officer Keith "Red" Wing began combing the city for Ken. They would work around-the-clock until Ken was caught.

Murder charges had yet to be filed against him. They would need more than Tina's body before that could happen. But at least they had an outstanding warrant for Ken for being a parole absconder. Farmington Hills police and Ken's parole officer had seen to that.

Zacks' first stop was Jerry's. He knew Ken better than anyone.

But Jerry was no longer in a very hospitable mood. Rather, he was "fucking fit to be tied." At least that was how Zacks would later recall the reception they got from Jerry that day.

Another Southfield police officer had been to see him the week before the body had been found and had threatened him, Jerry told Zacks angrily.

"I don't have to take this shit from you guys. I didn't do anything," Jerry spat at Zacks.

Zacks knew immediately who Jerry was talking about: Rochon. Rochon later confirmed he had made a house call to

Jerry's while on duty, even though it was officially out of his jurisdiction. But he insisted that he hadn't made any threats.

It was simply a mild warning, Rochon would say later.

"I told him, 'If you're involved, you will be prosecuted,' " Rochon remembered.

Jerry recalled the conversation a little differently. He claimed Rochon had screamed at him, "You know where she is. You helped him get rid of the mattress. If you don't tell me, you're going to rot in jail for the rest of your life like your buddy."

Jerry had responded by telling Rochon to "get the hell out of my house. I don't have to take this shit."

In any case, Zacks did what he called his "Barney routine," a song-and-dance scenario he used with contacts and suspects that he modeled after the cheerful purple dinosaur of public television fame.

"The 'I love you, you love me,' thing" was how he described it.

Not one to hold grudges, Jerry eventually thawed. He told them about Ken's favorite hiding places, golf courses, culverts, wooded areas. He also took Zacks' business card and promised to page him immediately if Ken called or paged him.

"Don't worry," Jerry assured Zacks. "If he shows up, I'll sit on his ass until you guys get here."

It was pouring rain when Zacks and Wing left Jerry's trailer. Still, they dutifully walked through every tunnel, overpass, and culvert in the city, shining their flashlights into dozens of dark corners. They got thoroughly drenched in the process, but turned up nothing.

Obviously, Ken wasn't sticking as close to home as was his usual custom.

Bill Biggar doesn't wear his heart on his sleeve. But at a press conference outside Farmington Hills Police Headquarters four days after Tina's body was found, he made his first and only statement suggesting he felt he may have failed his daughter.

"Things happen," said the commander with tears in his

eyes. "And what seems innocent at one point maybe deserves more attention."

There was no need for him to be any more specific. Everyone there knew exactly what he was referring to.

At the same time, Bill made it clear that none of what he'd discovered about his oldest child made him love her any less.

"We were blessed to have had twenty-three years with her," said Bill, who was standing behind a row of microphones, his hands clasped tightly behind his back. "Ninety-nine percent of us would do well to aspire to be a person like she was."

CHAPTER
31

While Zacks pounded the pavement looking for Ken, Cischke attended Tina's autopsy. The post-mortem examination began at 11 A.M. on September 22, almost twenty-one hours after Tina's body had been found.

Positive identification had been made from Tina's dental records, faxed from her dentist in Traverse City to the Oakland County Morgue.

Oakland County's Chief Deputy Medical Examiner Dr. Kanu Virani performed the autopsy. It was witnessed by Cischke, Pylkus, and two forensic specialists from the morgue.

Because all of them had attended autopsies on homicide victims in the past, they watched the proceedings with dispassionate interest. Yet this autopsy was somewhat beyond the ordinary.

There would be no usual Y-shaped incision from each shoulder meeting at the middle. There were no ravaged organs to uncover, no bullet wounds. There were no organs or flesh to speak of. Rather, it would be primarily a skeletal examination, which involved cutting away the clothing and examining Tina's bones in search of trauma.

Dr. Virani began by reviewing X-rays of Tina's remains. There were no bullet holes. No broken bones. Tina's skull hadn't been fractured.

During the autopsy, he dictated his observations to a morgue specialist, who transcribed the following:

1. The body was that of a female.
2. The body was 64 to 66 inches in length.
3. The body was clothed in the following:
   a. A light-colored, short-sleeved "Polo"-style Liz Claiborne shirt, size XL.
   b. Light-colored (light-blue) denim shorts, Francois Girbaud, size 9-10.
   c. 1 leather woven belt; brown or black in color.
   d. 1 pr. brown or black leather woven shoes, made in Brazil, size 9B.
   e. 1 underwire bra, size 36C, green or blue.
   f. 1 pair panties, size 7, green or blue.
   g. 1 watch w/leather woven band and blue face. Fossil brand.

After cutting free the clothing and bagging it for evidence, Dr. Virani inspected Tina's skull from outside and inside. He looked at all the other bones from the front, then from the back, separating them. All the vertebrae were intact. The only bone missing was Tina's hyoid, a small bone that sits in front of the voice box, along with the soft cartilages that make up the voice box, the larynx. He also pointed out that the body was absent any abdominal organs. For that reason, making swabs of tissue for forensic examination was impossible.

Dr. Virani took fingernail clippings from both hands, bagging them. Head and pubic hair samples were pulled and bagged, to be tested for alien fibers. Two rib bones were taken and bagged. All of the materials were turned over to the state police crime laboratory for forensic analysis.

To sum up his findings, Virani dictated: "Due to absence of neck features, it was not possible to make a conclusion regarding trauma to the neck. At this time cause of death, unknown."

On his own report after the autopsy and after talking to police, however, Virani noted the cause of death as "head and neck trauma" and pronounced it a homicide.

On Tina's death certificate, he added that it had been only "minutes" between "onset and death," meaning the amount of time that elapsed from when she suffered her fatal injuries to when she actually died. He would later say he was referring to the time it took to strangle someone.

The time of death, he wrote, was "on or after August 23." The actual place of death was "unknown."

In allowing Tina's remains to so wholly disintegrate, Ken had done himself a big favor—a very big favor indeed.

CHAPTER
32

After dumping Tina's body behind his aunt's house, Ken shopped for absolution.

For two days in a row, on August 24 and 25, he showed up on the doorstep of St. Alexander's, a church near his rented room, asking for "emotional, spiritual and financial help," the church secretary told police. When she gave him the name of a homeless shelter in Royal Oak, he complained he couldn't get there on his bicycle.

The church secretary noted that although he was looking for food he had a "nice bike" and "three diamond earrings in both ears."

After he left St. Alexander's on the twenty-fifth, Ken pedaled over to Divine Providence Church about a half-mile away, hoping for a better reception there.

He rang the church's doorbell shortly after noon, looking "sullen and about to cry," the woman who answered the door reported.

"Sometimes life isn't worth living," Ken told her, threatening to commit suicide and begging to see a priest. Since none of the clergy was available, the woman called in another parish volunteer.

A kindly older woman volunteer took Ken into the rectory dining room where she counseled him that "all of us sometime in life have to go through hard times, yet with God's help, we can do it."

She shared some of her own personal misfortunes with Ken, and then gave him the number of a suicide crisis hot line. They hugged before he left.

In the days and weeks that followed, Ken didn't venture back into the church. But he often walked past it or sat outside on the church steps. As Ken's favorite band, the Cranberries, put it in the song "Free to Decide," maybe he wasn't "so suicidal, after all."

In the first week or so after Ken disappeared from Jerry's, fleeing from the interview with the FBI, he slept in wooded lots and parks in Southfield and Detroit during the day. The one exception was the night Mark Hawthorne put him up at a hotel.

Apart from that, Ken roamed the streets, looking like any other homeless person, picking up bottles and cans for cash, money he spent on food at all-night restaurants.

Tired of hustling for change, he began applying for jobs. He knew restaurants desperate for service help would hire almost anyone.

He filled out an application for a dishwasher's position at a Ram's Horn restaurant in Detroit on Telegraph Road. As a personal reference, he listed one name only: Tina Biggar. He gave Tina's pager number—the pager he'd stolen and by then had already thrown away or sold—as her contact number. But he never took the job. Things were getting too hot along Telegraph.

Ken began to notice marked and unmarked police cars wherever he went, even at night, and especially along Telegraph Road.

It was time to disappear into the abyss. He took a bus to Detroit's Cass Corridor.

An area of several square miles near Detroit's city center, the Cass Corridor has the dubious statistical distinction of having the highest mortality rate of any neighborhood in metropolitan Detroit. Rife with street life, it contains a half-dozen or more transient motels and twice as many abandoned, burnt-out buildings, perfect for squatters, even though sleazy landlords often tried to charge rent on some of the decrepit buildings, latching on to the Social Security checks of Detroit's most vulnerable citizens.

Prostitutes, crackheads, alcoholics, and mental patients call the Corridor home. It's a place where people go to pursue their vices anonymously, free from the eyes of prying strangers. For true urban derelicts, the Cass Corridor provided a perfectly anonymous haven.

But Ken was a suburban derelict. He stuck out like a sore thumb on the Corridor's streets. It took him all of about two days to get mugged, beaten, and robbed of the few dollars he'd managed to take with him from Jerry's.

Not one to face adversity on his own, Ken turned to the Neighborhood Services Organization for help on September 13.

His name was Sandy Wilson, he told them. He was willing to work, but he needed a place to live.

The agency found him both. An employment service that contracted out laborers for day jobs and temporary work, mostly in the suburbs, put him up in a decent, albeit dingy, studio apartment in Nottingham Apartments, an older, multistory building on Selden Avenue in the Corridor.

His rent was taken out of his wages. The arrangement didn't leave much money for food or clothing, but he had a roof over his head and an apartment with walls, windows, and its own bathroom. That was more than he'd had at Gloria's.

More than Tina would ever have again.

Also, the employment service didn't ask a lot of pesky questions or bother him about things like proper ID or a Social Security card.

By September 18, his new life was official.

Each day Ken was transported by van with several other men to Plymouth, an upscale community in western Wayne County, where he worked as a landscaper at the Fox Hills Country Club, mowing and weed-whipping the club's forty-five-hole golf course.

The subject of a nationwide manhunt, his photograph nightly flashed across more than a million Detroit-area TV screens, Ken was hiding in plain sight, soaking up the Indian summer sun on the grounds of a suburban country club.

CHAPTER
33

With the publicity firestorm surrounding Ken's disappearance, people began crawling out of the woodwork to tell Farmington Hills and Southfield Police tales of previous contacts with Ken.

The mysterious mattress was the focus of a good deal of the attention.

One man reported seeing a single-sized, blue-green mattress with striped ticking in the driveway of the Plum Hollow Golf Course in Southfield on August 31 between 6 and 9 P.M. It had a large brown stain at its center. The mattress was gone the next morning, he told police.

A 12-year-old girl described how a man fitting Ken's description pushed a mattress and box springs on a dolly down Shiawassee Street near Gloria's, sometime in late August. "The mattress was white with pink flowers. And ther [sic] was 2 big blood spots on the mattress or maybe more," the young woman wrote in her statement to police.

Yet another observer had spotted Ken pushing a mattress and box springs down Shiawassee around the same time. The man knew Ken. Often, they both used the same pay telephone in the area. He described the dolly in detail as being "green and rusty and one wheel was falling off." Ken had told him he was "taking the mattress to his sister's for her kids to play on," the man told police.

Wary of all the trouble Ken had already brought to their

lives, Ken's family members were at first reluctant to talk to police after Tina's body was found. They knew better than most people the price one paid for getting involved in Ken's affairs.

But in dribs and drabs, they began to come forward to report whatever limited contact they might have had with Ken during the past month. Each morsel of information provided another piece of the puzzle.

Partly, they cooperated out of fear. Ken was still out there somewhere. He'd turned to them in the past when he was in trouble. They certainly didn't want him showing up on their doorsteps now. Mostly, though, they just felt terrible for the Biggar family. Paul had children, including a little girl. He knew the only place for Ken was behind bars. He persuaded Ken's other relatives to tell the police everything they knew.

On Paul's advice, Ken's Aunt Helen called the Farmington Hills detectives and recounted her story.

By chance, she'd been in Southfield visiting relatives the week before Tina's body was found. Nostalgic for her little white cottage on Nine Mile Road, she'd driven past it on Saturday, September 16, she told police. Ken had been in the driveway, pacing back and forth. There was a car, parked by the porch of the house, facing east toward the fraternity, with the trunk open.

Ken's Aunt Mary also told police about a bizarre encounter she'd had with Ken around the time Tina was last seen.

On August 22, just before she'd left for an out-of-town trip, she'd received a surprising collect telephone call from Ken, whom she hadn't heard from in more than two years.

"Where's Mother?" he had demanded.

Mary thought he must be losing what was left of his mind.

"Ken, your mother has been dead for almost twenty years, and you know it," she told him. That was pretty much the extent of their conversation.

But when she returned home on September 10, she found four strange messages on her answering machine, three from Ken and one from an unknown woman.

In the first message Ken said they "lost Mother." Ken had

called back almost immediately to say he'd "found Mother."
The woman had then called and left a message, saying
"We've found Mother."

The unknown woman added that Ken had lost his job and
had no money or place to live and that he was staying with
her for a few days. She also left a telephone number, urging
her to call as soon as possible.

Tina, frantic that the car deal wasn't going as planned, was
obviously trying to check out Ken's story about "Mumsy,"
his late wife's mother, police theorized. Directed by Ken, she
may have also been going along with a scheme to wring some
sympathy from his aunt.

To cover his tracks, Ken had left one last message on his
aunt's machine: "We found Mother. I'll call back and explain
later."

Mary had inadvertently erased all the messages after she'd
gotten them and had not noted the time or day they'd been
recorded. But the content of the messages had been too
strange to forget.

Slowly, the pieces of a murder case against Ken were starting to fall into place.

Police now had a motive: Ken wanted to silence Tina after
she began complaining about the car loan's not coming
through. After all, she'd been upset enough about the loan to
call one of Ken's relatives, someone she'd never met. And
everyone who knew Tina knew that she couldn't stand being
lied to or taken advantage of by a man. She defended herself,
even if it meant fighting back.

Now the police also had a modus operandi: Flush with a
little cash from his income tax check, a lonely Ken had started
calling escort services. The problem was that once he started,
he couldn't stop. It was too good a deal. Classy, pretty women
like Tina—women who'd never before given him a second
glance—were willing to service him sexually. And all they
expected in return was cash.

He didn't have to have a good job or be smart or even look
good. He just had to keep coming up with the dough. And if
he couldn't, he'd just lie about it. And he was great at that.

It was simple enough to tie Ken to where Tina's body was found, before and after he'd killed her. No one else Tina knew had connections to that house.

The only missing piece was exactly *how* and *when* Tina had died. But only Ken could tell them that. And Ken was nowhere to be found.

CHAPTER
34

The problem with being a pathological liar on the lam is that it leaves fewer people to lie *to*.

Ken could manage only so long without looking for sympathy or spinning his twisted yarns for someone. Anyone. Fortunately for the police, it wasn't long before he was overtaken by his need to deceive.

Ron Welker, a mechanic at Fox Hills Country Club, was a Christian who liked not only to "talk the talk but walk the walk," as he liked to say. Which was why on Friday, September 22, 1995, Welker brought two lunches to work instead of one.

The day before he'd noticed a dark-haired man, one of the workers being trucked in daily from Detroit to help mow and weed the golf course, going without food on his lunch hour.

When he'd asked the man—Sandy Wilson he'd said his name was—why he didn't have food, he'd said he didn't have any money.

"Don't worry about lunch tomorrow," Welker assured him. "I've got you covered."

Welker could imagine how difficult it must be trying to make ends meet as a day laborer. He knew that once you'd hit the Cass Corridor, you'd really hit bottom.

The next day he asked his wife to pack an extra lunch for

Ken. It was no big deal: a sandwich, a bag of chips, a piece of fruit.

But when Ron delivered the lunch, Ken went overboard in thanking him, far more than what the simple gesture merited, Welker had remembered thinking at the time.

"You'd have thought I'd just given him my truck, instead of a sandwich," Welker recalled later.

"Sandy" invited Welker to eat with him. He told Welker he was 42 and originally from Pontiac, a northern Oakland County suburb. He'd been homeless for a while, but had recently found a place to live in the Cass Corridor. It was tough down there, he confided to Welker, especially for drug users and prostitutes.

"I met this one prostitute. I feel so sorry for her," he said. "I hate to see someone in that condition. We're friends now. My heart just really goes out to her."

You gotta respect a guy who's down on his luck and still has compassion for other people, Welker mused as he drove home from work that night.

On Saturday, September 23, Welker was tuned into the evening news when a photo of Ken Tranchida flashed on the screen.

"Oh my God, I don't believe it," Welker yelled to his wife, Cathy, who was in another room. "Come here, you've got to see this. It's the guy I brought lunch for this week. He's wanted for murdering that pretty college student."

"Are you sure?" Cathy asked, skeptically stepping into the living room just as the news segment on Ken had ended.

"That was him," Welker insisted. "There's not a doubt in my mind, unless he's got a twin brother somewhere."

Welker immediately called the Southfield Police.

"I know where that guy Tranchida is," he told the dispatcher excitedly. "He's going by the name Sandy Wilson. He's working at the Plymouth Hills Country Club, and he's living in the Cass Corridor in Detroit. I had lunch with him Friday."

The dispatcher dutifully transcribed all the information on

a complaint form, noting the time as 10:25 P.M.

After calling the police, Welker was sure "Sandy Wilson" wouldn't be showing up for work on Monday. "Don't pack an extra lunch today," he instructed his wife. "I'm sure they got him by now."

CHAPTER
35

The sun had yet to set on the evening of Monday, September 25, when Oakland University students began assembling outside Pryale Hall for a candlelight vigil in Tina's memory. By 7 P.M., close to 200 students, faculty, and administrators had gathered. Bill, Todd, and Aimee stood near an entrance to the building, facing the crowd. The mood was somber. Many students hugged and cried.

The service began with an invitation from Sister Mary Bodde of Auburn Hills' St. John Fisher Chapel. Light your candles, she suggested to all those present.

"Light is one of the first elements of creation," she explained. "It's the symbol of new life. So when we light candles, we are symbolizing our dear friend's new life."

At Bill's request, Sister Bodde read Tina's favorite prayer, "A Prayer to St. Francis."

> *Lord, make me an instrument of your peace . . .*
> *Where there is injury, pardon;*
> *Where there is doubt, faith . . .*
> *It is in pardoning, that we are pardoned*
> *And it is in dying, that we are born to eternal life.*

Bill spoke next.

"In the two years Tina was here, she enjoyed it very much," he told the sea of mostly young faces before him. "I

know that. And those of you that knew her, knew the enthusiasm she generally shared with others and her zest for life.''

Todd echoed Bill, describing how Tina felt ''she found her
home in the psychology department. That's where she was
happy.'' Tina, he added, also found her calling in academia.
''She wanted to pursue graduate studies and to go on to teach
and to inspire other young minds as she had been so in-
spired.''

Neither Bill nor Todd made any effort to hide the pain and
sadness they were feeling, honest displays of emotion that
clearly touched those around them.

But the most dramatic moments of the evening came when
a tearful Aimee, clutching a tissue in her right hand, read a
tribute to Tina written by her younger sister, Julie, then 16.
It was written two weeks after Tina had disappeared, when
there was still hope that she would be found alive.

Julie described how she and Tina stuck together whenever
their brothers ganged up against them; how much it meant to
her whenever Tina came to watch her swim or play softball
or perform in a play; how hard it was for her when Tina left
for college; and how afterward, she missed having someone
''to crawl into bed with when I got scared.''

Her family, Julie concluded, is ''my security blanket.'' But,
she added, referring to Tina, ''a part of my blanket is missing
at the moment.''

''Please, God,'' she pleaded, ''keep her safe and bring her
home.''

Aimee, choking back sobs, was barely able to finish.

As the vigil began to wind down to a close, Sister Bodde
requested that everyone join hands. She then led the group in
a moving recitation of ''The Lord's Prayer.'' The service
ended with Oakland University's gospel choir singing an a
cappella version of ''If You Can Use Me, Lord.''

To those who knew Tina—and all that she had to offer the
world—it only seemed fitting.

Tina's death continued to reverberate through the Oakland
community long after she last set foot on the campus where
she'd found her direction.

The day after Tina's body was found, Mary Beth Snyder, Vice President for Student Affairs, issued a statement expressing sympathy to the Biggar family and mourning a "promising young life" that ended needlessly.

Tina's mentor, Algea Harrison, who, according to police, had not been especially forthcoming, eventually weighed in as well.

"I had the utmost respect for Tina," Harrison said the day after the vigil. She went on to praise Tina as a serious and hard-working student whose work on the CDC study was "first-rate" and who, she believed, would succeed in graduate school.

Tina's enthusiasm, Harrison said, "made her a great person to know and to work with. I will miss her greatly."

Finally, despite the fact that Tina's academic pursuits gave her entree into a world that ultimately claimed her life, David Downing, Oakland's dean of arts and sciences, maintained that the school had no intention of limiting undergraduate field work.

"It's important for the university to provide research opportunities for students," he said.

But, Downing added, "I also think it's important for us to look at these opportunities, as we do through the Institutional Review Board, on a case-by-case basis to make sure the appropriate protocols are in place and students are not exposed to situations where they would be at risk."

CHAPTER
36

Ron Welker's jaw dropped Monday morning when the van from the Cass Corridor pulled up and Ken stepped out.

Through crossed signals, his telephone call to police about seeing Ken on the golf course had never received attention.

As Ken started his maintenance duties, Welker confided his suspicions to his supervisor.

The two men dug out a newspaper and compared a mug shot of Ken with the guy who was at that moment mowing the grass just a few feet away. "You're right," Welker's boss agreed. "It looks just like him."

Call the police again, he urged Welker. Insist that they come out.

By Monday afternoon, Welker's second message finally reached Cischke. Ken sightings were now a dime a dozen, but Cischke promised himself he'd visit the golf course personally the next day, September 26, to check out the tip.

He never made the trip.

Welker wasn't the only one of Ken's new acquaintances who watched the news.

That Monday evening, one of the men who supervised Ken and who lived below him in the Selden Avenue apartment building also had spotted Ken's photo on TV.

He called a 911 operator, who alerted Detroit's Thirteenth Precinct. The call came in to the precinct at 10:50 P.M.

Four uniformed officers in two police cars sped over to

Selden, arriving in a matter of minutes. Unfortunately, they'd been given the wrong address by their dispatch desk. But street information being plentiful in Detroit, it took them less than a half-hour to nail down the right place.

James Bennett, Ken's supervisor, met the officers at the door. Bennett was positive the man living in Apartment 103 was Ken Tranchida. "He looks exactly like the picture on TV. And he moved in here, like, three or four days ago."

One of the officers, J. B. Lawson—no relation to Calendar Girls' Debbie—knocked hard, several times, on Ken's door and then yelled "Police." He put his ear to the door. He heard movement, but whatever it was, it wasn't coming toward the door.

The four Detroit officers secured the windows and exit doors of the apartment building and called for a supervisor. The owner of the building brought them the key to Ken's apartment. Two more marked police cars arrived on the scene. Selden Avenue was humming now. Ken had to know something was taking place outside.

The eight officers and supervisors who arrived on the scene were told to wait for even more backup and to call the homicide desk. They did both.

A Detroit homicide investigator notified Cischke, who subsequently reached Zacks. Also called was then-Lieutenant Dennis Richardson, head of the Violent Crimes Task Force, who was on the scene in a matter of minutes.

Ken was hemmed in, and he was hemmed in by the best. Known as the toughest, smartest special unit of the Detroit police force, Violent Crimes was the worst enemy of murderers, thieves, and drug dealers in Detroit.

And the head man himself, "Denny" Richardson was there. Cischke had asked Detroit to wait until he got there to confront Ken. But with Richardson on the scene and God only knew what going on inside the apartment since the officers' first knock, waiting any longer became too dicey.

A few minutes after midnight, Richardson and the four uniformed officers used the key and let themselves into Ken's apartment.

"Police, freeze!" they screamed, jumping inside, guns drawn.

Ken was standing in the bathroom, bleeding from both wrists. He held his arms up to show them, like a schoolchild showing off his latest finger painting. Blood was splattered everywhere. The walls, the floors, the bathtub, the toilet, and the sink were covered with it. A blue disposable razor, safety shield removed, was lying on the floor. Pieces of another floated in the toilet.

Ken had used the thirty minutes or so since the initial knock on his door for another of his half-baked suicide attempts; taking apart the disposable razors and running the dull blades horizontally several times across both his wrists. He wasn't going to die, but he'd need stitches. Lots of them. He was bleeding like a stuck pig.

"Get down on your knees," police ordered.

Acquiescent and silent, Ken dropped to the bathroom floor, still holding up his wrists.

One of the officers grabbed a sheet and some towels and put them around Ken's wrists to stop the bleeding. They pulled him to his feet to lead him out, dispensing with the handcuffs. It was clear Ken wasn't going to put up a fight. The only immediate problem he posed was sullying their patrol car en route to the hospital.

"Ken, is that you?" Southfield Detective Mark Zacks asked as he poked his head through the curtains in a partitioned area of the emergency room at Detroit Receiving Hospital.

"Yeah," Ken replied. Lying in bed, he looked pale, both wrists taped, as he waited to be sewn up.

"What's your last name?" Zacks asked, just to be certain.

"Tranchida," Ken responded.

Zacks explained to Ken who he was. His voice was kind, even sympathetic. Zacks was doing his best "Barney" number.

"You're under arrest for parole violation, Ken," Zacks advised him. "We also want to talk to you about an open homicide."

Zacks asked him a few questions about the room on Selden—if he shared it with anyone, whether the police could take his belongings from the apartment. Ken said it was okay. He asked Zacks to bring him his Bible.

"You're going to be all right," Zacks assured the obviously shaken Ken. "Everything's okay. No one's going to hurt you. We just want to ask you a few questions."

Detroit Police Officer J. B. Lawson, who'd helped bring Ken in, was standing outside the partition guarding Ken. He chuckled as Zacks walked out after the brief interview.

"Brother, you ain't from Detroit homicide, are you?" Lawson asked Zacks, doubling over with laughter.

He found Zacks' tender approach to Ken hilarious compared to the treatment murder suspects usually got from Detroit homicide detectives. Averaging about 450 homicide investigations a year, city cops have neither the time nor the inclination to coddle suspected killers.

"Yeah, this is the Oakland County soft-sell, buddy," Zacks conceded, high-fiving his Detroit counterpart in blue as he left.

The emergency room physician advised Zacks that Ken needed dozens of stitches. He could probably use some painkillers, too.

Zacks nixed that idea. "Nope, don't dope him up. Give him a local. He needs to be bright-eyed and bushy-tailed. He's got some talking to do."

It didn't take long for well-sourced police reporters and camera crews to find out that Ken Tranchida was in custody. While he was being stitched up, a phalanx of print and television reporters had assembled in the emergency room of Detroit Receiving. Zacks got hit with the bright camera lights the minute he stepped outside the area where Ken was being treated.

Before they could scream any questions at him, he ducked back in. *Damn*, he swore under his breath. The last thing he needed was a pack of news jackals nipping at his heels.

They'd jam the station with their cameras and their notebooks and their annoying questions. Then the brass would probably get involved. There was already enough pressure swirling around this case. There had to be another way out of the hospital.

As it turned out, there was. The head ER physician informed Zacks that a tunnel ran under Detroit Receiving, connecting it to Grace Hospital, another facility in the huge medical complex.

Zacks hatched a plan. They would smuggle Ken out through the tunnel to an entrance at the rear of Grace, where an unmarked Southfield Police van would be waiting for them. From there, they would head to Southfield.

He needed the ER chief to do him just one small favor.

"Wait two hours, and then tell all the news hounds out there that Ken's been transported to Farmington Hills," Zacks instructed. A parting shot to Southfield's sister Oakland County police department.

It worked like a charm.

By 7:30 the next morning, swarms of Detroit media had collected in a throng outside the Farmington Hills Police Department, all clamoring to speak to the chief.

By then, Southfield detectives had heard Ken's confession and were going out to buy him a hamburger and french fries for breakfast.

CHAPTER
37

While the interview room in the Southfield Police Station is small, it is comfortable and modern, just like the rest of the suburban police station. The room contains a small table and three cushioned chairs. A hidden video camera allows others to listen and watch the proceedings by tuning into a video monitor in another room.

Despite the fact that Ken's wrists were wrapped in huge white bandages, he seemed to settle comfortably into his new surroundings, visibly relieved to be back in the suburbs.

He also seemed alert and, in fact, eager to talk. Zacks read him his Miranda rights and noted the time. It was 3:35 A.M.

Zacks spent an hour or so going over Ken's background with him. Ken began with his favorite lie about having two children in Great Britain, that old prevarication he absolutely refused to drop unless someone called him on it. Zacks wasn't about to. Ken's children didn't concern him at the time.

About an hour or so into the interview, Zacks began to ask about Tina. If Ken was at all nervous, he didn't show it. But he refused to tell Zacks anything. Exhausted from lack of sleep, Zacks finally ran out of things to say.

Zacks went to get Cischke and Sergeant Leonard Goretsky of the Michigan State Police, both of whom had been watching the interview on a monitor in another room.

"Look, you've gotta do this," Zacks told Cischke, an acknowledged interrogation pro. "You live for this stuff. This is yours. I'm beat. I can't talk to him anymore."

Cischke took his pipe out of his mouth, popped in a stick of gum, and rolled down his sleeves. Cischke had watched on the hidden camera as Zacks had soft-soaped Ken during his interview. The guy had eaten up the buddy-buddy stuff, using it as a sounding board for more obvious lies. Ken's constant theme of self-pity had astounded Cischke. Ken *wallowed* in it. But unless Cischke was able to snap him out of it, the interrogation was going to end up being another version of *The World According to Ken*. They'd already seen that movie.

Zacks, who'd formed what he thought was a tentative bond with Ken, introduced Cischke to Ken as his boss. Goretsky, Zacks told Ken, is "a guy who saved my life when I was a young troublemaker. He's a great man."

Zacks had never met Goretsky before in his life. But Ken seemed to buy it.

Cischke's interviewing style is conversational and laid-back. He then uses that easygoing familiarity to crawl inside the brains of suspects. But that wasn't going to happen with Ken if he went skipping down his own yellow brick road again. They needed to start and to stay within the bounds of reality. This guy needed parameters and Cischke intended to give him some right from the get-go.

"Let me get this straight," Cischke began with Ken, his voice level. "You killed Tina Biggar, and you're going to tell me how it happened. And you're also going to quit this self-pitying crybaby rot and tell me the truth."

It worked like a tonic. Cischke started asking questions, and Ken's replies came pouring out.

He didn't really have a wife and children in England, he admitted. And he'd been in prison before.

Ken told Cischke about writing to women in mail-order bride magazines. He even bragged how easy it was to get the women to come to the United States. In fact, he had quite a way with the ladies, he boasted. He could pick up women whenever he wanted.

"You never know until you try," he said, revealing a twisted half-smile.

Cischke didn't respond. What Ken was saying was delusional self-aggrandizement from a guy who didn't have much of anything going for himself, as far as Cischke was concerned.

But Cischke didn't stop him. Ken was on a roll. And he and Goretsky were faithfully recording it all in their notes.

Ken said he'd first met Tina at an upscale bar in Bloomfield Hills called Hogan's. She was sitting with a man. When the man got up to go to the men's room, Ken approached her, telling her, "You're the most beautiful woman I've ever seen."

She thanked him, told him her name was Crystal, and wrote down her telephone number on a piece of paper. It was the number of the escort service.

"Call me some time," she said, tossing him a smile like a puppy treat.

Two weeks later, still beguiled by the beautiful blonde, he called the number. Someone at the escort service answered. Ken had never used an escort service before, so he was nervous, he said. When the woman told him how it worked, Ken then scheduled an appointment. "Crystal" met him at Gloria's and took him to the Blue Bird Motel on Telegraph, where they had sex. It wasn't intercourse, he admitted. Just oral sex.

During the month of August, he continued, they met at least two more times through the service.

"I-I-I was in love with her," Ken told the detectives. Ken said he begged Tina to tell him her real name. She did, and they then became friends. Ken saw this as a sign that Tina was "falling in love with me, too."

"We stopped using the service after that," he told them. They had "at least ten" paid sessions after that, with Ken giving the money directly to Tina.

"How could you afford that?" Cischke interrupted.

"I was working at the car wash and I got some landscaping work, too. I didn't eat very much, just candy bars. I would have done anything to be with Crystal."

She continued to have oral sex with him, but she told him that most other bedroom activity was off-limits. Still, he wanted more. He wanted to kiss her, have intercourse with her, and perform oral sex on her, too. But that was all taboo. Once or twice Tina had let him massage her back or feet, and she even allowed an occasional kiss. But she flatly refused to have intercourse with him.

"She told me it was Tina who did those things and I would have to wait if I wanted Tina. That kind of relationship took time."

"And you believed her?" Cischke asked incredulously.

"I would have gotten Tina someday, I know. She was telling me about herself, about school, her research. I know about her family, about her boyfriend, Todd," he boasted pathetically.

Ken said Tina had given him her pager number and her home telephone number. She allowed him fifteen minutes to get to a pay telephone that accepted incoming calls when she paged him. He'd then page her back with the pay phone number.

Once, he'd called her directly at home and Todd had answered.

"She was really mad at me for that," he confided.

"Did you ever order any other girls from the service?" Goretsky asked.

"Yes," Ken answered sheepishly, adding, "Tina didn't mind. That was business."

He explained that if he wanted sex with Tina, he would have to pay Crystal. The act itself was always very methodical, as Ken described it.

Tina would always place a condom beside her on the bed and put it on him before she performed oral sex.

"Once she started without it, and I thought, 'She must be falling in love with me,'" Ken said. But when she realized her mistake, she got up and got one from her bag, he admitted.

Amazing, thought Cischke. In his mind, Ken had split Tina into two separate people: Crystal, the no-nonsense hooker, and Tina, the college student. He wondered if Tina had sep-

arated her dual personalities as wholly, too, or if it was simply
Ken's shaky logic at work.

Ken said he knew that Tina's boyfriend Todd "was on the
way out." Tina had taken Ken to her old apartment at Muirwood, and he helped paint her new apartment in Ferndale.

He admitted that he told Tina he'd help her buy a new car
and that he'd lied about the loan from his former mother-in-
law. But he insisted that when the loan didn't come through,
Tina hadn't been concerned.

She *was* upset about her money problems, however, and
began complaining about them a lot.

"I was the only one Tina had in the world," he stressed.
"She didn't get along with her parents. She wanted to get
away from Todd."

Cischke could see Ken spinning off into his own private
orbit again. It was time for a reality check.

"You never had sex with Tina," Cischke hissed at him.
"You *paid* to have sex with Crystal."

"She was falling in love with me, but I had to wait," Ken
argued. "I did only have sex with Crystal, but I wanted more.
I wanted Tina Biggar. I was willing to wait for her. I wanted
to do everything I could for her. I wish I could have done
more."

More of his humanitarian bullshit, thought Cischke.

"You know what, Ken, she was using you," Cischke said,
his tone growing more scathing. "And you had no idea how
badly. She didn't care about you at all.

"But when you finally did realize you didn't mean jack
shit to her, that's when you decided to kill her." Cischke's
voice rose and fell like that of a masterful prosecutor's caught
up in the heat of a closing argument.

"No, I loved her," Ken started to say, but Cischke interrupted.

From the case file, the detective had removed a stack of
Polaroids of Tina's badly decomposed body. He had been
sitting shoulder to shoulder with Ken, but he now stood up
behind him and threw one of the Polaroids down on the table
right under Ken's nose.

"Is this love, Ken?" Cischke demanded. Ken looked off to the side.

"Look at her, Ken," Cischke yelled. "Look at the condition she was in when we found her. You dumped her body on top of thorns and sticks to rot. And you call that love."

Cischke threw down another Polaroid, a brutally graphic close-up of Tina's skull.

"Look at what you did to her, Ken. Did Tina Biggar—the Tina Biggar you say you loved—did she do *anything* to deserve this?"

Cischke then threw down Tina's high school graduation photo for comparison.

Ken finally turned to confront the Polaroids. The horribly decayed skeleton. Next to those pictures lay the high school photo, Tina smiling up at him, wide-eyed and radiant. He started to weep.

Cischke knew he had him. It had taken two and a half hours, but he'd done it. Still, he didn't let up.

"What's this all about?" Cischke went on, waving his hands over Ken's bandaged wrists. "What *exactly* is this shit, anyway, Ken?" Cischke asked, his voice thick with disgust.

"I was punishing myself."

"For what?" Cischke pressed.

"I didn't want to face it," Ken started, then stopped. "I took sleeping pills."

"You killed her, Ken, didn't you?" Cischke demanded.

"Yes," he said weakly. "I wish Michigan had the electric chair," he moaned.

Goretsky took over. Cischke was the guy who had been able to corral Ken's emotions, but Goretsky was the precision man. He wanted details. He wanted the stuff that would nail Ken's ass in court.

Dancing to the tune of Goretsky's terse, bulletlike questions, Ken spilled the whole grisly story.

Tina had changed the last week of her life, he said. She became obsessed with her financial problems. Her credit cards were maxed out. She needed money for school, for the car.

After the Ferndale apartment was condemned, she was worried about where she would live.

On August 22, he and Tina had gone to Oakland University. He'd watched television in the student union, while she'd gone to class and taken care of research business. After they left, they had dinner at a bar. Tina had "dumped him off" at home at around 5 P.M., Ken said, almost complaining.

The next day, Tina came to Gloria's at about 9 A.M. He was expecting her. They talked in the living room for a few minutes, and then went into his bedroom.

"What were you fighting about?" Goretsky asked, trying to pry information from Ken about any friction between him and Tina.

"We weren't fighting," Ken insisted. "It was a happy conversation."

He described what Tina had been wearing, the shorts and shirt and earrings.

"She always wears earrings," he said.

Tina's happy mood vanished once they got in the bedroom, Ken said.

"She got in my face," Ken told them.

Tina was standing about a foot from him, yelling at him. "I wanted to calm her down. You know, comfort her," Ken said.

Ken was silent for a moment.

"So what'd you do, Ken?" Goretsky prodded.

"I pushed her," he told Goretsky.

Tina fell back and hit her head on the safe, Ken said. After she hit, she "bounced to the floor."

He remembered standing over her, panicking. He then picked her up from the floor and put her on his bed, where he held her in his arms.

"Did you know at that point that she was dead?" Goretsky asked.

"Yes," Ken replied. Still, he said he checked her pulse. He held his hand to her mouth. He shook her.

He told her he was sorry and started to cry. He got a wet washcloth and put it on her face, but nothing would revive her. Her eyes were open, fixed in a horrible, accusatory stare.

Her lips "got black spots," he said, "and that made me panic even more."

Ken's answers were coming even faster now. He seemed almost relieved finally to be telling someone about that day in his room.

He'd left Tina on the bed for "two or three hours," he said, while he checked the house and outside to see if anyone had heard what had happened. No one had. About noon, he carried her body out to the trunk of her car and drove to his Aunt Helen's house. He'd placed her sideways, with her head lying toward the passenger side of the car.

Once there, he backed into the driveway and carried her to the side of the house, where he set her down. The bushes concealed her. He didn't know that he'd left her lying on thorns and sticks, as Cischke had told him earlier.

"I was so panicked. I just didn't want anybody to see me."

Then he stopped, looked at Goretsky, and his eyes went flat, emotionless. "What did it matter, anyway? She was already dead," he said, his voice cold.

This was the real Ken talking, Goretsky thought, a man capable of murdering someone with his bare hands. It sent chills up his spine.

After Ken dumped the body, he went home. He got sick on his mattress and took it outside to air. He didn't know what happened to the mattress after that. He drove Tina's car for a few days before leaving it at Angie Apartments.

He also used her telephone for a few days and then "threw it away." He sold both of their pagers. He denied ever seeing Tina's laptop computer.

Cischke and Goretsky told Ken they were just about through. It was 7:30 A.M. They had everything they needed.

But Ken wasn't ready to stop talking. He wanted something to eat and he wanted to continue the interview. Now he had an audience. Where the hell did they think they were going?

Zacks, who'd marveled at Cischke's and Goretsky's stamina during the four-hour session, offered to go get burgers for Ken.

After Ken finished eating, he agreed to help them make a

written statement with questions and answers and sign it, which he did, initialing each of his replies. Again, Goretsky nailed down all the specifics, all of the elements a prosecutor would need. The signed document included the following:

Q: Why did you grab her, Ken?

A. To basically give her a little comfort. At least let her know somebody's around.

Q. How much time passed from the moment she fell to the floor until you realized she died?

A. Gosh, 15 minutes, maybe.

Q. Who was at 27103 Shiawassee when this occurred?

A. Gloria Johnson.

Q. Did she ever know what happened?

A. No.

Q. Why did Tina bleed?

A. I honestly never knew she did.

Q. Did Tina bleed on your mattress?

A. No.

Q. Where is the mattress? Do you know where it is?

A. No. I left it in the backyard.

Q. Were there times when you were Tina's client and paid for sex with her?

A. Yes.

Q. How much did it cost?

A. $170.

Q. Is there anything else you can add to this statement?

A. That I still love her. I look up in the sky and ask God to take good care of her.

Even after signing the statement Ken wasn't ready to call it a night or, more accurately, a morning. He wanted to explain more about trying to sell Tina's car. He wanted to diagram the route he'd taken to get to his aunt's house and the location where he'd thrown away Tina's pager.

It was as though he couldn't bear the idea of being back

in a jail cell, alone. But the detectives needed sleep. It was 9:15 A.M. They'd been up for more than a day. They would continue the next day, they promised Ken, when he'd agreed to take a polygraph test to verify the truthfulness of his confession.

Ken wasn't pleased. "He couldn't stand the idea of anyone walking out on him," Cischke would later recall.

Practically in tears as he was led away from Cischke and Goretsky, Ken noticeably perked up when the state troopers who'd come for him informed him that he was being transferred to the Oakland County Jail.

Hell, that was almost like going home.

CHAPTER
38

O nce Ken Tranchida started talking, the police couldn't
shut him up.

About noon the day after Ken was taken into custody, he
was scheduled to take the polygraph examination. When sheriffs brought him into the Southfield Police Station, he began
crying and begging to talk to Cischke and Goretsky.

''I deserve to die,'' were the first words out of his mouth,
as the two detectives stepped into the interview room.

Cischke, who'd managed a few hours of sleep and who felt
slightly more charitable toward Ken than he had the night
before when Ken had been reeling off lies to Zacks, again
reminded Ken of his Miranda rights.

''You don't have to talk to us without a lawyer, Ken,'' he
said.

But Ken launched into another one of his self-pitying jags,
replete with all the hand-wringing intensity he could muster.
Even Cischke, who didn't much care for Ken, felt a tiny stab
of sympathy.

''I deserve to die,'' Ken said, gulping back sobs. ''I killed
her. If Michigan had the death penalty, I'd volunteer for the
electric chair. I know I'm going to jail for the rest of my life
and I deserve it. I'll die in jail. I'll have to live with what
I've done for the rest of my life.''

''Calm down, relax, Ken. It's going to be all right,''
Cischke assured him.

Ken managed to collect himself, but he wasn't ready to take the polygraph, he told Cischke. He wanted to clear up a few more details about Tina's death.

Again, Cischke read him his rights. They launched into another exhaustive session of everything they'd gone over the night before. Ken was basically repeating himself.

When, after two hours, he refused to be more specific about how he'd killed Tina, Cischke had had enough. Ken was jerking their chains, anything to hear himself talk.

"Ken, there's nothing left to talk about, unless you want to tell us exactly what happened in that bedroom." Cischke and Goretsky both got up to leave.

"No, don't go," he begged. "I'll talk."

"Think hard, Ken," Goretsky coaxed. "Think about exactly what happened in that room the day Tina died."

Again, Ken said he "pushed her" and she fell, hitting her head against the safe. As he stood over her, he said he "blacked out."

"I was in a daze. I'm not sure what happened," he told them.

When he put her on the bed, her limbs started to stiffen up but her neck was "looser," he explained. He insisted there was no blood.

"Describe exactly how Tina came to strike her head on the safe, Ken," Goretsky instructed him.

Ken agreed to demonstrate using Goretsky as a stand-in. The two men got up from the conference table and stood about a foot apart. Ken put his hands on Goretsky's chest, near his shoulders, and shoved hard. Hard enough for the detective to stumble back and lose balance.

Ken said he had no idea what he did after Tina hit her head on the safe.

"I could have choked her. I could have punched her," Ken said, punching the air in front of him. "I could have beat her," he added, catching himself, realizing what he had just said only after the words had escaped his lips. "But I don't think so."

He couldn't remember there being any wounds below Tina's neck.

"Why did you do this?" Cischke wanted to know.

Ken seemed to ponder the question for a moment.

"Did you ever love anyone so much—" Ken started and then interrupted his own thought. "I mean, not like your wife, I know you love her. . . . But did you ever love someone so much you wanted to put them out of their misery?" Cischke was in awe. He realized he may have just heard one of the sickest, most twisted self-justifications for murder ever to come out of a killer's mouth.

"Is that why you killed Tina?" Goretsky managed to ask.

"Yes," Ken replied. "I'd never seen her like that before. She was so sad, nothing like the Tina I knew. I made a sudden decision to end it for her and put her out of her misery."

Hot damn, both detectives thought at the same time, although they both wore their best poker faces. Ken had just said he'd "made a sudden decision to end it for her." That indicated a premeditated act. They had him on first-degree murder. Ken was going to go to jail for a very long time.

"What kind of misery was Tina in?" Goretsky wanted to know.

"She was breaking up with Todd. She had so many bills. She was desperate for money."

"Just tell us what happened after Tina's head hit the safe, Ken," Cischke urged.

"I can't," Ken whined.

"Why, is it too private?" Cischke asked.

"Yes." Ken hung his head.

Goretsky tried another avenue. If Ken said he couldn't remember what had happened in the room, maybe he'd be more willing to talk about how Tina *had* looked after she left the room. It might be another way of finding out exactly what he had done to her.

"What did Tina look like at the time you dumped her body?"

"She looked, kinda"—Ken struggled to find the right word—"kinda lost."

"Is that why you covered her face with her shirt?" Goretsky asked.

"I don't remember that. I just remember telling her I loved her and that I was sorry. Then I remember looking up in the sky and asked God to take care of her. I still love her. I always will."

The two detectives had heard quite enough. They gestured for the sheriffs. "He's ready to go," Cischke instructed them.

He headed back to his office, where he took his pipe out of his back pocket, tucked a pinch of Langoline tobacco in its bowl, and struck a match. He leaned back in his chair and put both of his feet up on his desk.

Ken Tranchida, Cischke mused, puffing on his pipe, has got to be one of the most selfish, self-pitying bastards I've ever met in my life.

Ken was still in his characteristic self-pity mode when he was arraigned on Thursday, September 28, in Southfield's 46th District Court on first-degree murder charges in connection with the death of Tina Biggar.

"I'm guilty," he blurted out to the startled media-packed courtroom. Cameras rolled. Reporters scribbled furiously.

Attired in orange prison garb, with his wrists still swathed in white bandages, Ken begged Judge Stephen Cooper to waive his preliminary examination and bind him over to trial.

"To be honest, I'm willing to pay my dues," Ken told Cooper, hanging his head.

Because Ken didn't have an attorney, Cooper refused to accept his plea. Instead, he entered it as a "not guilty" plea and ordered that Ken be returned to the Oakland County Jail and held without bond to await his preliminary examination.

Ken, however, wasn't without a lawyer for long.

The day after he was arraigned, criminal attorney Michael Modelski was appointed Ken's public defender.

A bearded, conservative Republican and an Abraham Lincoln look-alike with a wicked sense of humor, Modelski said he got the case because he "just happened to be hanging around the Oakland County Courthouse at the time."

Modelski was always hanging around the courthouse.

Intelligent, restlessly curious, and extraordinarily facile with words and thoughts, the 45-year-old attorney had been an Oakland County prosecutor for fifteen years. Then, in May 1993, he became tired of serving as what he described as a buffer zone between a staff that was scared stiff to do its job and then-Prosecutor Richard Thompson.

After Modelski quit, he became one of Thompson's most vocal critics. The media knew they could count on Modelski to use Ken's case as a bully pulpit to rail against the "idiocy" of the prosecutor's office. They also knew that he would have a field day with any holes or imperfections in the case the police had built against Ken.

He didn't disappoint on either count.

Modelski met with Ken that Friday afternoon at the Oakland County Jail. Ken struck him as a "sad individual, somewhat depressed. You couldn't miss the bandages on his wrists."

Modelski decided to try to drum up a little of the sympathy he felt for Ken in the media, as well. It couldn't hurt, he reasoned, given what had been in the newspapers and on television during the last month. Ken had been painted as a "crazed drifter and ex-con," Modelski would later say.

If Ken stood any chance at all of even getting a reduced charge, Modelski needed to turn that picture around, to pound home Tina's image as a prostitute while emphasizing the "loving," vulnerable side of Ken.

The first bone he threw the media was his pronouncement that Ken's confession had been forced. He had been beaten and drugged, he told the *Detroit News* in a story that ran the Monday after Ken's arraignment. Modelski claimed that Ken was also exhausted and weakened from loss of blood when he had confessed.

Detroit police had "kicked Ken in the ribs," when they'd broken into his apartment on Selden, he was quoted as saying. "They questioned him almost nonstop for three days and when he asked for a lawyer they wouldn't give him one. It's no wonder he confessed."

Modelski also said that Ken "was madly in love with Tina. He said he would trade places with her in a minute, if he could."

When Modelski wasn't throwing barbs at the police or the prosecutor's office, he was trying to keep up with the discovery material that had started to pour into his office in great mounds—more than 800 pages in all.

The police had been as busy as ants since Ken had been captured, nailing down every corner of the Ken-and-Tina tale in an effort to build a coherent timeline the prosecutor could sell to a jury.

The confession was a tremendous boon, but the case had to stand on its own without it. They went back to every last person who had been tied to either Ken or Tina in any way in the last several months, getting new statements from all of them. Bill, Todd, Jerry, Phil Black, Mark Hawthorne—they were all interviewed again.

From the international telephone number Ken had called when he used Phil Black's telephone at the car dealership, police tracked down Sandra Brown, Ken's pen pal from Coventry, England.

Sometime around August 16, Brown told them, Ken had telephoned her and asked her to transfer money from an unknown bank account into her account, then send the money to America.

She refused. "It sounded like bullshit," she told police.

Brown was also instrumental in providing a glimpse of Ken's candid thoughts toward Tina during their 12-day friendship.

Brown said Ken had also been calling her in the last month or so asking for advice. He wanted to know whether he should "financially support a prostitute named Tina so she could quit working as a hooker."

It hadn't surprised the 34-year-old Brown that Ken had been consorting with prostitutes; he frequently talked about "titty dancers," she told police.

Southfield's Zacks, meanwhile, went to Oakland University to meet with Professor Algea Harrison. He wanted to know precisely what Tina had been studying and what, if anything, it had to do with her work as a prostitute.

Ken had been charged with first-degree murder, but it was Tina who would be put on trial. Like it or not—and Tina's family certainly would not—putting the victim on trial is common in cases involving rape, sex, even murder. Nicole Brown Simpson's battered image was merely the most recent high-profile example.

During his few-minute chat with Harrison, however, Zacks discovered that she seemed to know little about the study on which she'd served as Tina's academic supervisor.

"She just kept saying, 'Danni knows this' and 'Danni knows that,'" Zacks recalled later. While he was on campus, Zacks also managed to hook up with Danielle Lentine, who was visiting from Atlanta. Yes, she admitted sheepishly to Zacks, she had been doing most of the work on the project—and continued to do so—even though she had moved out of state.

Danielle talked openly about everything Tina had told her over the last year: the affair with Nelson, the foursomes with Steve and Valerie.

Meanwhile, Detective-Sergeant Ted Monfett, a homicide investigator for the Michigan State Police, was interviewing all the L.A. Dreams personnel. If Ken were ever to go to trial, the police also needed to know exactly how the escort service operated and how Tina had become involved in the business. Ken's attorney was sure to stress Tina's escort activities and, again, the state didn't want to be blindsided.

Debbie and Donna were accommodating, even though they suspected it might eventually cost them, but they wanted Ken put away.

Monfett also was charged with nailing down Ken's last days before he was apprehended in Detroit. The police needed to prove that Ken had run from the law and was living under an alias. That wouldn't be too difficult, though. Ken's landlord from the Cass Corridor apartment said he'd be happy to testify against him.

The Farmington Hills Police, too, were still doing what they could to gather the threads together. But during their search of Ken's room at Gloria Johnson's, they ran into a stumbling block.

Tiderington had discovered that Bill, Todd, and Jerry had broken into the safe.

"What did you guys take?" the detective quizzed Todd. Todd told him about the photos of Tina, the roller blades, and Tina's cell phone battery.

"I understand why you did this, Todd, but this is not good."

Tiderington's boss, Doug Anderson, was even less pleased. They were being crucified by the press for not having taken this case seriously enough, and now it turns out that people had taken things from Ken's room while the case was still in the department's hands?

"Find out what they took," Anderson demanded, "and get it back."

CHAPTER
39

B ill Biggar was dressed in his neatly pressed officer's uniform, his patent leather shoes spit-polished to a high shine.

He had come to court to nail the man who had killed his daughter.

It was October 12, almost two weeks since Tina had been buried. Bill was scheduled to be one of the first witnesses to testify at Ken's preliminary examination before District Court Judge Bryan Levy. This was the proceeding that would determine whether Ken Tranchida would stand trial for murder.

In the few minutes before the exam was set to start, Bill stood in the hallway of Southfield's District Court, trying to isolate himself from the more than a dozen reporters who had gathered. But even surrounded by police officers and by Oakland County Assistant Prosecutor Donna Pendergast, who'd been assigned to try the case, Bill Biggar looked completely alone.

Determined, but alone.

Once or twice, when Debbie Lawson or Donna Mehdi caught his eye, Bill tried to force a smile. But he wasn't able to manage a full grin. They might be able to forget why they were here. Donna and Debbie, after all, could go home to their families. Even Todd could walk away, find another girlfriend. But he'd never be able to leave this hell behind. His oldest daughter had been senselessly murdered in the prime of her youth. He'd have to live with that forever.

A crisp, efficient professional, Donna Pendergast had handled twenty-five murder trials in the nine years she'd been with the prosecutor's office. Ken's would be her twenty-sixth. She was buzzing inside as she stood outside the courtroom with Bill, reminding herself of a million little details while trying at the same time to calm him.

At 37, Pendergast was one of an elite corps of prosecutors who almost exclusively tried high-profile murder cases. A slim, pretty blonde who was driven and aggressive, Pendergast was a Felix Unger, Type-A sort who drove some opponents crazy. The daughter of a Detroit beat cop, she didn't conceal her scorn for criminals. But her open disgust with some of the lowlifes who drifted through Oakland County courtrooms didn't endear her to criminal attorneys.

Nonetheless, her foes knew better than to underestimate her. If Pendergast didn't have a word or a law at her fingertips one moment, it would surely be there the next, dredged up from the depths of one of the voluminous black binders she lugged around. They contained every report and law even remotely connected to the case at hand, each page meticulously tabulated and indexed.

She also hated surprises, and prepared furiously to lessen the chances that any would occur. Still, she knew from her exacting research that the case against Ken Tranchida had quite a few wrinkles.

For one, Shankin had never read Ken his Miranda rights when he'd picked him up in Southfield. It meant that anything Ken said to Shankin that day would likely be deemed "fruits of the poisonous tree," or inadmissible, according to the law. The state needed to work in the fact that Ken had been carrying Tina's keys when he was picked up. More importantly, they needed the car itself, or rather the blood in the car. It was the only physical evidence against Ken that Pendergast had.

Pendergast, though, had found a way to work around this lapse. She would argue that the car was an "inevitable discovery," that its existence would have, at some point, become known without Shankin interviewing Ken. The apartment manager would have eventually called the police about the car, she'd argue. She'd even checked with the manager to inquire about the complex's policy on unknown cars found in the lot.

Still, she saw trouble ahead. Even before the examination was officially underway, her eyebrows were furrowed, her lips drawn into a thin line.

She planned to studiously avoid any mention of Tina's escort work. After all, Ken was on trial, not Tina or her lifestyle. And Bill was adamant that his daughter's private life be kept out of the proceedings. But Pendergast knew that wouldn't be easy. It's not often that the escort industry airs its dirty laundry in court, and reporters were more than eager to expose some of the more unseemly details about an illegal business that seemed to go unchecked in Metro Detroit.

In a way, it would have been strategically more savvy for Pendergast to take the wind out of Modelski's sails on the escort front by acknowledging it, by making it a non-issue and moving on to Ken and all his sick lies. But Bill had insisted it be left out altogether.

In addition to *all this*, many of Pendergast's witnesses were either media-shy, or just plain sick of all the attention the case had garnered. Bill, Todd, Debbie, and Donna had each asked her to request that cameras be banished from the courtroom. She knew that Judge Bryan Levy would probably turn her down, but she promised to ask anyway.

There's got to be a better way to make a living, she told herself, sighing, as she pushed open the door of Judge Levy's courtroom. For Pendergast, though, there wasn't. She ate, slept, and breathed this stuff. And it was all worth it to put guys like Ken behind bars.

While Pendergast had been keying up in the hallway, Modelski was playing court jester for the media inside the courtroom, ignoring the usual walls of decorum most lawyers hide behind once they step beyond the gate that separates the participants from the observers. He stood up at the lawyer's table, gabbing and joking with reporters in the audience, as he flipped through his notes.

But Modelski's preliminary exam public relations ploy was to pass out copies of Ken's signed confession and the poem Ken had written to Tina. It was proof positive, he told reporters, of Ken's "undying love" for Tina.

The signed statement, which wasn't as revealing as the detectives' interviews with Ken—neither of which had been tape recorded—was a more accurate view of Tina's death than what the detectives *claimed* Ken had said in his second interview about "making a sudden decision to end it for her," Modelski argued to reporters.

In Ken's signed statement, he only admitted to "grabbing her," so that he could "comfort her." Her death had been an accident. The police had concocted the "made a sudden decision" quote just so they could nail his client for first-degree murder. He and Ken now agreed that it was involuntary manslaughter, tops.

Modelski's preachings were misdirected. If his client wanted to cop a plea to lesser charges, he'd need to negotiate that with the prosecutor's office. But he knew the chances of that happening were virtually nonexistent.

Richard Thompson would *never* accept a plea.

Led in by sheriff's deputies just before the exam started, Ken again was dressed in orange prison garb. But by this time, the bandages on his wrists had been removed. He had gained weight, too—a good ten pounds since his capture. Jail was apparently more fattening than the streets.

Todd was the first witness to take the stand. He looked unsure and frightened. The court reporter had to ask him to speak up.

Pendergast steered Todd through his last days with Tina, what he'd done once he discovered she was missing, and all the particulars of Tina's life that played a part in the murder, including her car problems.

Ken sat staring straight ahead or scribbling on a yellow

legal pad. Occasionally he would whisper something into Modelski's ear.

Todd described his and Bill's search for Ken and the confrontation that took place at Duns Scotus.

"What did you say to him when he asked if you were going to kill him?" Pendergast asked.

"I said, 'No, all I want is Tina back.'"

"Mr. Nurnberger, can you indicate for the Court how the defendant acted during the course of your conversation with him? What was his demeanor?"

Todd replied, "He was quite nervous. He was—"

Pendergast interrupted. "What do you base that assumption on?"

"He had a pop bottle, a Mountain Dew bottle that he fiddled with all the time, had a hard time getting the top off it. He stuttered a lot and then ultimately when we told him that we had checked the airline log and that Tina didn't fly out on an American Airlines flight that day, he became very anxious, started coughing. That eventually became vomit.

"He started vomiting, and then started vomiting blood, falling to his knees. At that point, we became very alarmed for what he may have done."

In his cross-examination, Modelski went straight after Todd on Tina's double life and their disintegrating relationship.

"In fact, you were separating, isn't that right?" Modelski asked.

"Right," Todd replied. "We were getting two different apartments."

When Todd admitted that he hadn't known or remembered that Tina's apartment in Ferndale had been condemned, Modelski went in for the kill.

"In fact, there were a lot of things about Tina's life that you weren't aware of, isn't that true?"

"It appears to be true," Todd said sullenly.

Modelski kept hammering on the theme of Tina's double life, asking Todd about calling the Chop House and finding out that Tina hadn't worked there since June.

He finally snapped. "I still have a lot of questions for

Tina," said Todd. "But I don't have the opportunity to have those questions answered."

Todd's eyes bored into Ken, who stared right back, unblinking.

Todd equivocated about the duffel bag, but Modelski finally cornered him. He admitted there had been credit card slips in the bag.

"What else was in that bag?"

Todd blushed lightly. "Cigarette lighters, condoms, K-Y jelly, an envelope."

Looking to underscore Ken's relative helplessness against all the people who had teamed up in the search for him, Modelski pounced on a reference Todd made to "girls" from the service showing up at Duns Scotus to confront Ken.

"Are you talking about little girls?" Modelski asked with mock innocence.

"Girls approximately my age."

"Why did you call them?"

"Because they had been a substantial part of our search for Ken as well as added manpower. I was scared to face Ken alone."

"So you asked some *girls* to help," Modelski asked, his voice dripping with sarcasm.

"I wanted to get more people there." Todd was getting frustrated.

About midway through Todd's testimony, Pendergast got one of those dreaded surprises. The safe. She hadn't known that Bill, Todd, and Jerry had broken into it. If any one of them answered Modelski's questions about the safe, they could be incriminating themselves. She certainly didn't plan to prosecute them for damaging the safe, but she couldn't promise them she wouldn't.

They'd have to take the Fifth. It didn't look good, but there wasn't any other choice. This wasn't a trial. Surely Judge Levy would understand the three men's questionable judgment call didn't change the fact that there was enough evidence to try Ken for murder.

"What did you do at the gas station with the safe?" Modelski asked Todd.

Todd took the Fifth.

Modelski objected. "Your Honor, at this time I would ask that the prosecution indicate that in fact they in no way intend to prosecute this man and therefore he has no jeopardy problem."

Modelski was yanking Pendergast's chain. He knew she didn't have the latitude to make such a promise. He'd worked for Thompson before.

Pendergast tartly reminded him of that fact.

"As Mr. Modelski well knows," she said, "I cannot make those type of representations."

If it was odd seeing the comparatively clean-cut Todd take the Fifth, it was downright bizarre witnessing Bill Biggar—who was decked out in full U.S. Coast Guard officer's regalia and who asked to be addressed as "Commander" while on the stand—do the same. In fact, Bill sought protection under his Fifth Amendment rights not once, but eight times when Modelski questioned him about the safe.

Modelski had gone easy on Bill when it came to introducing facts about Tina's double life. He knew he wouldn't score any points with the judge or with the media by hounding a man who had just lost his daughter.

And Bill seemed as determined as ever to make all his public statements about Tina's escort work as obtuse as possible.

"You confirmed with the escort services that in fact Tina worked for them, is that right?" Modelski asked him.

"I wouldn't use the word confirmed. They were aware of her, yes," Bill answered.

"I'm sorry," Modelski said, raising his eyebrows and facing those seated in the courtroom so they could share in his skepticism. "They didn't indicate to you that she worked for them?"

"No, I didn't say that," Bill said, struggling to keep his frustration in check and maintain his dignity. Modelski wasn't

THE COED CALL GIRL MURDER

going to get the better of him. "I said that I wouldn't say that they confirmed it. I said they knew her and indicated she had."

It was confusing. But it was probably the closest Bill would ever come to admitting that his first-born daughter had worked as a prostitute.

As Pendergast predicted, Shankin got beaten up pretty badly by Modelski for not reading Ken his rights when he first questioned him on August 31.

Shankin explained how he found Ken at Plum Hollow after Ken had called the escort service.

"Did you at that point advise him of his Miranda rights?"

"No."

"Did Sergeant Anderson advise him of Miranda?"

"No."

"And how long did this interrogation take?"

"We were talking to Kenny for approximately six hours."

"And during any of that time, was he told that he had a right to an attorney and that he didn't have to say anything, and that anything he did say could be used against him?"

"No."

Shankin wasn't going to lie. He was willing to face the music. He just prayed that because of his mistake Ken wouldn't walk.

Pendergast escorted Bill out of the courtroom just before Dr. Kanu Virani took the stand to testify about having performed the autopsy on Tina's remains. She'd read the autopsy and morgue reports. Even though he was a thick-skinned military man who had seen a great deal, it was too much to ask that a father hear his own daughter's autopsy report. And Donna Pendergast planned to elicit every last horrific detail.

Dr. Virani testified that Tina's body was "skeletonized" by the time it was found. "Most of the decomposition was in the upper half, mainly torso, neck, and head area of the body where most of the bones were completely exposed leaving no soft tissue whatsoever."

"There was no skin tissue whatsoever?" Pendergast asked.

"Not on the head, neck, and chest areas."

"What about the organs? Were there any organs left in the body?"

"No, there were no internal organs left. The brain was completely decomposed. There was no soft tissue left in the neck area. The thoracic or chest organs including heart, lungs, and abdominal organs, including all intestines, liver, spleen, kidneys, were completely decomposed."

Dr. Virani further testified that Ken's explanation that she had died merely from hitting her head on the safe didn't wash with the fact that there had been no damage to Tina's skull.

"I would expect to see some indentation mark or a fracture in the area where the head is striking, if she is supposed to die from that injury alone," he said.

Because there was no skull fracture, Dr. Virani pronounced that the cause of death was head and neck trauma.

The two other principal factors he considered in rendering his opinion, Virani explained, were the information he'd gained from Ken's confession to the police and the missing hyoid bone and other soft cartilages from Tina's voice box.

"She might have been strangled," Dr. Virani testified, causing that area of the neck to hemorrhage.

"It started to decompose sooner than the rest of the body and that is why the small animals had been feeding on those bones."

Modelski wasn't buying it. He pushed Dr. Virani into acknowledging some of the vagaries of forensic medicine, especially when it came to pronouncing a cause of death on a body as badly decomposed as Tina's had been.

Boxed in, Dr. Virani finally admitted that technically he didn't have "absolute proof" as to how Tina had died.

Modelski had scored a significant victory in Ken's defense.

As vague as Todd and Bill had been about Tina's escort work, when Donna and Debbie took the stand they blew open the doors to Tina's double life, and, to some extent, to the whole shadowy escort industry.

Before they did so, however, they wanted some guarantees of anonymity. Judge Levy directed that the television cameras not be directed at them. He also asked that their names not be used.

The assembled reporters knew better than to say anything. Nobody was going to cut an anonymous sourcing deal with a judge in open court. It was within his power to shut down the cameras, yes, but everything else was fair game. Judge Levy knew as much, even admitting that the names issue was open to the media's "discretion." He was just passing on a request from the witnesses.

Pendergast used Debbie Lawson to highlight Ken's double-talk and some of the many incriminating statements he had made to all the people who were searching for Tina.

Debbie testified that Ken had told them two separate stories about the mattress: first, that he had gotten sick on it and later, that it was out being cleaned.

But Debbie proved much more useful to Modelski, who led her through every inch in the world of escorting.

"What kind of job is being an escort?" Modelski asked, again in mock innocence.

Pendergast objected. It was irrelevant, she argued. "I don't think it figures into the facts of this case, Your Honor."

Modelski shot back, "The prosecution's theory is that my client met Tina Biggar through the escort services. To say that the business of the escort service is irrelevant I think is—"

Judge Levy had heard enough. "Overruled," he said, adding that Lawson could take the Fifth if she perceived a question as incriminating.

Modelski continued. "What is the function of an escort, what services do you provide?" he asked.

"We can—we provide female companionship," Debbie said primly.

"What is the extent of that companionship?"

Pendergast cut him off. Once again, it was irrelevant, she argued. Again Judge Levy overruled.

Modelski *was* going to get some answers about the escort business, or grow old trying.

"We provide female companionship for dinner dates, concerts, theaters," Lawson said, as a packed gallery tried to stifle snickers.

"What about for sex?"

"No, sir."

"No sex at all?"

Debbie's own attorney asked to approach the bench. After a sidebar with the judge, Lawson agreed to change her answer to the sex question to a Fifth Amendment plea. Her attorney advised her that testimony in a trial would undoubtedly show that L.A. Dreams and Calendar Girls escorts routinely engaged in sex with clients and that Lawson had just perjured herself.

Modelski soon moved away from the sex issue and went on to the basics of the escort industry.

He led Debbie through the whole escort operation, asking what the escorts charged and how the money was divided between the service and the escorts.

In all of her answers, Debbie referred to the escorts as "females."

A state police detective later said of Debbie's use of the word "females": "It was so offensive. It was like she was talking about animals."

The notion of escorts as livestock arose a second time when Debbie described how the "females" were shopped to perspective clients, who are given an escort's height, weight, bust, waist, and hip measurements, as well as their eye and hair color.

When Donna Mehdi testified, she spelled out Tina's involvement with escorting even more clearly.

"Did Tina work for you?" Modelski asked Mehdi, who followed her sister on the stand.

"Yes, she did. She was an independent contractor."

"When did she start working for you?"

"Approximately May 26 of 1995."

When the court broke for lunch, Bill, Todd, Donna, and

Debbie all ate together at a small grill on the city's public golf course, which sits behind the courthouse. Todd and Donna and Debbie laughed and joked, while Bill sat quietly at the end of the table.

Cornered by a reporter in the courtroom hallway, Bill deflected a compliment about his efforts during the search for Tina.

"I did what any father would have done," he insisted modestly.

He refused to acknowledge that Tina had been working as a prostitute. "There are only two people who know whether Tina was doing what people have said she was doing, and one is dead and the other one is a pathological liar."

Besides, Bill added, Tina's conduct wasn't an issue. "My daughter is not on trial here. This is about the sonofabitch who killed her."

Shankin also caught Bill in the hallway. Bill shook the detective's hand.

"Sorry we didn't find her," Shankin told Bill.

Bill's eyes locked with Shankin's.

"Ron, I know I did my best," Bill said. "As long as you know you did your best, you shouldn't be concerned."

"Bill, I did my best," Shankin told him as the two men parted. Shankin left wondering whether the doubt he read in Bill's eyes was the commander's misgivings or a reflection of his own self-doubts.

The second day of the preliminary exam seemed somehow less fraught.

Modelski wore a tie imprinted with Odie, the character from the *Garfield* comic strip. Even Pendergast seemed to have softened somewhat, now that the bulk of the testimony was behind her.

Jerry Holbert, the proverbial good ol' boy, described Ken's comings and goings from his trailer and laid out in detail the entire effort to break into Ken's safe, even after having been advised of his Fifth Amendment rights.

"How does an air hammer work?" Modelski asked disingenuously.

"You hook it up to an air hose, you turn it on, and it goes to town," Jerry said with a proud smile.

"After you did that, would the safe still close? Could you still lock it?"

"No, it was in pretty bad shape when we were done with it."

Jorge Luna-Gen placed Ken at the field behind the house on Nine Mile on August 29. But he also added that he'd met Ken before. Five years earlier, Ken had come to the Luna-Gens' home saying he would be getting mail at their house. Ken had given their address to a woman overseas and had later received about four or five letters, Luna-Gen remembered. Another one of Ken's endless scams to impress a woman had come back to haunt him.

Modelski tried to keep Ken's confession from being entered into evidence by claiming that Pendergast hadn't shown corpus delicti, in other words, that she hadn't shown all the facts constituting a crime. The attempt came just before Michigan State Police Sergeant Leonard Goretsky was about to testify about the statement.

Modelski argued that all the prosecution had was a dead body and a medical examiner who claimed he couldn't figure out how Tina Biggar died.

Pendergast sprung to her feet: Oh, no you don't, she, in effect, told Modelski.

"We have much, much more," she said. "We have a sudden disappearance of an otherwise healthy young girl. We have the location of a body in an overgrown area that had a connection to the defendant. It's no coincidence that the defendant called his brother one of out of two times in three years and asked about this same location, where his Aunt Helen lived."

Pendergast's voice rose. She was on a roll.

"You have the defendant trying to sell Tina's car four days after her disappearance. You have blood in the trunk of a car consistent with Tina's blood type. We have the defendant's aberrational behavior saying he knows where Tina is, she's in Dayton, she is at a Hilton, which nobody was able to locate. We have further the unusual behavior on behalf of the defendant of vomiting and extreme nervousness. You have his evasive efforts on two separate occasions when the police tried to confront him.''

Pendergast continued to enumerate all the threads of evidence that tied Ken to Tina's death until Judge Levy raised his hand to stop her. Corpus delicti had been shown, he ruled. The confession was admissible.

During Goretsky's testimony, Modelski made a spirited effort to discredit Ken's confession. The two detectives had worn Ken down, he charged. The lights in the interview room were intimidating. Ken had been doped up.

Goretsky, however, was ready at every turn.

Ken's sad and sick statement wouldn't wash away, no matter how hard Modelski tried.

"I made a decision to put Tina out of her misery." There it was. It was Ken's statement, and Goretsky must have repeated it five times.

In the end, Judge Levy's only question to the prosecution before ordering Ken's case sent on to Circuit Court for trial was why the prosecution was arguing first-degree murder. Quizzing Pendergast, he asked her what elements showed premeditation.

"The defendant made a conscious decision to put Tina out of her misery and end it for her," she answered. "Those are key words. They show the defendant clearly had a conscious plan."

But had there been time enough between Ken's decision and when Tina had died to constitute premeditation? Levy wondered.

Even a nanosecond between stab wounds was all it took, Pendergast stressed. "I've had cases like that before," she told him. The elapsed time between decision and action was something for a jury to decide, she urged.

In his rebuttal, Modelski chided the prosecutor's office, claiming Ken should be charged with open murder. This would enable Modelski to argue for a lesser charge than first-degree murder at future court proceedings. He said the prosecution should never have come over with a first-degree charge in the first place.

Modelski argued the prosecutor's office, in hotdogging it, had trumpeted that a defendant in a high-profile murder case had been given the top charge and as a result, had painted themselves into a corner that would force them to prove premeditation.

Modelski charged that they had failed to do so.

Judge Levy disagreed. The state's proofs of premeditation were compelling enough, he said.

"The defendant indicated he made a decision. The word implies a weighing of factors."

Ken Tranchida would go on trial for Tina's murder in Oakland County Circuit Court.

CHAPTER
40

"I miss Tina, just like you do. If I had my way, I'd still slice my wrists because I know you guys are hurting." These words, mumbled almost inaudibly by Ken Tranchida at his May 3, 1996, sentencing hearing, offered little solace to Bill and Connie Biggar, who had driven more than four hours to see the man who had murdered their oldest child punished for the deed. If anything, the words demonstrated only that Ken's thinking, after more than seven months in prison, remained as twisted as ever.

The hearing took place less than three weeks after he agreed to plead guilty to a reduced charge of second-degree murder.

In the end, the Oakland County Prosecutor's Office *had* cut a deal with Ken. It wasn't a deal they relished cutting. But once more, Bill Biggar proved to be a formidable force.

"The family came to my boss and literally begged him to let Ken plead guilty to a lesser charge," Pendergast later explained. "They said a trial would be devastating and that they were in enough distress already."

Apparently, Oakland County Prosecutor Richard Thompson had taken the Biggars' plea to heart.

"There's always room under the terms of our no-plea bargain policy for a case to be evaluated on an individual basis when extraordinary circumstances present themselves," Pendergast said. "Mr. Thompson, in this case, did that. He took the family's wishes into account."

Pendergast also admitted that she would have had a "difficult" time making a first-degree murder charge stick.

"Our case for premeditation was based on actions he took and the statement he made to police after the murder," she says. "We didn't have any statements he'd made in advance indicating any intent to kill Tina."

Modelski said Ken agreed to the plea bargain for two reasons. The first was to spare the Biggars any additional pain. "He didn't want to hurt the family," the defense lawyer explained.

Secondly, Ken had plenty to lose by rolling the dice at trial. "Because he was charged as an habitual fourth offender, if he were to be convicted of any felony punishable by a sentence of five or more years, he was facing a possible life sentence," noted Modelski.

"Even if we'd gone to trial and he was found guilty of manslaughter, he'd still be facing life."

Ken, for his part, hadn't changed in the least. Even after his guilty plea, he continued to maintain that he never intended to kill Tina. He was as devastated as anyone by her death, he insisted.

"He was in love with her," Modelski said. "It pains him every day to think about the fact that she's dead."

But Ken managed to overcome this pain long enough to try—the morning of his sentencing—to wriggle his way out of the deal he had already made with the prosecution.

Just after 8:30, Ken, outfitted again in a bright orange prison uniform, was brought into the Pontiac courtroom of Oakland County Circuit Court Judge Rudy Nichols. As he stood in the juror's box looking down at the floor, Modelski informed Judge Nichols that Ken had told him just prior to the court session that he wanted to withdraw his guilty plea.

Ken was still trying to pull everyone's strings.

"He doesn't feel he's guilty of murdering Tina," Modelski said later that day. "He said as he was going over the speech he wanted to make to the court, he thought, 'I can't say I'm sorry I murdered her because I didn't.' ''

For many years, Michigan judges allowed defendants to withdraw their pleas right up until the time of sentencing. "There was a very loose standard," Modelski would later explain. That's no longer true today. "Now it's more of a question of what would be in the best interest of justice."

In Ken's case, Judge Nichols decided that Ken had waited too long to change his mind. His request was denied.

After Nichols' ruling, Bill Biggar stood and walked from the third-row bench where he was seated with Connie, to the front of the courtroom. He was dressed in street clothes—a gray sportcoat, navy blue dress slacks, and a paisley print tie—as opposed to the Coast Guard uniform he'd worn when he testified at Ken's preliminary exam.

Speaking quietly but firmly, Bill told the judge that neither he nor his family wanted "to see this man on the street again to supposedly help somebody by killing them and putting them out of their misery." He was referring to Ken's claim that he had accidentally knocked Tina down while trying to comfort her.

Modelski spoke next, addressing the court on his client's behalf. The attorney reminded the judge that Ken "has always had remorse" about Tina's death and that her death "was a tragedy for him, too." He also reiterated the statement Ken made following his arrest, the one in which he said he wished Michigan had the death penalty "so he could die and be with Tina."

Finally, it was Ken's turn.

"I'd like to apologize to the family," he said sheepishly, turning to the gallery to face the Biggars. "I know they really don't care, but I'd still like to apologize to them."

Ken's statement held little sway with Nichols. He wasted no time in sentencing Ken, who stood emotionlessly, to life in prison. However, just how many years Ken ultimately would serve was unclear at the time, thanks to a court battle then being waged over a controversial and convoluted Michigan law that requires parolees who commit crimes to finish the sentence for their previous offense, or offenses, before they begin serving their new sentence.

Ken's life sentence in and of itself would have made him eligible for parole in fifteen years. But because he was already on parole for larceny, breaking and entering, and embezzlement charges when he killed Tina, under Michigan law he'd have to finish serving his sentence for these crimes before beginning the life term. This would have added another twenty-five years or so to his imprisonment, meaning he wouldn't be eligible for parole until the late 2030s.

On May 29, 1996, however, the Michigan Supreme Court of Appeals ruled the law unconstitutional. No higher court could consider the law because it was a Michigan statute that was at issue. The ruling meant that Ken could be eligible for parole as early as 2011.

Ken's entire sentencing hearing lasted approximately fifteen minutes. The Biggars hurried out of the courtroom immediately after Nichols pronounced sentence, with about a dozen reporters, photographers, and cameramen hustling after them. Outside the courtroom, Bill Biggar ushered his wife down the hall, and then turned, quite unexpectedly, to address the media.

His stinging words that day weren't directed at the man who had murdered his daughter. Instead, they were aimed at the horde that stood in a semicircle before him.

"Since this thing has started, it has been my desire, as Tina's father, as the father of my other children, and as a husband, not to have any more tragedy in this family, not to have any more people hurt," he said, his voice quivering with anger. "I'm looking right now at the major hurt of my family.

"I realize that you think you're doing your job and I realize you take a paycheck home. But if you ever, ever could feel for an instant what you've done, what you perpetuate in the guise of free speech, how you hurt people that are hurting already, I'm not sure you'd be in this business.

"Bitterness begets bitterness. I'm not bitter. I feel sympathy for a profession that feeds off people's hurt and makes people hurt more.

"Put your name in the headlines. Put your daughter's name in the headlines. Put your son's. Your husband's.

"The sustaining hurt," he said, gesturing at the reporters and photographers who faced him, "is right here."

CHAPTER
41

K en Tranchida still has some things he wants to get off his chest. Things he's never told anyone, not even the police.

It is September 6, 1996. Tranchida is in a conference room at the Gus Harrison Correctional Facility in Adrian, Michigan.

The relatively new low-slung red-brick prison in western Michigan roughly resembles a college campus from the outside, albeit one where the buildings lack windows and the perimeters are marked by cyclone-wire electric fences. Inside, the facility bespeaks a spartan-like efficiency. Security is airtight. If you're a visitor, even your shoes are checked.

Behind bars for almost a year, Ken has had some time to think about things.

The scant eleven days he knew Tina Biggar have grown so large in his mind that when he speaks of that time, it sounds as though he were talking about a much longer span, years even. Or as if those days were suspended in time all together.

As full of self-pity as ever, Ken plans to appeal his sentence. He thinks he deserves "five years, maybe," he says, clinging to the story that Tina's death was an accident. He has, however, rearranged the tale and some of its elements since he last told his version of events to detectives Cischke and Goretsky.

He has gained even more weight, and is oddly lifeless.

Yet he's excited at the same time. He clearly enjoys the attention. He gets few visitors: his Uncle Pete, once in a while, and, of course, Jerry Holbert. The tow truck driver still stands by his friend.

Ken seems to revel in the opportunity to tell yet another version of the events surrounding Tina's death, although even he admits that the veracity of anything he says is highly suspect because of all the lies he's told in the past.

"They [the rest of the world, presumably] ain't going to believe me no matter what I say."

And rightly so. With little prodding, he admits to a lifetime of lies—beginning with the stories he told his wife, Theresa, about being a state police officer—"I wanted to make her proud of me," he intones—to the loan he had promised Tina for her new car.

"It was a con," he says about the car loan, not a trace of remorse in his voice. "I wanted to buy some time with her."

Didn't he think it would blow up in his face?

"I wasn't worried. I knew that would happen down the road."

He claims to get no thrill from lying. "It's just that I can't stop myself," he says. "If I could have, I probably wouldn't be in prison."

Ken blames his childhood and family less for his troubles during this prison stay than he did when he talked with prison psychiatrists during his past stints, although he says he's "never really" told the truth to jailhouse therapists. "They don't care," he says, gloomily.

Joe was "verbally abusive" and "sometimes threw hammers and stuff at me," he insists. But gone are the razor stories he once told to Marta Showalter. "He's my father and I still love him no matter what."

The extent of Ken's lies, it becomes quickly apparent in speaking to him, depends a lot on his audience's willingness to suspend disbelief.

Tina wanted to believe that she was getting a new car.

When she stopped believing, she was dead.

Ken says he joined the Army to "get away from home."

Despite being washed out of the military in less than a year, his childhood dream was to someday be an officer. Just like, ironically, Tina's father, with whom Ken shares no observable characteristics.

"I wanted to be a general," he says with a shy smile, sounding like an eight-year-old boy daydreaming about his toy soldiers.

The reason he was never successful in the military or in any job, was, of course, through no fault of his own. The world at large simply never recognized his talents.

"I could never find someone to give me an opportunity," he maintains. "I would have worked in a factory job, but I could never even find one of those."

He is childlike, too, when talking about sex or women, embarrassed or incapable of finding the words to express himself. Still, hints of braggadocio creep into his conversation.

His wife, Theresa, was the first woman with whom he ever had sex. But she was the aggressor, he claims. She was plain. He wasn't that attracted to her. She came after him.

He lied to her about being a state policeman and wrote bad checks to impress her, never concerned about what would happen when she found out. He never thought about going to jail.

"I never worry about the long-term consequences," he explains. "Maybe that's the problem. I don't worry about the end. I'm in it for the day."

After he began bouncing in and out of prison, the only women he felt comfortable with were topless dancers. No, he didn't have sex with them. He "mostly just watched."

"I just went in those bars because I was lonely. I never thought bad about them dancing or anything. They were do-ing—like Tina—what they had to."

But Ken admits that the anonymity that comes with relationships with women you pay to take off their clothes suits him perfectly.

"They lie to you and you can lie back," he says, laughing.
Like Tina?

"Tina was completely, totally different from anyone I've
ever known," he says, his words drifting off.

It's not so much that Ken stammers as it is that the words
seem to catch in his throat. And he still hasn't shaken the
verbal tic that Ron Shankin noted: his habit of using such
phrases as "I swear to God" or "honestly" or "Let's put it
this way" as preambles to his lies.

He claims that Tina was the very first prostitute he ever
had sex with.

"I was nervous. We talked for quite a while," he recalls,
thinking back to their first encounter. "I told her, 'Be patient,
this is the first time I've made love to a girl in about four or
five years. I might have forgot how to do it.' "

Tina, he said, was "kind, sweet."

No sooner had she left him that first day than Ken found
himself wishing she hadn't. "I didn't want her to leave. I
kinda missed her already," he now says.

When the escort service sent Ashley instead of Tina, he
was disappointed. Apparently Ashley was "the hurry-up
type."

Bypassing the escort service after his and Tina's second
date had been his idea. "I didn't like going through the service," he says. "You had to tell them who you were and
stuff."

He and Tina stopped having sex when he told her he
wanted to get to know Tina, not Crystal, better.

And he stresses that there was a clear split in Tina's personality.

"Crystal was the hooker and Tina was the schoolgirl," he
claims. "There were these two people you were dealing with.
Tina had relationships, you know. She was the wholesome
girl next door. Crystal was the hooker. Crystal used to get
dressed up, wear sexy-looking stuff, nice dresses, short skirts,
low-cut blouses."

Ken now says Tina never got angry with him about the car

loan because she never put it together that he was conning her.

"Tina never knew I didn't have the money. She never knew the car wasn't coming. If she had, I wouldn't be here today. She would have blown up at me and walked out. That would have been it." He looks and sounds almost hopeful as he says this, an imagined scenario he's probably played out in his mind hundreds of times.

In fact, he wants the world to believe that Tina hardly ever bugged him about money.

"She might have brought it up once or twice, but it was never like she got mad or anything."

Ken also says he took as many as twenty amphetamines in the twenty-four hours before Tina died, something he claims not to have told the police.

"They were yellow. I probably took about five of 'em the night before and another ten or fifteen that day."

It was another pathetic suicide attempt, he claims, brought on not by finding himself in Tina's disfavor, but because "I go through spurts like that."

The drugs, he said, made him "racy."

"My mind was racing, like I wasn't sure what to do, like I was going fifty miles an hour."

Racy enough to strangle Tina and not know it?

"I've never choked anybody. I would have known if I choked her. I know how she died. She hit her head."

Ken rejects completely the notion that Tina's skull would have shown evidence of trauma were his story true.

After having breakfast at a Big Boy, they came back to Gloria Johnson's and were joking around in his bedroom playing "grabby." He grabs at the air to illustrate his point. Just as he was about to pull her leg out from under her, she said, "Be careful." But by the time those words came out, it was "too late." He had already grabbed her leg.

She fell. She hit her head on the safe. She was dead.

"She kinda fell over and laid there, for, it seemed like

minutes. I said 'Tina, get up.' She didn't move. She wasn't breathing. Her eyes were open.''

Ken says he's still haunted by that image.

"I can still picture her laying there."

Why didn't he run out of the house, call the police, get help?

"I don't know."

Isn't that a normal reaction when someone gets hurt?

"I'm not normal, never claimed to be," he replies. In his voice there is almost a sense of pride.

Surely you're with it enough to know that something is terribly wrong at this point, Ken?

"I don't know if I was with it or not," he says. He believes that the speed clouded his thinking, he claims.

One of the reasons he didn't call the police, he says—once again, in his childlike guise—was because he thought he would "get in trouble because I was an ex-convict."

"I wish I would have done a lot of things differently," he continues. "I wished I never would have got involved in the escort service. Had I never called the escort service, she'd still be alive."

After she died, he paced around the house. It wasn't until 10 P.M. that night that he moved the body to the field behind his Aunt Helen's former house. (Originally, he had told police that he'd dumped Tina's body at noon that day.)

"I put her over by the fence and I got the hell out," he says.

"I didn't plan Tina's death," he insists. "If you planned something out, you wouldn't leave a body on your own relative's property."

He maintains that he called for another escort from the Plum Hollow Bowling Alley because he "just needed someone to talk to."

Someone with a specific hair color?

"I don't know." He shrugs.

He knew that once he left Tina's body in the field he would get caught. "It was only a matter of time."

He wasn't afraid of Bill Biggar or anyone else who had been searching for Tina. He avoided them, he claims, because he was afraid he would tell them about Tina's death.

"I thought Bill was a nice guy. I was more afraid of Jerry than Bill."

Ken now says the reason he vomited blood at Duns Scotus was because he had been drinking peroxide out of the Mountain Dew bottle.

"I'm drinking the stuff right in front of them hoping to die. I didn't care."

Ken denies that his suicide attempts are just pitifully lame cries for attention.

"I've tried plenty hard," he insists. "But it never seemed to work. I twice tried with sleeping pills when I was in the Cass Corridor. They screwed me up. I fell asleep, remembered my heart jumping a couple of beats. I've tried a lot of times, over the years."

After he dumped Tina's body in the field, he says he went back to visit her twice because "he missed her." He went once late at night, and another time early in the morning. Both times he stood at least thirty feet away from her body, apologizing, talking to her, "hoping she'd wake up."

Tina finally "answered" him while he was in Oakland County Jail awaiting sentencing.

"It was at night," he says. "I heard her talking to me. She said she forgave me. I remember her telling me, 'It's okay, I'm happy now.' She was nice, sweet, you know, where she's not pissed off at me."

But didn't you say she never got angry at you, Ken?

"I still killed her. It's still my fault. Had I not been playing grab—grabbing each other . . .'' His voice trails off again.

Still one more time, he reiterates his desire to kill himself so he can be with Tina.

"Hopefully, I won't have that much time in here. Someday I'm bound to get it right."

What makes him think that if one day he finally does get it right, he's going to be wherever Tina is?

"I will be," Ken says with complete confidence. "God is a loving and forgiving God."

CHAPTER
42

B ill Biggar maintained a seemingly unassailable strong front throughout the month-long search for his daughter, confiding his innermost fears to virtually no one.

But if the words of comfort offered by the Reverend Edwin Thome at Tina's funeral told any story at all, it was that the private military man had taken on at least one confidante.

Jesus Christ, he reminded the overflow crowd, "ate with prostitutes and those known as sinners. And he, too, suffered the consequences. The self-righteous did not understand. Eventually, they put him to death.

"Tina had that spirit of adventure, which took her into uncharted waters. And she died for something she believed in."

September 27 was a sunny, unseasonably warm Wednesday in northern Michigan. It was also the day close to 700 people packed Christ the King Catholic Church in tiny Acme, just outside of Traverse City, to pay their respects to Tina. Family members and hundreds of Biggar family friends were there. So, too, were most of the 125 Coast Guardsmen stationed at the Traverse City air station, and dozens of children from Grand Traverse area Catholic schools, which all of the Biggar children, including Tina, attended.

Mourners walked past a ten-man Coast Guard honor guard

as they entered the church where Tina had worshipped with her family.

Bill, dressed in his Coast Guard uniform, and Connie greeted loved ones in a room off the church's vestibule, which was decorated with dozens of elaborate floral arrangements. Also on display were about thirty pictures of Tina. In one, she was wearing a graduation gown. Another showed Tina at a birthday party. In yet another, she posed with her father in front of a Coast Guard aircraft.

Tina's light blue casket was positioned nearby.

The ninety-minute service began just after 11 A.M. From the start, those gathered made full use of the boxes of tissues that had been placed on the pews.

After an initial hymn, Bill and Connie and Tina's brothers and sister entered the chapel. Tina's casket, covered with a beige cloth, was wheeled in behind them and placed near the altar.

In his eulogy, the Reverend Thome spoke of the senselessness of Tina's death.

"In my observation, over many years of ministry, I find that death is particularly difficult to assimilate when it happens to a teenager or a young person who has already taken a giant step into adulthood, as did Tina," he remarked. "This incomprehension is heightened whenever there is a violent death."

Thome also led mourners in a number of hymns. A singer, accompanied by piano, organ, two guitars, and timpani, performed a moving rendition of "Wind Beneath My Wings." It was, Thome said, "a special request by the family."

Several speakers moved mourners with their remembrances of Tina. Todd, introduced by Thome as "Tina's special friend," spoke briefly. "Tina may be gone from our lives," he noted, "but she is not gone from our hearts."

Also offering solace was Commander Eric Fagerholm, commanding officer at the Traverse City air station. Fagerholm, a longtime friend of the Biggar family, spoke of how Coast Guardsmen from all over the country had called the base to express their condolences.

"I'm here to tell you that those of us in this beautiful church are not alone in our grief," he said.

Fagerholm also presented a folded U.S. flag to Bill and Connie, explaining that it was in recognition of Tina's membership in the Army Reserve.

Without question, mourners were most deeply touched by a reading of Julie Biggar's tribute to her big sister, the same one Aimee Vermeersch had read at the vigil at Oakland University two days before. Many mourners, smiling knowingly, openly cried.

The Biggars, walking behind Tina's casket, were the first to exit the chapel upon the service's conclusion. They walked slowly and solemnly down the center aisle, Connie clutching the folded flag to her breast.

A Mass of Christian Burial was celebrated for Tina three days later in Bill's native Elkton, South Dakota, which bills itself on a sign posted in its tiny downtown as "a community that cares and shares." The service took place at Our Lady of Good Counsel Catholic Church, the same church where Bill and Connie had been married a quarter-century before.

Father Charles Mangan reminded mourners that in spite of Tina's tragic death, she was not "gone for good."

"This is not what we believe as Catholics and Christians," he noted. "The body can be taken but the spirit continues. Our sister is not gone. She lives in the communion of saints." Following the Mass, Tina was laid to rest beside her brother, Matthew, and her maternal grandmother at Elkton's St. Mary's Catholic Cemetery, in an area surrounded by rich farmland and shaded by towering evergreens.

While in South Dakota, Bill Biggar, who had been close-mouthed around the press in Michigan, was more forthcoming with reporters from newspapers in Elkton and in Brookings, Tina's place of birth.

In the *Elkton Record*, he spoke of how much he and Connie appreciated the kindness they'd been shown by even strangers throughout their ordeal; a kindness, he said, that "comes from way down deep."

He told the *Brookings Register* that Tina "would have made a great psychologist." His daughter, he said, "had a special talent as a listener."

Not surprisingly, Bill had only harsh words to say about Ken.

"He's a habitual liar," he declared in the *Register*. "The only thing I believe that he has said so far is that he killed my daughter."

One question he does not ask himself about Tina's death, Bill told the newspaper, is "Why?"

He and Connie and their children stopped asking "why," he explained, after Matthew's death.

"There are no answers to 'why' questions," Bill said. "God only knows. Someday, we'll find out."

CHAPTER
43

Tina has been gone for more than a year.

But to Aimee Vermeersch, it seems like only yesterday. Some days, while working at the Chop House, she finds herself waiting for Tina to sweep through the door, just in time for her evening shift, chattering excitedly about something she'd learned in school that day or about the research project that meant so much to her.

"I'll see her in my mind," Aimee explains one day, choking back tears. "She's just so alive."

But then something will snap Aimee back to reality.

"There's this void in my life," she sighs, shaking her head. "I can't believe she was taken away, not just from me but from everyone."

Like Aimee, Todd Nurnberger also often finds his mind filling with thoughts of Tina: whenever he pulls on a shirt she gave him, whenever he glances at a knickknack that once sat in the apartment they shared, whenever he does something he and Tina used to do together.

Hurt, anger, self-doubt, and sadness are among the emotions that accompany these recollections.

"More than anything, I wish I could ask her, 'Why?'" he says. "But I know I'll never have that chance."

Even after Tina's body was found, Aimee had refused to consider the possibility that Tina had been leading a double life, that she may not have known her close friend as well as she thought she did.

"I could see how Tina could get a little anxious and maybe she did go out on her own," Aimee conceded after learning that Tina had begun contacting escorts even though her research project had yet to be approved. "But if she did, it was to further her study, not to become an escort or a prostitute."

Aimee also dismissed reports that several escort service owners admitted that Tina had been working as a high-price call girl. She wanted to believe that they were just angry at her for trying to interview their employees, she wanted to believe.

"Maybe Tina upset those people," Aimee theorized, sounding more than a little as though she were trying to convince herself at the same time. "Maybe Tina was talking to some of the girls and the owners became angry and that's why they're saying, 'Hey, she was in it, too.' "

Aimee eventually came to terms with the truth: Not only had Tina worked as an escort for close to a year, her friend had also told her one lie after another, doing whatever it took to keep her escorting career a secret.

The more she thinks about things Tina said and did over the last year of her life, the more obvious it becomes to Aimee that nothing added up. Aimee knew about Todd's infidelity. Tina had even told her she was ready to shop around for a new boyfriend.

"If Mr. Right or some good-looking guy had come along and asked her out, she wouldn't have hesitated to go out with him," she says.

Aimee also knew Tina was "extremely bitter" about Todd's having cheated on her. "She was so angry about it," explains Aimee. "She was beyond angry. And she was always swearing she'd get back at him one day. She said she was going to do to him what he'd done to her."

At first, Aimee sympathized with her friend. There was Tina, about to move in with her boyfriend when she learns he fooled around behind her back. But after a while, Aimee

began to feel Tina was letting her obsession with revenge rul
her life. It didn't seem healthy.

"One of the last times I saw her, we went out for drink
with another friend of ours, a guy named J. T.," she recall
"Tina began going on about Todd. I said, 'Tina, I understan
your being bitter and angry. But it's been almost a year tha
you've been talking like this. You have gone out with othe
people. Don't you think you've gotten him back?' "

"Absolutely not," Tina declared, dismissing her friend'
concern. "I'm going to do to him exactly what he did to me."

J. T. put in his two cents as well.

"You know, Tina, if you don't want to be with Todd, don'
be with him. But don't stoop to his level," he told her.

Her feathers clearly ruffled, Tina immediately changed th
subject.

Aimee also recollects being somewhat puzzled when, th
previous January, Tina cut back on the number of shifts sh
was working at the Chop House.

"How are you going to be able to cover your bills?" sh
asked her friend.

"I'm getting paid for the research I'm doing at school,'
Tina replied.

"Some grant or something," Aimee remembers Tina tell
ing her.

Around the same time, Aimee asked Tina about a numbe
of new pricey possessions.

"We were sitting around her apartment one day and sh
brought out a cellular phone and a pager.

"You cut back on your shifts and you've still got all thes
new toys!" Aimee exclaimed. "It must be nice. How abou
setting me up with whatever you're doing?"

Tina, she says, "just laughed."

Unlike Aimee, Todd, who had discovered evidence o
Tina's secret life only days after her disappearance, had littl
time to assimilate the shocking truth.

"I would have bet my life that I knew her inside and out,'
says the young chemist. "If someone would have told m

Tina was working as an escort, I would have said, 'There's no way in hell.' ''

Todd still can't believe, either, that some people who have followed the case think he was aware of Tina's moonlighting all along.

"How could anyone think I would have let that go on?" he asks incredulously.

For Aimee, coming to terms with the truth about Tina has also meant learning to forgive her.

"It doesn't make me love her any less," she says, referring to Tina's having lied to her over and over again. "But I do wish that she had come to me. Basically, that's all I think about."

But that doesn't mean Aimee thinks she—or anyone else—has the right to judge Tina.

"I know it's an old cliché," she says, "but until you walk in somebody else's shoes . . ."

As for the money Ken had promised to lend her, Tina probably believed he really had it, Aimee now thinks.

"Tina was neither naive nor gullible," Aimee maintains. "But I can see how she may have been duped. He obviously fed her some kind of line and she fell for it."

Aimee is convinced Tina called Ken's bluff when she finally realized he was scamming her about the loan, probably the morning she died.

"I think she confronted him," she explains. "I think she said to him, 'You don't have this money, do you?' He must have become enraged. He didn't know what to do because he was losing control and, most likely, about to lose her as well."

Though not a cynical person by nature, Aimee has found herself wondering, even after Ken's sentencing, if anything positive can be wrought from Tina's death.

She's come to the conclusion that, if so, perhaps it's that young women who hear Tina's story will think twice before becoming escorts themselves.

"It's a lonely, sad, dirty world," Aimee says. "And you don't know who you're going to meet up with.

"It could be a Ken Tranchida."

EPILOGUE

JERRY HOLBERT continues to drive a tow truck. H writes to Ken and has visited him in prison.

PAUL TRANCHIDA has received several collect cal from his half brother Ken. Each time, he has refused to accep the charges.

RON SHANKIN remains a detective with the Farmingto Hills Police Department. He was awarded a citation for hi work on Tina's case.

AIMEE VERMEERSCH is still a manager at the Roch ester Chop House.

DONNA MEHDI and **DEBBIE LAWSON** were arreste in November 1995 and charged with prostitution, operating business without a license, and operating a business within residential zone. They pled guilty to prostitution and wer fined $350 each and sentenced to probation and communit service. Around the same time, Debbie Lawson was diag nosed with cancer. She died in April 1996.

TODD NURNBERGER works as a chemist for a phar maceutical firm in the Virgin Islands. He shares his home wit a mutt named Kodiak.

BILL BIGGAR retired from the Coast Guard in the sprin of 1996. He and Connie still live in Traverse City.

KEN TRANCHIDA filed a petition in March 1997 wit the Michigan Court of Appeals, seeking to have his second degree murder conviction overturned. Tranchida's attorne argued in her brief that the prosecution failed to prove Ken' guilt and that the court denied his rights in not allowing hir to withdraw his guilty plea the day he was sentenced. H remains incarcerated at the Gus Harrison Correctional Facilit in Adrian, Michigan.